M000268630

"This time in history has driven people of conscious to embrace a consistent and systematic system of oppression and inequality aimed at subordinate populations in America, and disproportionately against black people. The cry that 'Black Lives Matter' does not exclude the importance of all humanity but shines the light on the elephant in the room that black lives have not and are still not perceived or treated with equality.

For the past 40 years, Abiodun Oyewole, in the tradition of the West African oral historian has spoken truth to power, and has been on the front lines using his weapon of art to challenge white and black America to examine themselves and do better. In this anthology, we are not only given the opportunity to celebrate those in the struggle, but are given a directive to continue the struggle. *Black Lives Have Always Mattered* honors the ancestors, and gives hope for peace and justice for future generations where through policy and a new collective consciousness, all lives will truly matter!"

— Dr. Linda H. Humes, Executive Director Yaffa Cultural Arts Inc.
Assistant Professor John Jay College of Criminal Justice,
Africana Studies Department Chair of Education
National Association of Black Storytellers

"Part of the value of this important new anthology is that it keeps our pursuit of justice in America in historical and political perspective. It reminds us that "Black Lives Matter' is not a new revelation but a continuation of the black social gospel proclaimed by Richard Allen, Adam Powell Sr., Marcus Garvey, Malcolm X, Martin Luther King Jr., and the many more. To value black life is part of our legacy. in a very real sense the reason we will never be defeated is that at the very core of our existence is the firm belief and understanding that *Black Lives Have Always Mattered*."

— Bob Law, National Radio Personality

"The power of story unleashed in these pages penetrated my soul. No history book, no single black story, has yanked the rug of comfortable white ignorance from beneath my feet as these readings have. Taken one by one, these essays and poems offer conversation starters, sermon elements, and curriculum deepeners. Taken as a whole, *Black Lives Have Always Mattered* tells the story of America's silenced racial trauma in a way that will fuel the movement to speak the unspeakable."

—Debby Irving, racial justice educator and author of
Waking Up White, and Finding Myself in the Story of Race (2014)

BLACK LIVES HAVE ALWAYS MATTERED

BLACK LIVES HAVE ALWAYS MATTERED
A COLLECTION OF ESSAYS, POEMS, AND PERSONAL NARRATIVES

EDITED BY
ABIODUN OYEWOLE

2LP EXPLORATIONS IN DIVERSITY
Sean Frederick Forbes, Series Editor

NEW YORK
www.2leafpress.org

P.O. Box 4378
Grand Central Station
New York, New York 10163-4378
editor@2leafpress.org
www.2leafpress.org

2LEAF PRESS
is an imprint of the
Intercultural Alliance of Artists & Scholars, Inc. (IAAS),
a NY-based nonprofit 501(c)(3) organization that promotes
multicultural literature and literacy.
www.theiaas.org

Copyright © 2017 by The Intercultural Alliance of
Artists & Scholars, Inc.

Edited by: Abiodun Oyewole
Copy edited by: Carolina Fung Feng and Gabrielle David

Cover art design: Richard "Vagabond" Beaumont
Cover photo: The UNITAS program on
Fox Street in the South Bronx, 1983. Copyright © Ricky Flores.
Book design and layout: Gabrielle David

2LP EXPLORATIONS IN DIVERSITY
Series Editor: Sean Frederick Forbes

Library of Congress Control Number: 2016958430
ISBN-13: 978-1-940939-61-2 (Paperback)
ISBN-13: 978-1-940939-62-9 (eBook)

10   9   8   7   6   5   4   3   2   1

Published in the United States of America

First Edition | First Printing

2LEAF PRESS trade distribution is handled by University of Chicago Press / Chicago Distribution Center (www.press.uchicago.edu) 773.702.7010. Titles are also available for corporate, premium, and special sales. Please direct inquiries to the UCP Sales Department, 773.702.7248.

This anthology is dedicated to all the freedom fighters every-where: the Black Panther Party and The Republic of New Africa, to the Marcus Garvey philosophy to the NAACP and CORE; CBTU and Union 1199; to the Nation of Islam and Yoruba; to every black studies department and every black institution of higher learning; to the Civil Rights and Black Power movements, SCLC, SNCC and Black Lives Matter; and especially to all of the children who participate in demonstrations for black equality.

Finally to my children: Pharoah, Aina, Sowande, Obadele, Ebon, Ademola, Donjimen, and their mothers; and to all of my adopted children who mean and matter so much to me.

—Abiodun Oyewole

CONTENTS

∎∎∎

MOURNING BLACK LIVES
THAT MATTERED // 5

BLACK SKIN / WHITE MASKS // 47

BLACK SPACES / BLACK PLACES // 99

THE LEGACY OF
BLACK PROTEST CONTINUES // 207

"Words like 'freedom,' 'justice,' 'democracy' are not common concepts; on the contrary, they are rare. People are not born knowing what these are. It takes enormous and, above all, individual effort to arrive at the respect for other people that these words imply."

James Baldwin "The Crusade of Indignation," *The Nation* (July 7, 1956)

SERIES EDITOR'S NOTE

■ ■ ■

I MAGINE IT'S THE FIRST DAY OF CLASS. You don't know anyone. Your eyes begin to scan the room quickly; it's instinctual to do so, to scope out the space for familiarities, for oddities, for the closest exit. You won't be graded in this class, but you're invited to be active listeners and speakers. Amongst you are fellow classmates with a range of feelings and narratives in regard to the topic of diversity in American society. In your hands is the anthology *Black Lives Have Always Mattered: A Collection of Essays, Poems, and Personal Narratives* in which seventy-nine contributors have contemplated and written arduously and eloquently about the meaning of black lives and that they have always mattered. It will be the primary text for this class.

Some members of the class are angry, apathetic, bored, fed-up, frustrated, incredulous, indifferent, petulant, uncertain, unwavering in their beliefs; the list is endless. There are those who have never spoken openly about race matters and there are those who have always spoken openly about it. There are those with college degrees and there are those without. There are those who think they should be the only ones to talk about race matters, and there are those who desire to talk about race but don't think they should. There are those who have been taught to feel as if they are superior to others by virtue of their skin color, gender, sexual orientation, ethnic, national or regional origin, religious belief, or political affiliation, and there are those who have been taught to feel as if they are inferior. There are those who are self-deprecating and self-loathing, and there are those who are self-centered and self-preserving. There are those who hold onto the beliefs that the laws of a land are fair and just, and there are those who can't hold onto these beliefs in the law. There are those who think they have all of the answers and solutions, and there are those who know that no one person can. There are those who will read these very words, who will read this entire anthology and feel as if they have learned something meaningful, and there are those who will scan the title, my words, the editor's Abiodun Oyewole's introduction, this anthology, and think this was a waste of energy, time, and paper.

In this classroom setting the discussions to be had will *sound* familiar, they will *sound* like they needn't be revisited or spoken of again. Will someone state that another member of the class is being impossible to reason with, or is being unrealistic, or not living in reality, or is misunderstanding what has just been said, or is putting words into another's mouth, or is being over dramatic, or is being too sensitive or not sensitive at all? Yes, these statements will be voiced. Will someone be accused of inciting hate speech, of being ignorant, of further dividing the class, of not being a team-player? Yes, these accusations will happen. Will someone leave the room in a huff, or want to drop the class, or refuse to acknowledge the members of the class when they speak, or roll their eyes at every statement, or continue to be apathetic and bored? Yes, these behaviors will happen. I have undoubtedly engaged in these types of statements, accusations and behaviors many times, and while I would like to think I won't succumb to them again, it's highly possible that I will. I have learned from these moments and will try my hardest to continue to engage in conversations that are uncomfortable. Perhaps one of the greatest flaws of humanity is that one has to be reminded constantly of one's humility, but these constant reminders, if one acknowledges them, have the power to affect great change.

There are many who will unabashedly say, as has already been said and spoofed before, that all lives matter. Of course all lives matter, but to state that "black lives have always mattered" doesn't mean that other lives have *not* always mattered. I suspect that some of the animosity, misunderstanding, and negativity many have toward the term "Black Lives Matter" and its movement has more to do with the word "matter" than "black lives." The American Heritage dictionary defines "matter" as "something that occupies space and can be perceived by the senses" but also as "the substance of thought or expression; a subject of concern or action; trouble or difficulty [*what's the matter?*]; an approximated quantity [*a matter of years*]; something printed or written; to be of importance." The multiple meanings and ways in which this singular word is used can create many confounding anxieties and fears. For instance, if I were to say my life as a gay Afro-Latino American "matters," someone might take my statement the wrong way and think that I mean their life and identity markers don't matter, when in actuality I am asserting my own selfhood, and not devaluing another's selfhood.

I have read *Black Lives Have Always Mattered* three times and each time I was intrigued by the wide range of voices and experiences presented. It is a much needed anthology that complements and strengthens the core goals of the 2LP Explorations in Diversity series of fostering dialogue that goes with and against the grain. The first anthology in the series, *What Does It Mean to Be White in America? Breaking the White Code of Silence: Personal Narratives by White Americans,* co-edited by Gabrielle David and I, features eighty-two contributors who respond honestly and openly with the title's question. A forthcoming anthology, *The Beiging of America: Personal Narratives About Being Mixed Race in the 21st Century,* co-edited by Cathy J. Schlund-Vials, Tara Betts, and I, features thirty-nine contributors whose personal narratives articulate the complexities of interracial life.

It's easy to get information from a singular source and then proclaim that one knows all there is to know about a given topic. As a poet, teacher, constant learner and reader, I am always on a quest to gain more knowledge and to question myself and others every step of the way. Sometimes one may falter, sometimes one may not listen to another view point immediately, or one may be reluctant to hear the other side, but what matters is that conversations need to *matter* again and again.■

—Sean Frederick Forbes
Thompson, CT
May 2017

INTRODUCTION

■ ■ ■

Abiodun Oyewole

Why We've Always Mattered

WHEN I WAS ASKED to be the editor of this anthology, I took issue with the book's initial title, "Black Lives Matter." I felt then as I do now, that black lives have always mattered. I was a child of the sixties, and a product of the Black Power movement. To endorse the idea that Black Lives Matter as a new thing was rather feeble to me, because having been an activist for most of my life, the concept that black lives matter preclude my life and the lives of every living black person everywhere; from the moment they brought us to America's shores in chains, to the world we find ourselves living in today. This in my mind is a given. Since I did not entirely agree with the book's title, and was asked what I would call this anthology, I proposed *Black Lives Have Always Mattered,* which embarked my journey in the compilation and editing of this book.

After my initial meeting with the publisher, several thousand poets, writers and activists were contacted to solicit poems, essays and personal narratives, and more than 200 people responded. While I was shocked and pleased by the response, I did not foresee the painstaking ordeal of reading each submission to decide who was going to be in or out. It was a process that did not make me very happy because as a teacher, I like to give everyone a chance, but it had to be done. In fact, the last time I read these many papers was when I was teaching an African American history class at the College of New Rochelle at the Co-Op City branch over twenty-five years ago.

I must admit, however, this has been a wonderful learning experience. Even though I am a poet and travel around the world performing, teaching remains my passion. So as I combed through all of the submissions, I read them with a teacher's eye and a black man's soul. I was touched by the outpouring of deeply personal stories in poetry and prose, and the reaffirmation of the beauty of blackness. I was also pleased that the book's theme attracted the participation of people of white, mixed race, and Latino descent; voices from the LGBT community; people from the African and the Caribbean diaspora; and multiple generations of people, from millennials to older folks of diverse occupations including a number of college students, who are represented in this volume of work.

While I initially did not conceive creating sections for the book, the submissions dictated otherwise. The anthology is divided into five sections: "Mourning Black Lives That Mattered," "Black Skin/White Masks," "Black Spaces/Black Places," "Black Lives Remembered/Reclaimed," and "The Legacy of Black Protest Continues." Because I received a number of works that discuss the fear of being black and the loss of black lives, which is at the forefront of "why we matter," I felt it was fitting that the anthology opened with "Mourning Black Lives That Mattered." The section, "Black Skin/White Masks," which acknowledges Frantz Fanon, goes straight to the heart of the matter of how skin color determines our destiny. "Black Spaces/Black Places" exudes just that, where people talk about how those spaces and places are undervalued and discriminated against. By the way, those "spaces" and "places" are also meant to be looked at figuratively as well as literally. I thought it was interesting that I received a number of pieces in remembrance of people—some famous, some not—and felt they required a separate section, "Black Lives Remembered/Reclaimed." Finally, "The Legacy of Black Protest Continues" is where different thoughts and ideas converge into one space that tackle the questions; "What are we doing?" and "Where do we go from here?"

As a poet, I was also very happy to see so many great poems. I thought it was important to include poetry in this anthology because of its direct connection with cultural history and politics, and its ability to restore order out of chaos. I bring this up because the opening poem for the book, "Table Talk" by Angel Dye, and the closing poem, "Healing" by Shirley Bradley LeFlore, in many ways represent not only the pages of work that appear between the two poems, the poets who wrote these works are equally symbolic to this volume. Dye is an upcoming poet, a student at Howard University; and LeFlore is an older poet who was very much involved in the Black Arts movement of the sixties. It is this generational overlap of both emerging and established artists and activists that is essential to help give rise to movement, which we desperately need in our communities today.

Black Lives Have Always Mattered offers a thorough insight into the lives, dreams, aspirations, victories, defeats and recognition of black people in America. Considering the times we are living in these days, this anthology should serve as a mental compass for how we value ourselves and each other, and how we manifest our own destiny. I am very proud to have been a part of this project. I know for years to come, this book will matter more and more for each new generation that follows. ∎

—Abiodun Oyewole
Harlem, NY
April 2017

MOURNING BLACK LIVES
THAT MATTERED

"To be black in America is to exist in haunting, mundane proximity to death at all moments."

— Hannah Giorgis, writer, organizer

Angel C. Dye

Table Talk

"The race card is an
imaginary joker
placed by the dealer."

"#BlackLivesMatter is
a blind, disruptive attempt
at freedom papers."

Rasaq Malik

How Do I Tell My Son?

That he should run whenever he hears
sirens blaring in the streets, that he is a
black boy whose name resembles the name
of a black man called Alton B. Sterling, 32,
shot by police officers in Baton Rouge, LA
How do I tell my son that nothing is more
saddening than reading about how a girl
watches how a Minnesota police officer
sprays bullets on her father, how she
comforts her mother as they handcuff her.
How do I tell my son that he is not safe
whenever he walks the streets and someone
calls him a nigger, and someone curses his
skin as he tries to explain how being
black is not a threat. How do I tell my son
that love is fragile in a country where people
wake up every day to see bullets lurking in
the sky, to bury their black beloveds, to pick
the broken bones of their dead relatives,
to see smoke spiraling in the sky. How do
I tell my son that the world is dead and
it needs a revival, that everything that
remains is a memory of how every
black child struggles to exist.

Kimberly Garrett Brown

A Mother's Fear

RARELY WRITE ABOUT HOTBED TOPICS. The two sides are polarized and uninterested in understanding one another. Consequently, joining the conversation feels akin to preaching to the choir. Unfortunately, that phenomenon is the very thing that keeps a lot of people silent on some very important issues. That certainly was the case for me as it relates to the Black Lives Matter movement. Though I understood and agreed with the tenets of the campaign, I kept my thoughts to myself. But a seemingly casual occurrence between my son and I made me realize how important it is for me, a black woman writer, to write about a fear shared by every mother of a black son. And while I generally avoid superlatives, this is one instance where I know what happened to me happens repeatedly across this country.

The evening started innocently enough. I pulled into my driveway to find my son's car parked in his spot. He'd been away on business for the last three months. The buzz of the television greeted me as I came into the house. Nostalgia washed over me. It had been years since one or both of my boys were downstairs watching television while I worked in the kitchen. Back then, the noise got on my nerves. Now it was a welcomed relief from the quiet and often lonely evenings I spent waiting for my husband to come home from work. While being an empty-nester had its advantages, it also heightened my grief. The silence amplified the reality of my older son's death.

As I unpacked my groceries, my mind waded through the memories. I was moments away from tears, when my younger son, Nick, came upstairs, wearing a pair of basketball shorts and a T-shirt with the arms cut out.

"What are you cooking?" he asked.

"Chicken and squash stew."

"Are you cooking for me?"

"Who only cooks enough stew for two?" I asked.

"Well, you said you weren't cooking for me anymore and you're a woman of your word."

Prior to him leaving for his assignment in Texas, I had gotten frustrated by the amount of food thrown away because he ate before coming home. But all was forgiven. I was glad to have him back.

"I'm cooking for you. Just let me know when you have other plans."

"Will do," he said as he headed out the door for his evening run.

With little thought to the time, I seasoned the chicken, and tossed it into the pan to be sautéed. As I diced the various vegetables, I noticed it had gotten dark outside, and Nick had been gone for a while. Much longer than it took to run a few miles.

I told myself not to worry as I added chicken stock and vegetables to the pot. As I let the stew simmer, panic rose in my chest. George Zimmerman and Trayvon Martin floated through my mind.

What if one of my white neighbors saw my black son with long dreadlocks, wearing a cut-off shirt and basketball shorts, running down the street? Would they see a young man exercising after work? Or would they see him as an imminent threat to their home and family?

I tried to calm my fears. We lived in a nice, safe neighborhood. And while we weren't friends, the neighbors were friendly. We were the same basic socioeconomic demographic, each wanting a comfortable and safe place to raise our families and live our lives. But that description could also be said about the gated community where Trayvon Martin was shot. Suddenly, all the names of the young black men shot by white police officers came to mind.

I paced around the kitchen, debating whether to call Nick and tell him to come home. But that felt wrong. Why should a young man be afraid to go out for a run because his neighbors might perceive him as a threat based solely on the color of his skin? He wasn't hurting anyone. It was his neighborhood, too. He had a right to be there. We paid our taxes just like everyone else.

But then I had a vision of him trying to explain himself to a local police officer. I saw him against the police car. Of course, that would be the best-case scenario since the current trend with black young men and white police officers is to shoot first, and *maybe* ask questions later. My heart sank. I envisioned my son dead in the middle of street. I began to cry. I couldn't lose another son. He had to come home.

How much longer are you going to be out, I texted.

A half hour, he texted back.

Though I was relieved he responded, I still felt anxious that he wasn't closer to home. *Come home,* I typed into my phone, but deleted it. It wasn't right to burden him with my fear.

Instead, I prayed for his protection, and begged the Lord to bring him home safely. My fervent prayer went on for the next twenty minutes or so until I happened to notice his car wasn't in the driveway.

Where are you? I texted.

The gym, he texted back.

The tension in my shoulders thawed as I whispered a prayer of thanks. Then, I texted Nick and told him how worried I had been when I thought he was running in our neighborhood.

It's crazy that you'd be more worried about me running in the suburbs than you were when I ran at night on Georgia Tech's campus, he responded.

Truth is, as a mother of black sons, I'm always worried. Though my sons were raised in upscale neighborhoods steeped in influence and money, neither one of them could behave badly in public without the potential for dangerous repercussions. On more than one occasion I feared for their lives because they both grew up believing, and rightly so, they were American first and protected under the unalienable rights promised in our Constitution. My fear tripled when we moved to the South. What if they got stopped for speeding? Or something happened when they were at the bar on the weekends? Would the police single them out? Would people perceive them as a threat and act accordingly?

Even with that fear, I stood somewhat aloof when the Black Lives Matter movement began. I believed teaching my sons to be respectful and responsible would protect them. I even shifted some of the blame to the victims, believing the lessons of respect and compliance passed down since the time of slavery from black mothers to their children was the safest way to react. But that belief is built on the assumption that one group of people deserve more respect than another. For centuries, blacks in this country have been dehumanized and subject to heinous acts of violence propagated by a belief that skin color is a determining factor of worth. And so, parents tried to protect their children by teaching them the "right way" to behave. But deference and obedience doesn't stop the real problem of racism and hatred.

There is still a deep-seated mistrust and fear of African Americans. It's easier to accept an over-simplified belief that all black people are the same than to take the time to understand the individual with his or her own characteristics and history. And when we don't understand, we make quick judgments about why people do what they do or react a certain way.

When my oldest son was lost to suicide two years ago, I began to see how much people hid their pain. For some, like my son, the anguish becomes too much to bear. Others are downtrodden and barely surviving. There are others who lash out at the world to protect themselves from further hurt. We may believe that they can change their lives if they tried harder without considering the social and institutional systems that actively work against them. We judge based on our own experiences, rather than seeing their experience from a place of compassion. Love heals. And as Maya Angelou says, "We are more alike, my friends, than we are unalike." Imagine what we could do if we spent more time meeting our collective needs than fighting about our differences.

Unfortunately, the current administration wants to keep us divided as we blame one another and fight amongst each other, because then we won't pay attention to the ways in which their behavior and actions are helping to shape our nation's biggest economic and social problems. Once we stop being distracted by all the rhetoric, we may discover how powerful we can be if we engage in serious dialogue about real problems and work together.

That may sound lofty, but it's achievable. The fear that mothers feel for their black sons isn't just a black problem. It's a human problem. As sentient beings, we can look deeper than the color of one's skin. We must be willing to step out of our comfort zone. For some, that means operating out of a place of compassion. For others, it's seeking to understand people outside of their own race or ethnicity. Either way, we must approach these uncomfortable topics with the goal of finding a solution. If we remain silent, we miss an opportunity to make a difference. ■

Ali D. Collins

Bargain of Life

In dedication to Rayquan Borum and Justin Carr

I REMEMBER THAT NIGHT like it was yesterday. The warmth of his blood that oozed through my fingertips as I tried to stop the bleeding and the cooling of his body after he struggled to breathe.

I swear that the evidence that I shall give...

I remember looking down at his lifeless body that I once called my brother, my friend. Only ten minutes prior to that, we were chanting, "No justice, no peace!" Ten minutes prior to that, I remember hugging him after tears of black sorrow. We were mourning a black father that was killed just for reading a book while waiting for his daughter. Had I not known that ten minutes later, I'll be mourning you.

Shall be the truth...

Had I not known, I'd be wrongfully accused as the coldness from their handcuffs attempted to cut my circulation. Had I not known, my face would hit the concrete as blood overpowered my taste buds. Had I not known, pancakes would be our last meal together. Earlier that day, we chanted, "The whole damn system is guilty as hell!" and it's true. It was a rubber bullet that traveled faster than the speed of light that robbed your life and my youth.

The whole truth...

The sound of the gavel births anxiety in my throat as a conversation occurred before recess had ended. "Remember, we can all make this go away if you plead guilty," my attorney said. I don't believe this as the killer sits in to watch, smirking and laughing, because he just returned from vacation. The killer raised his hand and swore to serve and protect us, but he pulled the trigger because we didn't look like him.

And nothing but the truth...

My mother watches me as her sister and community comforts her. The puffiness under her eyes shows sleepless nights while the redness shows countless hours of crying. She not only mourned over you, but soon she will be mourning over me too. Although, the media says I'm guilty, I will continue to plead innocent.

So help me God. ■

Melba Joyce Boyd

It Could Have Been Me

President Obama said in response to the killing of Trayvon Martin

"If I had a son,
he would look
like Trayvon."

He is hand-
some. Skin
the color
of coffee,
cream and
cinnamon.

Slight of build,
with a physique
yet to become,
he is shrouded
under hooded
myths and
shadows
of white guilt.

Grasping fists,
armed
with a
package
of rainbow
colored candy,
he is stalked
while striding

across grounds
of a gated
compound;
targeted by
imaginary fears
enforcing
Americanism.

How does Trayvon
stand his ground
when he steps
beyond borders
of the reservation?

What can a
black boy do
when "the man"
with a gun
comes?

How do you
walk away
from death
aimed at
your back?

"It could have
been me,"
the President
said.

"It could have
been me…"

Trayvon Martin was an unarmed, seventeen-year-old teenager, who was gunned down
in Sandford, Florida on February 26, 2012. The title of the poem is a quote from
the statement President Barrack Obama made in response to the senseless murder.

Ayshia Elizabeth Stephenson

Rooms of Murder

I'm not afraid of aliens
I'm afraid of those who shoot
Unarmed civilians in the back
Of sergeants who shoot and kill
A mentally ill and elderly
Woman in her room —
In her home
Of officers who gang rape
A teenager
And call it a hoax

I'm afraid of those who kill
Worshippers
In a room of God
Who murder teenagers
Because they're wearing a hoodie
Who open fire at the movies and
On first-graders in a classroom
I'm afraid of unborn futures
And that the America he
Protects is the one
Who makes me unsafe

Some people say all lives matter
And they do
But some people don't know
I'm black and afraid
Every time I see a cop —
When I'm sipping coffee

When I'm walking from
One class to the next
When I'm at the airport
And security touches my crouch
Because my *braids set off the alarm*
Some people don't know
There's a pain in my chest
From just
Being

My fear runs
From a long and steady
River of white hate
Immigrants aren't the problem unless
They become white.
No, I didn't march this time
In Boston or D.C. or anywhere else
I nodded when a friend said
I marched for you
Yes march for me
Thank you
It's your turn
I'm going to keep writing
And working and studying
Because when your excitement
About this cause dissipates
I still need to be better than you in order to survive.

They ask me how much more do I want?
I want to walk
into a store and not be followed.
I want to walk
on campus and not have white people
give my hair dirty looks.

I want a world
where I don't fear

for the lives of children
I don't yet have.
I want black to be fucking normal.
And for rooms of murder
not to be painted white and called clean.

Tara Betts

An Open Letter to the Voyeurs

KEEP TRYING TO WRITE A SENTENCE, simple and clear, but I keep writing the beginnings of poems that process the electricity and extinguishing of human charges, a persistent black light, a startling series of resistant sparks. The flashing clouds of shots fired puncture the flesh that we know, pinned down to this death language that they want us to speak like our first tongue, but it is a language without tone, a tongue of decaying then dissipating spirit. There are days when the songs of my dead seem to be the only notes that people trace with fascination, a morbid sort of savoring that ignores anything that helped someone like me live. This body of mine is alive and the product of being hugged, shared laughter, the dismantling of so-called textbooks. When you break me down to a product that purchases so many consumable goods, cut down my life and blame me for having babies so young, there is some equation where the pennies I make add up to someone else's vacation in the Antibes, and their children might reference it in an easily published poem. My poems must talk about the anglings of flesh in cell phone cameras, once breathing then red, still.

I must be fascinated with my own death, subsumed in grief I did not build. This sort of death is not old age, diet, smoking, alcohol, or drugs. This sort of death falls short of cancer, diabetes, and heart disease, and it is not an accident. Accidents require fewer bullets. Accidents are not just that call that startles you out of sleep. Accidents are never systematic, repetitive, and unloaded daily. Accidents do not extinguish parents in front of children, nor do they swing the pendulum toward a skin that catches a glinting sun in a whole other character.

No, this is the deliberate swing of phone books and pulled triggers that drop hammers. This is the dragging of bodies into warehouses to say "Look at how they kill each other." This is the shaking of heads that say look at their report cards, sex lives, and past records. These are the editors who will ask you can they publish another poem about your dead because your nihilism is spiced just right with hot sauce from your bag and some peach cobbler from the black restaurants that don't survive in rejuvenated neighborhoods. This is the paean that no one wants to find in a hymnal because the chorus points at who is holding the gun, instead of the dead on the floors, in graves, and left on the streets of America, a country known for jagged hurts waiting in its buck knife. Don't expect less from a two-sided blade ever.

This history tangles in the morass of Reconstruction bitten by Jim Crow and punctures like Carolina fields by Klan hoods and cotton bolls. This is a history wired, routed to eliminate, dim any charge that jumps clear off grid.

What some of you seem to forget is how I am a daily observer of electricity. ■

John Warner Smith

Why Being a Black Father in America Today Frightens and Angers Me

For it is not light that is needed, but fire;
it is not the gentle shower, but thunder.
We need the storm, the whirlwind, and the earthquake.

–Frederick Douglass, 1852

I am an American, a descendant of an African boy
who was stolen from his family, brought
to America and sold into slavery.
I am a father and grandfather of black boys
born and living in America,
doing honest work,
not committing crimes,
not hurting people.

    We walk and drive down city streets,
    get stopped by flashing blue lights, cars
    emblazoned with the word POLICE.
    White men who stop us step out of their cars,
    pull their guns, shoot, and kill us.

Twice this week, when I closed my eyes
to sleep, the rat-a-tat-tat of gunfire
and the screaming cries of mothers
rang in my ears. I saw blood
pouring out of a man's body, two men:
    Alton Sterling and Philando Castile,
    black, young – shot and killed
    by white police officers in two American cities.

In Baton Rouge, Alton Sterling was shot multiple times
at execution range after he was wrestled
to the ground and pinned down on his back
like a man being nailed to a cross.

Too often the purveyors of justice have seen
   such horrifying images and viral afterimages,
   far too many, but not enough for them
to see the guilt and dishonor
of militarized police officers
   who kill innocent African American boys and men.

Melissa Dunmore

Black Death

I need to talk about how no one is talking about
the elephant in the room
the big, bleeding, black elephant in the room
that trampled my rose colored glasses underfoot

I need to talk about how no one is talking about
Black Death
septic not skeptic Black Death
deep seated, mistreated Black Death

I need to change my voice mail greeting to
"can't come to the phone right now" because I'm grieving
set my Out of Office reply to "I've suffered a loss"
I am at a loss for words

water cooler talk is Jen and Ben
Courtney and Scott
who cares?
Kimye? I'm not okay

see, I can't come make the meeting today
because I'm screaming in my car
sobbing at the nightly news
shrieking at the radio
singing a spiritual in the shower

fearing the Grim Reaper is my black brothers' keepers
scythe blocking the light from reaching my eyes
this old genocide a rolling blackout

and I can't shout else I'm an angry black woman
any gross old epithet to make me less human

I need to talk about
Trayvon, Mike Brown, Marissa Alexander, Sandra Bland
am I standing in quicksand?
because I swear I'm sinking

I need to talk about
this living nightmare
being black in America in 2015
where hoarders of historical hate
fly Confederate banners of evil
that laugh in the sky above
pyres of black smoke
from black bodies

I need to talk about
how can you function?
what's it like to function amid the forever funereal?

I don't want to function at the junction
of ignorance plus privilege
if at the corner of apathy and apartheid
is where I must meet you
then I will never attend
my soul hasn't had a chance to mend

does it not give you pause?
not even a moment of silence
no grief counselor in sight
ignoring

people talk sardonically about a quarter life crisis
saying millennials aged 25 are
too anxious about making the wrong move
that we don't move

but I can't move because I don't want to get shot
can't move because I have not forgotten
can't move because I...I... dot dot dot

hands up, eyes down, mouth quivering to stay shut
holding back an Edvard Munch type scream
bursting at the seams
torn between wanting to be alive
and wanting to dive below the surface

I want to extract the empathy from you like rainwater from a cactus

when my kin wrinkle like raisins in the sun
modern day bullet wounds akin to being hung
strange fruit are the media's loot
demonizing the dead on CNN
innocence is a death sentence

headlines of "black killers" oppose "white shooters"
"mentally ill" versus "society's ills"
diction dictates decorum
diction dictates dissent
diction the prescription for my malaise
the black mayonnaise that coats my days
all the while I can't catch my breath
can't ignore Black Death

I

CANT

BREATHE.

Maria James-Thiaw

A Fuse Blew

A fuse blew the night we found out;
It was right before the rains came
beating on the glass panes
like fists, like heads on concrete.

A fuse blew the night we found out
so we sat in the dark, hot expanse
of a warehouse behind a coffeehouse.
Espresso and art energized the stage.

Sankofa was purple from passion and pain
Dustin took us there all night and all day
The Priestess struck us like lightning
Soul Cry made you want to taste the rainbow.

The unlit stage hooded Tiger's face
For no one can see a black boy
in the dark when the rains come.
No one can see a black boy
In the dark when the rains come,

and the night was as heavy and thick
as Shane's poems are true.
Indeed, we heard it then
from lips that had just spit
the deepest wisdom,
A Ghetto Issued proclamation,
a herald to we, the scribes,
and we almost clapped out of habit,

we almost snapped out of habit—
we almost snapped out.

Because we had heard it then.
Smart phones buzzed
like black women on the back pew.
We shared a gasp, exchanged curses, questioned
the verdict.
    George Zimmerman: NOT guilty!
NOT GUILTY?!!!

A fuse blew.

Yael Kenan

Mourning: Black Life, Black Death[1]

AFTER LOSS, THEN WHAT?," Judith Butler asks in the title of one of her essays.[2] In thinking critically about the prevalence of dead black bodies in the U.S. and the myriad of cases of violence and discrimination, the process of mourning, of what comes after, may often be overlooked. Mourning is, however, a central component of the racial dynamics in America, and plays a significant political role. In the following, I identify a theoretical framework of mourning, both in general and specifically in the context of black people in the U.S., through readings of formulations by Claudia Rankine, Fred Moten and Judith Butler. Thinking through their work about the dead body and its various representations, I seek to establish a notion of mourning in the face of precarity. Finally, I discuss a particular example of textual mourning in Marylin Nelson's *A Wreath for Emmett Till*, hoping to outline a way of reclaiming mourning, and employing it in a life-affirming politics.

In a mournful essay published five days after the Charleston church shooting in June 2015, Claudia Rankine diagnoses the state of black living in the U.S. as a "condition...of mourning," citing the words of a friend who is "the mother of a black son." This condition stems from the prevalence of loss in the black American experience, what Karla FC Holloway discusses as a phenomenon so central it has become part of the black cultural identity, almost part of the vernacular: "instead of death and dying being unusual, untoward events, or despite being inevitable end-of-lifespan events, the cycles of our daily lives were so persistently interrupted by specters of death that we worked this experience into the culture's iconography and included it as an aspect of black cultural sensibility"(6). This cultural sensibility can be seen in Rankine's list of daily occurrences, which for black Americans may prove lethal: "no hands in your pockets, no playing music, no sudden movements, no driving your car, no walking at night, no walking in the day, no turning onto this street, no entering this building, no standing your ground, no standing here, no standing there, no talking back, no playing with toy guns, no living while black." While some of these mundane actions may refer to specific cases in which black lives have been compromised (playing music may refer to Jordan Davis, the toy gun evokes Tamir Rice), they all illustrate how vulnerable all black lives are; the many who have in fact been targeted and/or killed while driving their cars (Walter Scott, Rodney King) or walking at night (Trayvon Martin), but also the many more who engage in such everyday activities and may be targeted at any given moment, "for simply being black" (Rankine).

Adding to this list, and the trend it illustrates regarding the prevalence of mourning, are Rankine's examples of numerous losses of black lives throughout history, recalled in the wake of the current shooting in Charleston: the Alabama church bombing which occurred "eleven days before [she] was born," slavery, the killing of Michael Brown and most prominently in her essay, the lynching of Emmet Till. The events are mentioned and discussed out of chronological order not due to a lack of historical awareness – indeed, a historical argument is very much at stake – but rather to demonstrate the never-ending sequence of violent events which permeate American history, their frequency itself challenging a sense of social progression. Rankine argues that violence regularly characterizes the way the black body is treated in American life, from slavery onwards: "Dying in ship hulls, tossed into the Atlantic, hanging from trees, beaten, shot in churches, gunned down by the police or warehoused in prisons: Historically, there is no quotidian without the enslaved, chained or dead black body to gaze upon or to hear about or to position a self against." Rather than discuss the differences between Middle Passage, lynching, police shootings and mass incarceration – a discussion which far too often leads to an eerie congratulatory conclusion that we have "come so far" – Rankine points to the terrifying ubiquity of these distinct but related historical events. The result of this ubiquity is that Dylann Roof, the Charleston shooter, "along with the rest of us, has been living with slain black bodies" (Rankine). The jarring effect of this statement does not derive only from the mention of dead bodies, but from their dwelling where they seemingly do not belong – alongside the living.[3] Rankine's contention in this piece, starting from its title asserting that "the condition of black life is one of mourning," is that life and death in the case of black people are not as distinct as we would like to believe, because "We live in a country where Americans assimilate corpses in their daily comings and goings. Dead blacks are a part of normal life here" (Rankine).

The persistent and haunting presence of death stems from the long history of institutional and racialized violence because, as Achille Mbembe explains in his article on necropolitics, "in the economy of biopower, the function of racism is to regulate the distribution of death and to make possible the murderous functions of the state" (166). In the context of race, violence and death are constituents of the political and not an aberration, demonstrating their regularity. What Mbembe's articulation – a response to Foucauldian biopower which challenges its normative view of the political – does not take into account is precisely the question of what comes after loss. It is the question of what living with the dead means for the living, how the dead are integrated into the life in their wake – the question of mourning. The presence of dead blacks in everyday life has a significant effect on the meaning of mourning. If dying – prematurely, unexpectedly, undeservedly – is a defining feature of black life in America, then mourning too is not an unusual time but rather an all-encompassing experience, one which does not have a definitive starting moment. Consequently, Rankine demonstrates that in the case of the black experience in the U.S., mourning does not only occur after death; rather, it is a reality of life, muddling the difference between the two. Hence, Mbembe asserts, for example, that "slave life, in many ways, is a form of death-in-life" (170). Thus, because of the precarity of black life in America, a paradox of mourning is created – there is constant need for mourning, but it is not sanctioned in public life. Black life is not considered worthy of grief by state authorities, and this in itself makes it vulnerable, rendering death an imminent part of life and mourning an inevitable but impossible task.

Grieving, especially in the context of precarity, is simultaneously inevitable and impossible – omnipresent and all-consuming on the one hand, and absent and forbidden on the other. The prevalence of death and the consequent paradox of mourning before death are manifest in a variety of ways, given the different circumstances. So, for example, John Calvin Marshall, the Martin Luther King Jr. figure in Julius Lester's *And All our Wounds Forgiven*, lives with a keen awareness of his imminent death, which informs his life with a sense of urgency and historical weight. In addition, the child murders in Atlanta depicted in Tayari Jones' *Leaving Atlanta* loom over the children in the novel, whose lives seem like a not at all child-like game of Russian roulette. Another example is Ernest Gaines' *A Lesson before Dying,* in which Jefferson awaits his death throughout the novel, knowing his fatal future and yet not having an option of preventing it or arriving at any redemptive denouement. One need not resort to allegorical readings to see these texts, and many others, as representative of entirely non-fictional current and historical events in the black experience in the U.S. In addition, characterizing this situation as a paradox is not merely an academic and philosophical observation. Rather, this paradox defines and marks black life and death, interlacing them and in effect perpetuating this condition.

In *Precarious Life,* Judith Butler explains that violence is not considered as such when it is perpetrated against those who are already excluded from the constitutive national group: "if violence is done against those who are unreal, then, from the perspective of violence, it fails to injure or negate those lives since those lives are already negated" (33). Consequently, "they cannot be mourned because they are always already lost or, rather, never 'were,' and they must be killed, since they seem to live on, stubbornly, in this state of deadness" (ibid.)[4] These ghostly figures are spectral while living and after they are killed, as the medical distinction between life and death is not what defines their state. The implications of this are significant because, as Butler asserts, the question of mourning and who merits the preliminary rite of a proper burial is pertinent to the definition of the human: "the derealization of the 'other' means that it is neither alive nor dead, but interminably spectral" (33-4). Therefore, Mamie Till Mobley's actions after her son's death amount to a "refusal to keep private grief private," as she recognized the importance of the public and communal aspect of grieving as a counteraction to derealization (Rankine). In this way, Mobley "allowed a body that meant nothing to the criminal justice system to stand as evidence" (Rankine). So, Emmett Till's body, whose legal status and state of existence were questioned in the trial of his murderers and in different ways in his killing and what enabled it, was put into public evidence by his mother as a body worthy of mourning. The presence of the body confronts viewers with its reality, and

Rankine therefore sees the decision on the part of Ferguson police to leave the body of Michael Brown out on the street for four hours after he was shot as compelling a choice by viewers: "a person had to decide whether his dead black body mattered enough to be mourned" (Rankine). This decision, this choice, is a reaction to the particular paradox of black mourning, and it is importantly located at the site of precarity itself, the black body.

Mon'in': Body, Image, Sound

RANKINE'S PRIMARY EXAMPLE is the event many consider a catalyst of the civil rights movement–the lynching of Emmet Till in 1955. In Holloway's terms, "the story of Till's lynching lingered like melancholy in the memory of black folk" (7). More specifically, Rankine pays particular attention to the state of Till's dead body as it was made public via Mamie Till Mobley's famous decision to bury her son in Chicago in an open-casket funeral, because she "wanted the whole world to see." Rankine cites Mobley's words and adds a pertinent sentiment: "I believe that the whole United States is mourning with me." Rankine is understandably incredulous about the veracity of the assertion, but claims it is nonetheless significant because in her decision to highlight her son's dead body, Mobley refused to participate in a long tradition in the white U.S. of disregarding the dead black body specifically by callously displaying it in public. "She 'disidentified' with the tradition of the lynched figure left out in public view as a warning to the black community, thereby using the lynching tradition against itself," Rankine explains, evoking the well-known images of anonymized black corpses hanging from trees. Mobley reclaimed her son's body after it was claimed by his murderers, Milam and Bryant, but also by generations of institutional racism which enabled his murder. In doing so, Mobley reclaimed her son's status as grievable, someone worthy of a funeral service and rites of mourning.

Importantly, mourning Emmet Till takes place via the viewing of his slain body, because "we need to see or hear the truth" (Rankine). Fred Moten, who is quoted by Rankine in her essay, also writes about the image of Till's dead body, demonstrating the affinity between the photograph, power structures and death. Linking the visual image to Barthes' *Camera Lucida* on the one hand, and the civil rights movement's critique of hegemony on the other, Moten relates the photo of Till's corpse to haunting and resurrection on several levels; Till's death is both haunted by previous and similar deaths and haunts those who view the image, and it is a disruption of hegemony, echoing Rankine's view of mourning black bodies as "intervention and interruption." Further, Moten explains the impact of the pivotal choice to leave the casket open: "Ms. Bradley opens, leaves open, reopens, the violent, ritual, sexual cutting of his death by the leaving open of the casket, by the unretouching of the body, by the body's photograph, by the photograph's transformation in memory and nightmare of which many speak" (64). The emphasis on repetition as a political act is evident in Moten's own repetitive sentence structure, but the impact of the photo as a form of resistance is perhaps clearest in the coining of a new word, "unretouching." This choice is not only counter-hegemonic but also underscores the agency and action involved, with the prefix "un" almost negating or undoing both the more customary 'retouching' designed to make death more palatable, and the word itself.[5]

For Moten the image is not only visual but audial, as he describes the "extreme and subtle harmonics of various shrieks, hums, hollers, shouts and moans" the photograph generates (66). This can be understood as the sounds captured in the moment of the image as well as the reactions it solicits in viewers, both of which are a form of mourning. The sounds mentioned are, importantly, not verbal expressions, but they nonetheless articulate and perhaps crystalize something about mourning. While Moten recognizes the tradition of philosophical debates on the primacy of sounds or written characters, which he says he "echoes" (66), his focus on non-verbal expressions bypasses that discussion and creates a different category. "Black mo'nin' is the phonographic content of this photograph," Moten explains, with his central term "mo'nin' " referring simultaneously to the sound of a moan and to mourning (in a spoken colloquial pronunciation) of which it partakes (ibid). Moten, too, identifies a blurring of the lines between life and death through the image and sound it provokes and discloses, which he sees as "the drama of life in the photograph of the dead" (69). Moten describes this drama in terms of life, death and art, linking them all together: "Black Art, which is to say Black Life, which is to say Black (Life Against) Death, which is to say Black Eros, is the ongoing production of a performance."[6] He then goes on to perform this ritual himself in the rhythmic articulation: "rupture and collision, augmented toward singularity, motherless child, childless mother, heart-rending shriek, levee camp moan, grieving lean and head turn, fall, *Stabat mater,* turn a step, loose booty funk brush stroke down my cheek, yellow dog, blue tran, black drive" (Moten 72).

Sites of Mourning

RANKINE'S ESSAY IS ACCOMPANIED by a series of images of various sites of mourning, in which we might also hear the loud (and sometimes silent) sounds of black mon'in'. These images include a memorial for Eric Garner on Staten Island, a line of mourners near the place where Michael Brown was killed in Ferguson, and a vigil in Charlotte, South Carolina. Perhaps most striking among these images is a famous one of Mamie Till Mobley, agonizing over her son's open casket. The casket contains her son's mutilated corpse, but is adorned with images of him in life: a regular, living boy. This juxtaposition demonstrates the imbrication of life and death, as well as the way the photographic image is haunted by the presence of life but is also markedly distinct from it. The images surrounding Rankine's piece not only depict acts of mourning but constitute mourning in their representation and reproduction. They lay bare acts of mourning, displaying them "unretouched," and while they do not include horrors like a de-faced and bloated body – and this is a significant distinction – they do display public acts of mourning. The violence is not present, but it is implied as the context and background of the images, as are the sounds of "mo'nin' ." Thus, in the second part of my paper, I discuss a textual instance of "black mo'nin'," that is, a cultural artifact which expresses, through various uses of images and sounds, grief over the loss of black lives.

Marilyn Nelson's heroic crown, *A Wreath for Emmett Till,* was published some fifty years after Till's lynching, but is still deeply entrenched in mourning. The book uses common tropes of mourning, such as flowers, but being a cycle of poems it consists not in the flowers themselves but in their names and verbal descriptions.[7] However, rather than a process of metaphorization, Nelson's poems are in fact an ongoing process of realization of metaphor, muddling the lines between real and representation, much like Moten's focus on the overlap of ontology and image. So, her wreath as it is presented in the first sonnet includes forget-me-nots, a colloquial name for a type of flower but also the poem's entire ethical injunction. The weight of this edict comes into full force in the following sonnet, which starts with a variation on the name of the flower as an imperative: "forget him not."[8] Similarly, in mentioning the "weeping-willow," Nelson reminds us of the origin of the metaphor but also realizes the metaphor by apostrophizing the plant and making it speak: "I'm sad," it says. This speech occurs not only because "flowers had/ a language then," but also because the wreath itself oscillates between flowers and words, ontology and images, and participates in both equally. However, this apostrophizing is thwarted soon after, when in the second sonnet the speaker laments: "if trees could speak, it could/describe, in words beyond words, make us see," casting doubts on words both through the conditional and the term "words beyond words" (2). These words are perhaps akin to the non-verbal expressions of grief in Moten, the shrieks and hollers of black mo'nin'.

Mourning is rendered more specific with the description of Emmett Till, whose name "still catches in the throat," a line that repeats itself in the next sonnet (3, 4). Like Moten and Rankine, Nelson evokes the bloated body of Till, known to the public by the photographs and the open casket. However, Nelson quickly turns from the corpse to the memory of it, perhaps knowing that there is still much work to be done in mourning. The fifth sonnet thus addresses Mamie Till Mobley, wondering about her famous role as a grieving mother and calling her "mother of sorrows" and "mother of a boy martyr."[9] This sonnet contemplates Mobley's role in preserving her son's "public remembrance," which later leads Nelson to imagine an alternative form of life for Till, imagining what it would be like for him to have "lived well and wisely" (7) instead of his "shortened childhood" (2). However, even this fantasy of life, with its national implications given the evocation of the World Trade Center, is only accessible through death, as the sonnet imagines an alternative Till not as he might have lived but as that other life might be mourned: "let's write the obituary of a life / lived well and wisely" (7). Moreover, in many ways such an alternative and positive life was likely not readily accessible to a black boy in the 1950s, and if it is more so today that is largely due to the strides of the civil rights movement emboldened by the death of Till.

Another form of lamentation pervading these sonnets, both explicitly and implicitly, is that of the country that allows for murders of children to take place. Most notably in sonnet 11, Nelson returns to the trees, which may seem like symbols but in fact have played a painfully literal historical role: "Thousands of oak trees around this country / groaned with the weight of men slain for their race, / their murderers acquitted in almost every case" (11). Again, the weight is both literal and metaphoric, and the trees' groans are once again reminiscent of Moten's "shrieks, hums, hollers, shouts and moans," adding to the list of expressions of "black mo'nin'." The tree becomes an aggregate of sorrows, as "one night five black men died on the same tree, / with toeless feet, in this Land of the Free." The American myth of freedom is exposed as a façade, or better yet as true only for some as it has a Janus face: "one mouth speaks with forked tongue, the other reads/ the Constitution." Nelson locates the duplicity specifically in the mouth as it utters words, demonstrating their importance but also the threat they may pose. Both of these sides are "[her] country" and she sings them both as a form of lamentation.

The final form of mourning in Nelson's *A Wreath for Emmett Till* is her choice to end the cycle with a return to the "gouged eye" and its injunction: "we must bear witness to atrocity" (14). Like Rankine, Nelson asserts the importance of seeing as a form of witnessing, because "people may disappear, leaving no trace,/ unless we stand before the populace." Those still present must speak for those made absent, Nelson opines, and insist that they leave a trace, and this is done through mourning. So, per the form of the heroic crown, the last sonnet returns to the first line of the cycle and to Ophelia's use of flowers as evocations of memory: "Rosemary for remembrance, Shakespeare wrote."[10] This line performs memory in multiple fashions: in its intertextual appeal to Shakespeare and specifically to a grieving Ophelia; in its notion of remembrance; and in its repetitive pointing to the beginning of the cycle, which amounts to a sort of ritual repetition which, as Moten explains, "leaves open, reopens, the violent, ritual, sexual cutting of his death."

Final Words

IMAGES OF DEAD BLACK PEOPLE seem to be a commonplace, raising important questions about documentation and desensitization. Videos documenting the deaths of Eric Garner, Keith Scott and Philando Castile, among many others, have been viewed by millions, though visual evidence does not guarantee neither legal repercussions nor even clear knowledge of the facts. Moreover, these documented deaths must also remind us of the many deaths and many bodies which remain out of sight—unseen, unheard, and too often unremembered.

Many formulations of mourning—theoretical, essayist and literary—explicitly grapple with questions of what mourning actually is, how they might perform it and what role memory and commemoration play in the life that remains after loss. This points to the reflexive nature of mourning but also to a sense of uncertainty about it, that might stem from the intangibility of mourning itself (as well as that of the person mourned for) and from the precariousness which marked the lives of the dead and continues to plague them in their death in many ways. This precariousness of the body, living and dead, and of memory, makes the importance of mourning that much greater. Rankine thus defines Black Lives Matter as a movement centered on mourning and sees it as "an attempt to keep mourning an open dynamic in our culture because black lives exist in a state of precariousness." She argues that it "aligns with the dead, continues the mourning and refuses the forgetting," meaning that in order to demonstrate that black lives matter, their deaths have to matter as well, and vice versa. In this sense, if there is such a thing as "successful mourning" it is that which obviates itself—mourning as a political movement which can make mourning somewhat less omnipresent. ∎

ENDNOTES

[1] The following is based on a paper written for Michael Awkward after a class on Representations of Black Dead Bodies taught at the university of Michigan in Fall 2016. I am grateful to Professor Awkward for his helpful remarks.

[2] The essay appears in Eng and Kazanjian's *Loss: A Politics of Mourning* along with Moten's essay, which I discuss here in detail.

[3] In addition, this juxtaposition may also point to the way we have all gotten used to living with slain black bodies, indicating the type of acquiescence which allows for this to continue.

[4] Butler's book, written as a response to 9/11, focuses on the lives and deaths of those deemed "other" and "dangerous" (which are practically synonyms) outside of a particular national group. However, this theoretical frame work can be extended to the black experience in the U.S., given its exclusion and othering. This alignment itself deserves further discussion.

[5]   Till's body was in fact retouched before burial, at least partially. Moten might be drawing on the famous pictures of Till's mutilated face, an image engraved in cultural memory.

[6]   The alignment of eros and sexuality deserves greater attention but goes beyond the scope of this present paper.

[7]   Since the book does not have pagination, I reference the sonnets according to their order in the cycle.

[8]   This is also the only sonnet of the 15 in the crown which does not end with any punctuation mark, rendering the link between "Forget-me-nots. Though if I could, I would" and the following "Forget him not" that much stronger, almost as if it were, in fact, one continuous sentence. This transition also amplifies the connection between the flower and the injunction to "forget him not."

[9]   Both terms obviously originate in religious and specifically Christian imagery, and are similar to Moten's mention of *Stabat mater*.

[10] Shakespeare's *Hamlet* is often read as the melancholic par-excellence, but usually in regard to the titular character. While the distinction between mourning and melancholy is the subject of much scholarly debate, it goes beyond the scope of this current paper. However, Nelson here chooses a quote from Ophelia, thus highlighting both a woman grieving and not the main character. Likewise, in the case of Till, a mother is mourning her son whereas in *Hamlet* Ophelia is here mourning her father.

WORKS CITED

Butler, Judith. *Precarious Life: The Powers of Mourning and Violence.* New York: Verso, 2004. Print.

Holloway, Karla FC. *Passed On: African American Mourning Stories, a Memorial.* Durham: Duke UP, 2002. Print.

Mbembe, Achille. "Necropolitics." *Biopolitics: A Reader.* Eds. Timothy Campbell and Adam Sitze. Trans. Libby Meintjes. Durham: Duke University Press. 161-92. Print.

Moten, Fred. "Black Mo'nin'." *Loss: A Politics of Mourning.* Edited by Eng, David and Kazanjian, David. Berkeley: University of California Press, 2003. 59-77. Print.

Nelson, Marylin. *A Wreath for Emmett Till.* Boston: Houghton Mifflin, 2005.

Rankine, Claudia. "The Condition of Black Life Is One of Mourning." *The New York Times,* June 22 2015. Web.

DaChardae Roncoli

Black Lives Matter

What's it going to cost to stop all these lives from being lost?
Hatred is flowing through veins and inequality rains.
How much more must we suffer before we can exhale?
When will we see an end to this horrific tale?
The media is being flooded about black lives being taken.
It should enrage the public, yet most aren't even shaken.
How many more lives will continue to shatter
Before the world realizes that black lives matter.

Carletta Joy Walker

Matter

THE DOMINANT CHORAL SONGS encircling horrors defiling humanity are mostly binary and discordant.

News streams in—live stream, on tape, in stills, in print—constant flow; it begins to feel like, and is a death dirge, an operatic lament. I am faced with how to speak, how to write from the intelligence my "heartmind" understands. In the weeks preceding this essay hundreds of Muslims, in the period of Ramadan (July 2016), have been killed by attacks on public gatherings by a very, very small sect of other Muslims who have claimed singular rightness in practice and interpretation of faith. Two black men have been killed by white police officers. The "reasons" for these killings is not known. I have little to no information about the mind-intellect-reason for these murders, or the heart-feeling-reason for these murders.

Matter—what and who matters—is central to refrains being sung out about shootings and killings in the United States. Listeners in a competition for misunderstanding of the lyric—black lives matter, all lives matter, blue lives matter, and do Muslim lives matter? Are women included in black, all, blue? Are children? My youngest sister once wrote, "We love as we love" in response to my writing in an email that I loved her. It rings true in this contemplation seeking understanding and change. We matter as we matter. I matter! What I do and what is done to me matters. You matter, what you do and what is done to you matters.

I do, you do, is done is the we in this one shared earth turf 'hood.

Black Lives Matter is a call-to-action that faces up to a haunting specter of inaction, numbness, powerlessness, and giving up claim to fairness in the face of the specificity of "attack black." All Lives Matter is reactionary. Blue Lives Matter following Black Lives Matter (and we will prove it with legislation), is a focused coordinated reaction.

Black Lives Matter then reacts to the reactions, and the truth in the specificity of this movement dilutes and rigidifies into false truths. Breathing inside hearing and understanding becomes thin.

From my experience, my reading, my listening and observations, the vast majority, if not all of us living, have been subject to some indignity, some behavior action/inaction that affronts us. Too many of us have been subject to horrors that defile us as human beings.

There is need for healing in the core mindheart/thinkfeel DNA. Binary and dualistic thinking will not achieve the oneness of heart that disallows the violation of self and another. The practice of holism requires unity of thinking, feeling and breathing.

Several days into the writing of this essay, five, then three police officers were targeted and killed, and two additional incidents of concentrated mass violence resulted in the deaths of children, men and women.

Weep and pray, pray and weep; be love, act love, see, hear, speak love. Respond, train reaction – compassion inseparable from wisdom; wisdom inseparable from compassion, a means, a model, an understanding to have results look like and be a world in harmony with itself. ■

Tim Wood

And Told That She Didn't See What She Saw

Craig Futterman, NPR Morning Edition, November 25, 2015

And the boy then is moving away
and trying to get away
toward a fence. And as he moved away,

the officer shoots him – shoots him,
spins him around. And he falls to the ground.
repeatedly shoots him while he lays on the ground,

to release this information and release it.
Holding it back and holding it back
demand after demand and request after request,

a witness to the shooting
who repeatedly screamed, "Stop shooting,"
as the officer emptied his gun into the young boy's body.

Where   this happened   cameras had
seven different video files. He erased
all seven of those files, surveillance video

running while the officer erased them.
And so there's a videotape of the officer erasing
the video. Thank you. Thank you so much again.

BLACK SKIN / WHITE MASKS

"I am black, not because of a curse, but because my skin has been able to capture all the cosmic effluvia. I am truly a drop of sun under the earth."

—Frantz Fanon, *Black Skin, White Masks* (1952)

S. Baltimore Jones

Black

Black from the day's chain in a pack
to the trip shackled in a stack
To Jim Crow riding in the back
living in America can be a trap
for those who nap trying to be something
other than black
wake up jack
The dark skin always a
Fact.

Jesús Papoleto Meléndez

Indentured

In
  The United State
        of America
  an old
    Black man
      in 21st Century
      125th Street
         Harlem,
   with a
      broom
        &
      dust pan
   in his hands,
         cursing
           while chasing
       this empty
          bag
      of potato
         chips,
      twirling
       round
     on the
       sidewalk
      in this
       circle

           ,blame
      the wind.

Dedria Humphries Barker

Was My Father Just Another Pig?

WAS SPEEDING DOWN INTERSTATE-96 EAST to Detroit. Business awaited me in the city, and I had just enough time to get there from ninety miles out. My hometown had changed over the three decades since I left to live in the state's capitol. In its time of duress, I was trying to help out, to give back by working with the Fair Housing Center of Metropolitan Detroit. Their office was in downtown Detroit. I didn't want to be late.

I was driving in the near lane. Fifteen minutes into my 90-minute drive, I saw the flashing emergency lights of a police car on the highway shoulder. A state trooper stood at the door of his vehicle, faced out to the road. He held a speed gun.

My eyes dropped to the speedometer. It hovered just shy of the seventy hash mark.

I looked up to find a second state police car pulled onto the interstate shoulder. It couldn't have been more than fifty feet from the first police car. It seemed that short a distance as I approached at nearly seventy miles per hour. The second officer faced the window of a vehicle pulled over on the shoulder. I traveled another few minutes, and then checked my rear view mirror to see a police car, lights on, closing in on my bumper. I pulled over.

The state trooper came to my driver's window, where, the U.S. Department of Justice reports, most Americans meet their police. He bent slightly from the waist to look into my vehicle. I greeted him through the open window with a smile in my voice.

"Hello officer."

"Where are you going?" he asked. He was lean, and white.

"Detroit. I'm going to a business meeting. I'm taking them this."

I showed him the cover of the *Fair Housing News*.

"What's the speed limit?" I asked. "I was doing less than 70 mph."

"Your speed was fine. You were doing 65 mph. But you failed to pull over into the next lane for the emergency vehicle."

I felt genuinely bad about that. "I always pull over for those," I said. "I am from a police family."

"Then you should be concerned about one of us getting hit by a car," he said.

"I was busy looking at your speed gun."

"But you also didn't pull over for my partner who also had his emergency lights on."

He held out his hand. His waiting palm was colored Easter pink and white.

I handed over my driver's license, registration and proof of insurance.

"Are you going to give me a ticket?"

"Yes," he said, turning away.

I was so angry, I hit the steering wheel with both hands, open. The force of the impact on that hard rubber steering wheel stung. I wanted to throw something, anything, but all I had was my bag full of papers. The car was in park, but still running. I switched it off just before bursting into tears.

Because of our troubled history with police, most African Americans distrust them, but not me; I love the police.

My father, grandfather, uncle and cousin were all sworn to the Detroit Police Department. I learned to drive on the streets of Detroit, smiling at the young black officers who stopped me for my errors. Many of them knew my family and I was able to charm them, and get out of a ticket, with the warning, "I am going to tell your father." Tickets were for other people.

Growing older I became a better driver and drove my cars less. I hadn't had an accident or been pulled over in years. This was so embarrassing.

But more than that, I was angry. The state trooper had sent mixed messages and me, a growing-old person, had not been able to multi-task on the two messages.

The flashing lights had sent the message "emergency, pull over, pull over," but the uniformed officer pointing a radar gun sent the message "check your speed, check your speed."

Doing both at once was against the mores of the road. I was bound to get one or the other of them wrong.

But why are these public servants doing two things at once? At virtually the same spot? I couldn't figure it out and then I realized, it was a sting. A trap. By the police.

That made me think.

In the time it was taking this officer to write my ticket, I wondered, had my father supported our family, bought us food, and clothes and paid the mortgage by tricking people? By victimizing people on the street? Had my father made sure his child knew her life mattered by doing things that told others their lives did not matter? First, intimidating them with his uniform, his badge and firearm, and then, legally robbing them, taking advantage of their confusion about what to do first, and next?

Most people will shrug their shoulders about this. Police are like that, they say. That's their job.

I know most people don't like police, but I love them. They are family.

This made me cry more. And scream.

Is this why my father was quiet about his work? He never regaled me with tales from the street. No heroics from him. The one story I knew was that he and his partner had caught a man between them in an alley and both fired. The chief of police never told whose bullet killed the man. My father got a week off, and desk duty for a month. Mama told me the story.

Otherwise, what I knew was my father wore his uniform to work (blue shirts: long sleeved in winter and short sleeved in summer). He left home at 3:00 p.m. and returned back at midnight. He put the .38 service revolver in his top bureau drawer and the bullets in a wooden box on his top closet shelf. Every other Friday was payday, when my parents went to the bank and paid bills. On paydays, my siblings and I ate popcorn for lunch.

I felt the state trooper approaching. I didn't bother to wipe my face. I wanted him to see my stress. My grief. My naked understanding.

I looked up past his black belt with the shiny buckle, up his blue-buttoned shirt to his face. A young face, maybe a new cop who was glad to have this good job. Police mostly come from families like my family: the working class.

I said in a voice thick with tears, "You're supposed to help people."

He thrust my papers, including the citation, through the open window.

"I'm supposed to be going home," he said.

I unfolded the citation. It was a full 8.5 x 11-inch piece of paper that looked freshly printed. There was no human handwriting anywhere on the paper. None. The contents: my name, his name, and the legalities. It was a misdemeanor: "Failure to yield to an emergency vehicle – stationary." According to it, the violation happened in Wheatfield Township.

It made me shake to read it.

Had my father given me money to buy pants suits that he earned victimizing people on the street? This is what the newspapers say people say. African Americans say this. Was it all true? Was my father just another pig?

I couldn't move.

I have a history of taking exception to how police officers treat me, and how I expected, as a police officer's daughter, to be extended professional courtesy. Sometimes I told police that in a loud and persistent voice. One time I delivered my criticism to the barrel of a shotgun.

■ ■ ■

IT WAS DURING THE 1970s. Angela Davis was on the run. All of America sought her, a light-skinned African American woman with a large afro. That generally described me, a university student, as well.

Detroit police stopped me, my boyfriend and another couple as we rode in a car on Eight Mile Road, the same road Eminem rapped about.

In those days, Detroit police rode four deep in marked cars, shotguns racked in the middle of the front seat. These patrols were called The Big Four. The four were always white men.

One ordered us out of the car. I was talking from the time I put my foot on the pavement. "Why did you stop us?"

"A bank was robbed by two couples who escaped in a car."

"It's not us," I said. "My name is Dedria Humphries. My father is Lt. Andrew Humphries. He works downtown at 1300 Beaubien. You got the wrong people."

"Shut up," one of the officers said. And he raised a shotgun.

I looked at it long enough to understand that a Detroit police officer was pointing a shotgun at me, the daughter of a Detroit police officer.

"Do you know who I am?" I demanded. "My father is a Detroit police officer. He is Lt. Andrew J. Humphries. He is in charge of the cellblock at the first precinct. We're on a date. You got the wrong people. We didn't rob a bank. "

He leveled the shotgun. "I said, shut up."

"Uhh, you need to lower that gun out of my face. My name is Dedria A. Humphries and my father is Andrew J. Humphries. He is a lieutenant at 1300 Beaubien Street downtown and he's not going to appreciate this. You need to lower that gun. Get it out of my face."

On my other side, my boyfriend finger poked me in the side. "Could you be quiet?"

I turned on him, looked him up and down. He looked scared.

I was too insulted to be scared. "This is police business," I told him.

Then I turned back to the shotgun and the police officer holding it.

"You need to lower that shotgun and show me some professional courtesy. My father is a Detroit police officer."

I wasn't hysterical. I was being reasonable. I kept referring to my father by his police title and formal name. I didn't cry, or shout.

Finally, one of the Big Four must have recognized my father's name or called downtown, or something. One came over and said, "You're free to go."

The shotgun barrel sank down until I could see the face behind it. Blue eyes cooler than Paul Newman's.

I held his gaze, seeing him, taking account, staring. He turned away.

My friends pushed me back into the car, and drove me, the crazy girl, straight home. My father and I had never talked about this event.

This was our pact: He was my father; he loved me, I loved him; he protected me. I took that out into the street.

I'm not crazy. I just expect more from the police. Because of that I was stewing in forty-year-old memories while waiting for the state trooper to deliver me a ticket.

At church we're advised to HALT: Do nothing when you're Hungry, Angry, Lonely or Tired. I was so very angry: at myself for not being quick in moving over one lane away from the working police. At myself for getting caught. At the officer for catching me. At my father who had continued to work a job that called his and my honor into question. A job for which I had loved and respected him. And which had given me a sense of self-worth I defended vigorously on the street. Angry with people who insinuated that the men in my family victimized others. And I was so lonely for my father, who I hadn't seen since his death nearly twenty years earlier.

There on I-96E, I sat not moving for several minutes. Checking the rear view mirror, I saw the state police car sitting there behind my car, still.

I felt the energy crackle between me and him, an electric current as powerful as the storm strike that brought Frankenstein to life.

Now that I'd been stung by a miscommunication of radar gun and flashing lights, and endured the past erupting into the present as I sat in a car on the side of the road, he wanted me to go on like nothing had happened. To move along. Get on my way. Go on with my business. Complain to them people in my world. Let them endure my grousing.

In due time – ten days, the citation said – tell it to the judge. If the judge would hear me. I might not be granted an audience because, really, this was not that big of a deal except to me, and this cop who wanted to go home.

In the rear view mirror I saw the trooper back up his patrol car, lights still bubbling. Perhaps he thought his vehicle blocked my view so I could not see when traffic cleared and it was safe to reenter the highway. The state police car was about 30 feet off my bumper.

Minutes passed.

"Motorist," his voice came over the loud speaker. "Please move your vehicle from the shoulder."

His voice broadcasted all over the highway.

"Motorist, please move your vehicle from the shoulder."

What would my father the police officer do with resistance? I'd been able to charm my father. And other police officers. All but this one.

This cop wanted me to move into traffic with my heart wrestling with things I didn't want to know. I was supposed to just move on, operate a two-ton vehicle with the fresh knowledge that my father may have, probably had, victimized people as part of his job. I was supposed to just move along. There's nothing to see here.

The key hung in the ignition.

In the rear view mirror I saw the door to the state patrol car open. The officer stuck his shoe out. Black leather.

Cops wear black shoes. Always polished. The lazy ones wear patent leather. Always shiny. I think it reflects on them, their attention to duty. My father taught me to shine my shoes with polish. "Puddin'" he called me.

The state trooper stepped onto the asphalt. His legs scissored apart on his way back to me. We were to meet again at the driver's window.

The state trooper's stride carried him closer. Just when I could make out his face – stern, frustrated, angry, impatient to go home to his little girl, a daughter or perhaps his wife – I finally understood what people said about the police.

Calm descended, a majestic eagle gliding into the front seat. I reached for and turned the ignition key, cranked over the engine, put the car in gear, and slowly reentered traffic.

Many Americans suspect the police, and respect them out of fear. I didn't. I don't think I ever will. I am hard-wired to love them. But, now I understand, a little more, about Sandra Bland in Texas, and what it means to say, black lives matter. ∎

JoeAnn Hart

Milkshaking

I N THE FALL OF 1975, Joe and I were at a block party in Stamford, Connecticut's South End, the old black neighborhood on the other side of the train tracks and Interstate 95. Joe owned a gently used blue BMW 2002tii at the time, which he had just bought on credit. An amazing feat considering he had no credit. But he was a recent graduate from Columbia University, had already ran for mayor of Stamford, and knew a loan officer at a local bank. So with no job, and no money, Joe had a late model BMW. With one arm resting on the open window as he steered with the other, we drove at parade speed down the street, which was not legally closed even though it was filled with large groups of people—all black, of all ages from babies to grandmas, to teenagers to moms and dads—and everyone had to move out of the way for Joe's fancy German car and white girlfriend. It was dusk, the air was loud with voices and music. Marvin Gaye's "What's Going On" flowed from a turntable that sat on a windowsill. A band was setting up equipment, running speaker wires around buildings and snaking them through open doors. Oil-drum grills were set up on the sidewalk, producing sweet and smoky smells, and metal garbage cans were filled with ice, soda, and beer. Older folks sat on folding aluminum chairs, the middle-aged perched on curbs, young bloods milled around, and children ran amok, which must have made the presence of a car not just annoying, but a hazard. People glared and Joe ate it up. He waved without smiling to a few people, and they reluctantly returned the favor.

I assumed that I was the real object of their scorn. This was early in our relationship, and I hardly knew what to expect from the black community. The white community, oh yes, I knew all too well, having lost both my job and a place to live in the first month we were together. Here in the South End I experienced what Joe did all the time: The knowledge that strangers might not like me for the color of my skin, and would make assumptions about who I was without knowing me. It took me all of a minute to see that the black community as a whole had as little tolerance for mixed race couples as did whites, but it was more complicated than a basic dislike of me and my skin, although there was certainly some of that. Over time I heard deeper concerns. Some elders felt that dating or marrying white folks indicated a lack of racial pride in their young men and women, or worse, self-loathing. They, of course, worried about their safety. Whatever the case, no one seemed happy to see me sitting next to Joe. But on reflection, even if I hadn't been there, parading about in a fancy car in hard economic times was in bad form. Joe was slumming, which was not lost on any of them. The fact that I might be seen as slumming was completely lost on me.

We had one face-to-face interaction at the party before we motored away into the night. A young black man walked towards us out of the crowd, and Joe stopped the car in the middle of the street to talk to him. He rested both arms on Joe's window and leaned in to have a look at me. He was thin, with a large puffy afro and a polyester shirt open halfway down his brown chest, the better to exhibit his medallions. On his fingers he wore silver rings the size of plumbing fittings.

"Where'd you get the pretty pink thing from, bro?" he asked Joe, while staring at me.

"JoeAnn," Joe said, by way of introduction, without looking at me or taking his eyes off of him. Joe was often reserved, even self-protective, in his interaction with his black friends in a way that he was not with his white friends, a semiotic dance of cool that served to respect space and face. After they exchanged a few gnomic comments on the scene – "Check it out…" "Heavy duty…" "It's out there…" – they performed a simple two-step soul shake and Joe drove slowly off through the crowd.

"Pretty pink thing, my ass," I said, and Joe laughed.

A few weeks later, Joe's BMW was totaled before he made a single payment. Not that he had the money for a payment. He slammed into the back of his mother's car late one night as we were following her home to Redding from a bar. Georgia had stopped her car on the dark rural road to get out and yell at a newspaper guy for stopping his truck to deliver bundles. She was just telling him how he could cause an accident in the middle of the road like that, and then we came around the corner and slammed into the back of her Cadillac. As accidents go, it wasn't a bad one. My head tapped the windshield because I wasn't wearing a seatbelt, but the Beemer's catalytic converter got stove-in, which in those days was enough to total it. Joe used the AAA number of an old girlfriend and had it towed away for the bank and insurance company to sort out. Georgia's Cadillac had an imperceptible dent on the bumper.

In the end, losing the BMW was just as well. Not only couldn't Joe afford it, he soon had his license suspended from an old DUI that had been pending in court around that time anyway. I didn't have a car of my own, but I had recently gotten my Connecticut license, so when Joe was able to borrow a car here and there, I began to do all the driving. Almost. Interpreting his suspension as being racially motivated, Joe took the wheel every now and again just to show them they couldn't keep him from driving. It turned out they could. One night, when we were driving through downtown Stamford, Joe got frustrated with what he called my pussy-ass driving, meaning, full stops at red lights and going the speed limit. We argued. "Let me drive," he said. Fine. I got out at a light, he got in, we drove one block and he got stopped by the police.

One block. Oh, the cops, they were always watching.

Joe got taken away in handcuffs. I tried to follow the police car, but they lost me, which Joe later told me pleased them no end. When I finally found the station, the officer at the desk lied and told me there was nothing to be done. This was before my parents found out I was engaged to Joe and severed our relations, so I drove all the way back to their house in New York, an hour away. Joe and I had no place of our own. For weeks, since our living situation abruptly changed when I lost my job, we'd been bumming rides and sleeping on floors and sofas not just in Stamford, but at his friends' homes in upstate New York and Boston, and on rare occasion at his mother's. It was amazing how many of Joe's friends accepted homelessness as a completely normal state. None of his friends would have been surprised if I had shown up without him, and told them he was in jail for a moving violation.

Regardless, I wasn't willing to sleep on Joe's friend's sofa that night without him. Joe was furious that I had left without posting bail, as if I had that sort of knowledge, or cash. He had used his one phone call at the station to contact yet another old girlfriend to bail him out. I didn't make that mistake again, and learned to carry a bondsman number with me at all times. Alan P. Fishman. I found his card in a wallet stored in a box with some old photos. It is one of the rare artifacts that survived from those days. And although I never needed to call upon the good graces of Mr. Fishman, Joe and I were stopped many times during the two years we were together. As Joe said, it just "went with the skin." Getting out of tricky police situations was something I had to learn on the job, which involved keeping quiet and agreeable when pulled over, regardless of which one of us was driving, regardless of what the stop was for. Keeping quiet and agreeable when the stop turned out to be for nothing, as when a broken tail light miraculously began to work again. Keeping quiet and agreeable not just for the police, but almost any time in public, even if someone shouted "nigger-lover" as we drove by. It was too dangerous to yell back, because then we'd soon have the police on our tail.

We were stopped so frequently by the police back then, that thirty years later, in 2006, when I returned to Stamford to find the library in a city I barely knew anymore, I had to roll down the window of my Subaru wagon for air. I had to keep telling myself that Joe was not there beside me. I had internalized the lesson that just being seen in public with him could be a dangerous activity in itself. I actually looked at my inspection sticker on the windshield to make sure it was up-to-date. My eyes kept darting down the side streets, looking for cruisers, but my worry was for naught. I arrived at the library unscathed. Of course. I was a middle-aged white woman in a station wagon. I had not been stopped by the police since Joe and I went our separate ways in 1977. For two years it seemed as if my life was defined by harassment. I cannot imagine having to live like that all day, every day. An entire life.

It would be nice to say that the times had changed, and that if Joe were in the car with me that day on the way to the library I would have had the same outcome. It would be nice. But a quick glance at the headlines across the country tells me that Driving While Black, or With Black – milkshaking as they used to call it in the South – is still a violation of some unwritten law, and Running while Black can get a young man killed. It is a gross injustice that has never gone away and could be getting worse. Since the November 2016 elections, it seems everyone feels entitled to express their own worst biases, as if shedding political correctness is now part of some white liberation movement. In the Massachusetts city where I live now, a young mixed race couple was driving through town last fall and a white male teenager on the sidewalk screamed "nigger lover" at them as they passed. And they kept driving on, without a word. ■

Clara B. Freeman

A Southern Woman Speaks Out About Black Lives Matter

'M OBSESSED WITH RACISM. My one desire is to expose it and eradicate it from the hearts, minds and souls of white folks; an arduous task that not even Martin Luther King Jr. could completely accomplish. While children are not born to hate, they are taught by their parents how to hate. Hate is a wall of ugliness worn like a shield by many white people. Some white people I have known in my lifetime have placed more value upon their beloved animals than they do a fellow human being born of black skin. If the tragedies of 2016 taught us anything, it's that the reality of racist hatred has reared its ugly head more vigorously and more maliciously since the dawning of slavery and Jim Crow.

I was born and raised during 1950s and 1960s in the Jim Crow South, and received an early education on the ways of white folks. Southern black children became intimate with white folks' demonstrative acts of a false and preconceived notion of superiority early on. Black people were automatically labeled because of the color of our skin. We were led to believe that we were a lazy, voiceless, and shiftless people who had little or no say in how we were treated and how we were forced to live our lives as Southerners in the flatlands of Dixie, the land of cotton. In fact, our school history books rarely had any pictures of people of color in it, unless it applied to slavery and George Washington Carver and his peanuts. In essence, it was a time where white supremacy ruled and colored folks accepted this notion although they were "free," with their minds and oftentimes physical beings bound to the white man's rules. Nevertheless, this blatant separation of the races could not keep me from knowing my own true self and self-worth. I defied what was being taught in school, and refused to live up to the expectations of how to live and what to believe.

The first time I really came into awareness and truly learned how people of color were viewed was when I was about eleven years old. I had accompanied my hard working mother to the country store to go food shopping. I remember loitering about as she made her purchases from the young white man behind the counter. After paying for our groceries, this young man asked my mother something to which she replied, "Yes sir." I was incensed. I remember telling my mama right there in the store that she didn't have to say "yes sir" to this person because she was older than him, and she was a grownup." My mother gently took me by the shoulders and ushered me out of the store without saying a word.

That experience awakened me to the ways of white folks, and how black folks didn't want to upset the applecart of how they were being treated. Although I was young and could not articulate it at the time, I knew in my heart that my life mattered, that the life of my colored parents mattered, and that all people of color mattered. I also recognized that this white attitude toward blacks weren't my truths, and did not represent the truths of an entire race of people. Of course, I know now what I didn't know much about as a child growing up in a somewhat sheltered lifestyle, that racism did not only happened in the South, it was happening everywhere. My parents, like most parents of color at the time, probably felt that in order to not rock the boat, they protected their families from retaliation by being respectful and cordial to white people. I decided I wasn't ever going to be like my parents. I was told that I came into the world screaming and hollering, and I'd like to think that even at birth, I was protesting.

By the late 1960s and early 1970s, I was more aware and observant of how things were not equal, and that racism was the foundation for which the majority of white America stood. Still, it was a time of hope for blacks when the Civil Rights laws were passed. These were basic demands for equal rights for all human beings, finally legislated and passed on the backs of millions of people of all races who lost their lives in the fight for freedom and social justice. White people in the South, who fought, maimed and murdered people who stood up and spoke out against hatred and bigotry, never accepted the fact that America is a country where we are all equal, regardless of skin color.

Dr. King became the poor people's savior, and black peoples' hope for equality in all things; their right to live and thrive freely as true

Americans, without being discriminated against because of the color of their skin. The Freedom Riders, many of them white, came to march in solidarity in protest against a white establishment that would hinder people's rights to vote. Medgar Evers, a civil rights leader and organizer was gunned down in his Mississippi driveway shortly after midnight, after a long day of fighting for black people's rights. Four little black girls died in a Birmingham church bombing. I was seven months old when a young fourteen-year-old Emmett Till was brutally murdered for allegedly whistling at a white woman in 1955, in the small Southern town of Money, Mississippi. Three young men traveling from the north to the south to help register folks to vote were found dead at the bottom of a Mississippi lagoon. I remember the anguish on my own brother's face upon hearing the news of his classmate's death, murdered on the street of a rustic Mississippi town by white guys out for a joyride; it was the night of my brother's twelfth grade graduation. We heard that his friend, who had been named valedictorian, was still wearing her graduation robe when she was shot three times in the stomach. A Mississippi jury took less than twenty-four hours to find them not guilty, and they would go on to live a life of white privilege.

I was in my teens when the soul singer, James Brown sang everything I was carrying inside my being, "Say it loud, I'm black and I'm proud!" At seventeen, I was inspired by the words of an outspoken activist named Angela Davis, who stood on a podium with a fist raised in defiance of the injustice carried out against the rights of people of color. This black activist was placed on the FBI's most wanted list because she, Huey P. Newton, Bobby Seale, Fred Hampton and so many other brave black revolutionaries of the Black Panther Party dared to stand up for people of color and against racists, including cops who murdered black men, women and children.

The twenty-first century finds America once again embroiled in race hatred and divide. The reality is that millions of people around the globe with brown skin, and who love the skin they were born in, must face the truth that racism has never died. Living with this reality, we need some questions answered in order to eradicate racism in this country. I want to know, for example, why white people are imploding from within with this seething hatred they've kept buried for so long? Why now? What upset the applecart of the privileged world of white folks in America? Why do black men and women have to wonder if they will be shot by a police officer? Why is white America so angry when black people and other minorities take a stand against hatred, murder and injustice? Why do white people think black lives matter so little?

Carol Anderson, in her book, *White Rage: The Unspoken Truth of Our Racial Divide*, says:

> The trigger for white rage, inevitability is Black advancement. It is not the mere presence of Black people that is the problem; rather it is Blackness with ambition, with drive, with purpose, with aspirations and with demands for full and equal citizenship. It is Blackness that refuses to accept subjugation, to give up. A formidable array of policy assaults and legal contortions has consistently punished Black resilience.

I recall all of the anger I felt toward white people as a young girl growing up in Mississippi. But, it wasn't just anger toward white people; I was also feeling a deep sort of pained disappointment in black people. I had witnessed how my parents and other black folk responded to whites and I wasn't happy about it. I was just a skinny little country girl, but I knew that I loved the dark skin I was born in, and I was proud of who I was. I had no reason to want to change that fact, and I wanted white people to respect me for who I was. It angered me that my people, for all intents and purposes, did not see who they were, and were accepting of and acted docile towards this racist environment. To be fair to blacks living under the umbrella of Jim Crow, I understand it was the sign of the times, and I get it, but, this did nothing to lessen the pang of injustice I was feeling. I kept this anger bottled up inside of me and it made me a "mean girl," to the point that I began fighting boys, girls and even my own siblings if they even looked at me the wrong way.

My parents taught my siblings and me what we needed to know in order to avoid confrontation with whites. When we went out, we were not to drink from white people's water fountains, swim in their pools or stray into their section of town. I remember an episode where this white property owner had a private lake, and we could see their families gathering for pool parties, food, music and swimming. Our parents had warned us not to trespass on this man's private property, but my older sister and cousins didn't take heed of that. One bright sunny Sunday evening, they went to that lake, made their way into that beautiful resort cottage, and had themselves a mighty grand time. That episode caused me to love my sister so much more, not only because she had taken an awful whipping for this, but because she had the nerve to defy white people. She was probably asking the same questions I'd been asking: "Who gave white people the right to tell black people what they could and could not do?"

There comes a time in our personal lives when we have to make the hard and oftentimes fearful choice to stand up for what we believe in. When we stand up, we're standing out from the crowd of those who might not think like we do, or who prefer to keep silent when faced with the probability of retaliation from the ugly hate mongers in our midst. We have to be brave to stand on the side of right. I wasn't always brave. There have been times where I haven't spoken up when I should have, but kept silent.

Not once, during those silent episodes did I sleep well. I felt less than who and what I am, and not worthy of the trailblazers who came before me, or the ancestors who fought and died for generations that fought for freedom. While I can't live in the hearts and minds of other people, the reality here is that all lives matter, but it's not white people's lives that are in peril. It is my black life, my black son's life, and other black mothers with sons and daughters living in this racial divide of the twenty-first century.

"We don't tell the truth about race and racism in this country and that's exactly why it's still happening," says Iyanla Vanzant, who is an author, Yorba priestess and television personality. She thinks that white people's feelings of superiority and black people's feelings of inferiority are at the forefront of racism, and until a meaningful conversation is had between the races, there will always be racism. I believe hatred exists because hate is a learned situation, and that white folks are raised to view black lives as inconsequential to theirs. Change will only happen when this old way of thinking is laid to rest. I plan to keep standing, keep protesting and keep fighting to eradicate hate and racism once and for all. ■

Erren Geraud Kelly

Loggerhead Turtle Skull...
After the Cynotype by Alexis Doshas

sometimes, i walk the streets
because i know if i stop moving
i'll become prey for predators
i'll become extinct;
god is my friend, though sometimes i
wonder if he hears me when i call
the cries rippling, echoing on
the waters, the turtle swims under

in the coffeehouse, my true habitat
i sit, listening to jazz or trance or dubstep
or electronic music, using any form of
art as ekphrasis, to strengthen
my own art, to toughen up
my shell, which is still soft
art toughens up every part of me
but always soften up my heart

the loggerhead sea turtle
has a life span of 47 to 67
years

the men in my family never live long
my father, daredevil he was,
managed to make it to 70
survived three automobile accidents
and three triple bypass heart surgeries

my baby brother, roderick
lived for 15 years waiting on a kidney
finally laid down 77on night
and made his grand exit

he told the world "fuck it"

as if life was a currency
that had lost its value
like the loggerhead sea turtle
i have brown skin, i am enormous
roaming the streets, like it roams the sea
my natural habitat
cops watch me, like undersea predators
cops watch me, like they shoud've watched adam lanza
before he walked into an elementary
school in sandy hook
opened fire and made kids eternal

cops track my movement
by satellite and gps, like
they should've stalked those russians
who bombed the boston marathon
and made sweet caroline
the mourning hymn of a broken city

but cops keep me under surveillance
because i'm brown
and because my pen and tongue are
liquid swords
words are the habitat i swim in
like my father and
brother, i know i will die
the men in my family
don't live to be old

but i can look at death, like a turtle
looks at larger prey
and laugh

cos i know there are
better worlds than this
better oceans to swim in
to make my mark, to leave my
legacy

the loggerhead sea turtle
has a low reproductive
rate
females lay an average
of 3 or 4 egg clutches and then
become quiescent, producing no eggs
for 2 or 3 years

the loggerhead sea turtle reaches sexual maturity
within 17 to 33 years
once, the turtles reach adulthood, their
formidable size limits
predation to large marine animals
such as sharks

i am fighting to exist
i am making sure
my name lives on
after i'm gone

after daddy died
i thought about kids
at first, i wanted a son
a nice little brown boy
who would carry on my name
who would have me and my father
inside him
who would be creative

if he wanted to play sports
i wouldn't stop him
but i'd prefer he
paint, write or draw
maybe play jazz
the way miles or monk did

the loggerhead sea turtle's
sex cannot be determined
externally until it
reaches adulthood, fully grown

i have been told i have feminine traits
i'm big but, i'm hypersensitive
i'm strong, but i'm vulnerable

in a coffeehouse
a man walks up to me and touches me
saying, "i'm just trying to be friendly"

i show restraint and do everything
humanly possible not
to beat him down into a grease spot
i have this thing about
men touching me:
it's a violation of my space

kinda like living on
the streets, isn't it?

survival of the fittest

i get up everyday
doing my best to be the lion instead of
the gazelle
i apply for a job and an interviewer
assumes i have a criminal record
never mentioning my b.a. degree in english

"you speak too well and articulate too good
for a black person"

some will accuse me of playing the race card
but that's only because most people
don't play the game fair

but i keep reading books
like they're oxygen

i look at women's breasts
for their fullness
their hips for their
roundness

i not only want a woman to love

i want a woman who
will keep the line going
who will swim with me
under the ocean and bring my kind
back from extinction

jason n. vasser

If/then

The European long gun introduced to Africans for substance
foreshadows their descendants placement in ghettos
inundated with corner gun stores and the introduction of crack

If it were not for
the trans-Atlantic slave trade
        or an anti-black ideology
or the killing, raping, then bringing
to kill, rape, and bring more—
        if it were not for names left on a shore

the picnicking of black bodies
resulting
in pieces of black flesh kept as trophies
        the hobbies of so many
is to go coon huntin

leaving stripes on the backs
leaving their bodies stacked
like logs readying for winter—

imagine if there were no such thing as a prison system
that uses black bodies as commodities for wealth
while the communities from which those bodies came from are left
with scraps to fight over like crabs in the bucket
using food stamps to buy crab legs for dinner
and the winner—is the hunter betting that the crabs would eat each
other
        or If black mothers didn't have to bury their young
        or If black fathers didn't have to bury their young

 or If black siblings didn't have to be parents
 or If black families didn't have single parent standards

Or if zoning laws were not enacted
keeping black families from the American dream
Or if blacks could say of their history as much as Jews that it
happened
without scrutiny –

then maybe, just maybe all lives would matter.

Karen Ford

White Privilege

TRY TELLING THE AVERAGE WHITE PERSON that he or she benefits because of white privilege and listen to the litany of comments denying it. The most common statement I've heard is the "I wasn't born privileged. My family was (whatever) class. We weren't rich." Those of us who understand the true meaning of those two incendiary words just shake our heads and walk away. We realize it is useless trying to explain what white privilege really is to folks who don't want to own up to it. Yet, I'm going to try or at least give you an idea of what it means to me.

Several years ago, former White Sox manager, Ozzie Guillen got into a pissing match with one of the sportswriters of a local newspaper that lasted several days. Under normal circumstances this would not be on my radar. However while watching the news, I heard a broadcaster mention that Ozzie's tirades were going to make it difficult for another Hispanic man to have the opportunity of managing a professional baseball team. I was so angry after hearing this that I screamed. My husband rushed into the room thinking that I'd hurt myself. Once I'd calmed down and told him what made me scream, he began to rant and rave himself.

Why is one person of color always made responsible for everyone else in his race? Why is it that whites take any opportunity to keep us from getting ahead by using the behavior of one person to condemn us all? Why is it someone white can do something, and it is understood that the behavior is by an individual and not an indictment of an entire race. After all, the man who shot up the theatre in Denver is an individual. The young man who shot and killed the people at Sandy Hook is an individual. The Oklahoma City bomber is an individual. Not once has anyone said that all young white men are killers or deranged. Why is that same reasoning not accorded to people of color? That's the million dollar question.

The original title of this essay was "Bobby Knight" because he is a perfect example of what I'm referring to. For years, Bobby Knight screamed, cursed, threw things, hit people and acted a natural fool on television, in press conferences and on the floor of the basketball court. He violated any number of collegiate rules and criminal laws (assault and battery immediately come to mind), and yet he has been revered by those in sports. If he were to indulge in that behavior anywhere else but on a basketball court, he would have spent more than a few weeks staring at the bars of a jail cell. Yet I never once, in the many years he coached basketball, heard anyone say that his behavior was going to prevent a white man from coaching college basketball in the future. Bobby Knight's behavior was attributed to one person—Bobby Knight. Why then are people of color held to a different standard? Ozzie Guillen, regardless of how you feel about his statements, represents one person and one person only—Ozzie Guillen. He is not responsible for what anyone else of his ethnicity does, nor is their behavior accountable to him. We are individuals like you with warts, foibles, talents and interests, and we should be accorded the singular respect that comes with seeing all people as individuals.

This is the luxury of white privilege—the right to be an individual without bringing an entire race along for the ride. ■

Michael E. Reid

Skin

W HEN WE ARRIVED IN KERALA, late in the evening after
a long flight, I felt as if I was coming down with something and had a near miss with the toilet. My husband, Bill,
thought it was because I had three glasses of detox juice at Dwarika's in
Katmandu. It was awesome! I should have known something was up.
The waiter looked at me funny when I asked for "one more." But there
was also a lot of coughing going on around me, and I just might have
been fighting a cold. Anyway, my defenses were down and I wasn't at
my best when the guy at immigration started to give me a hard time.
It helps to be at your best when facing discrimination.

No one passed out forms on the plane to fill out, and so we didn't
have any to present to the immigration official when we landed. When
we got to the head of the queue, Bill's agent smiled and quickly filled
out one for him, but I was thrown one and told to go fill it out on my
own. This is the third time I had an unpleasant entry into a foreign
country, while Bill (who is white) was greeted with open arms. Last
year it was in Sri Lanka. The year before, it was at the border in Laos.
I can still remember that awful feeling of dread, humiliation, and the
nagging question that seems to follow me wherever I go – why can't I
be treated like everyone else? Especially when I'm on vacation, away
from the States – and where all the locals are different shades of brown.

Discrimination by skin color seems to be everywhere in Asia, but
it's most obvious in India. In Delhi it got so bad that I shouted out an
answer to yet another question asked only to Bill by a hotel staff. Bill
turned and asked me why I was yelling. I was tired of being ignored
and wanted to be seen and heard. Invisibility and discrimination are
both blatant and nuanced in these places of former British colonial
rule, and where the majority of the people actually do (as it relates to
color) look alike. American blacks like me are certainly not exempt.

Photo spreads and ads in Indian magazines seem to be the exclusive domain of models with lighter skin. People in the media and Bollywood, whom most people absolutely adore, are invariably light-skinned. Darker-skinned Indians in the southern states like Karela and Tamil Nadu have created their own films and have established their own heroes. Bleaching creams are promoted everywhere. "You too can look beautiful and white" – the billboards read. And if you can't afford the cream, layers of talc will do the trick; that is, until you start to sweat. Faces have skin that is different from necks, which are different from hands, that are different from feet. Skin, on one body can look like the amalgamation of many. No telling what variations lay beneath clothing and out of sight.

It's staggering to witness and difficult to talk about. Pregnant mothers consume special drinks to ensure that their babies are fair skinned. Children are told to stay out of the sun, especially girls who hope to one day marry. Beaches are totally empty. No one is even thinking about getting darker, except for Europeans eager for a tan. It may not be surprising that online dating sites post specific skin tone requirements; but even job announcements include what we call "the paper bag test" in their list of qualifications for employment. People with dark skin need not apply. And it's all absolutely legal.

The good news is that there's an emerging consciousness about this unfortunate phenomenon. A conversation is beginning to take shape, initiated by Indian women who are young, gifted and "black." It's interesting for me (a Caribbean American) to observe this. It feels like the beginning of a renaissance, as if someone's looking west and taking our lead. A group of beautiful well educated fashion models who are tired of being type cast as "exotic" in their own country, has formed a coalition called "Dark and Lovely." They are lobbying advertising agencies and casting agents in India to see beyond their skin color and hire them too. Sound familiar?

But the solution goes beyond the advertisers. It sits in the hands of companies and marketers who are pandering to an ever increasing prosperity and social mobility. As a friend who lives in Asia said, "The problem is, you no longer have to live with your skin. You can change it," along with the color of your hair and eyes. By lightening your skin, you can become the person you think you want or deserve to be. Or worse, the person you are told you must become in order to be valued and have access to opportunity or simply respect.

No longer a secret, this slice of Indian culture is encouraged and reinforced by a complex system of discrimination once dictated by caste, and now driven by an economic prosperity influenced by the color of skin. It's 1960 all over again. This time on the subcontinent of India. But black lives are finally beginning to matter even here. And it's about time. ■

Mary McLaughlin Slechta

Leaving the Cave

RETIREMENT WAS THE SWEETEST GIFT of my life as an African American. For the past five years, I've stopped dancing to the unpredictable world outside the house. The working world where a white person, even a "kindly" one, might lob a grenade at any moment: trying to silence me with "humor" or by over-noticing my presence. And those were the recent years, the best of times.

When I hear people complaining about political correctness, I could throw something myself. I have vivid memories of being harassed as a woman, as a person of color. Over the course of my working years the battlefronts changed, the harassment more nuanced, but I fought back hard and loudly. Imagine each of these as an unhealed wound somewhere in the body and then multiply it: calling out the colleague who started a discussion group on *The Bell Curve* (no discussion!), the counselor who said I was one of the nice black people (expletives deleted), the union rep who lamented that "they"– crafters of an unfair evaluation–wouldn't let me retire with my dignity (don't get me started). The only time I didn't fight was when my blackboard was covered with swastikas and the Klan. In 1988, in a suburb outside my city home, my only choice was to leave.

I was a writer when I began teaching and never stopped. Never stopped writing, reading, being an editor, or seeking the company of other writers. The writing life developed me as a human being, made me a better teacher, and mended my injured soul. It didn't stop all the mental and psychological pain, didn't stop the repressed pain from manifesting as stomach aches, high blood pressure, and migraines. It did, however, like working with young people, provide for my "retirement." I left with my dignity intact, my humanity enlarged, and relatively hopeful.

It wasn't easy. The lowest points were when I had the terrible thought that my life wasn't my own. None of it. School, work, home.

Poetry. Surviving a racist terrain had forced me to detour so often that perhaps the idea of "choice" was laughable. Perhaps the school water fountain may as well have said "Colored Only."

The terrible thought may be the closest I come to understanding the condition of slavery without succumbing to despair: the terror of owning nothing, not even oneself. It is the loose thread that could unravel me, and I resist it by praising black achievement. We, not I, have made a way out of no way.

The best advice books on writing say, not to take rejection personally. I've never believed that entirely. The same people who wrote a petition to block my family when I was a baby, today step in front of me in line at the store, and just a few years ago mistook me for the assistant rather than the teacher. They run the government and control grant money and maybe tomorrow they'll open a document with my poem or story. I obviously don't announce my race in the cover letter, but I write as a black person to a black audience.

"Black people don't talk like this," says one editor. (Really?) *"Your ending offers no solution to [racial] conflict,"* says another, (I'll keep working on that). *"Doesn't transcend."* (Ouch!) The fact is I do take rejection seriously and revise/edit when an editor sends a reasonable suggestion. I *am* grateful to anyone who takes the time to think about something I've written, *but,* I also keep a small chip on my shoulder. My experience as an American tells me it's very possible that an editor is not interested in characters of color, situations involving race, black childhood, stories which might make them feel personally assaulted, blamed, etc., etc.

Archaeologists in New England have discovered stone shelters, self-made caves where elderly black slaves may have lived after their "usefulness" was over. What a bitter triumph to have survived slavery and to be "free" in such impoverished circumstances. I imagine the frailty of their condition, the aching hunger, the cold and damp worsening their rheumatism, muscles permanently strained from hard labor, blindness, depression at the loss of family and friends, the invisible scars of deep-down trauma. Was there any joy to be left alone, at last, or was it too late? The last bits of life wrung out of them. How can I begin to compare myself to those dear ones?

So lucky, such a gift to be alive and healthy. My cave is built of silence and private thought. It's lined with books that I never take for granted. I write almost every day and have stopped caring if part of the world doesn't find it transcendent, because I've transcended that part of the world. I communicate with very few people outside my family and close friends, and enjoy a community of writers, some of whom I've known for years, decades even, and others whom I've never actually met in person. I read my favorite journals, discover new ones, and joined the editorial staff of a press I admire. It's a safe and nurturing environment in contrast to the one I spent most of my life fighting.

I don't let myself turn bitter with what was taken from me/us or what was made more difficult. I've had a second birth, a reinvention of my engagement with the world and for the long struggle still ahead. ∎

Brittny Ray Crowell

How to Play Dead

Inspired by Jamaica Kincaid's "Girl."
Dedicated to Charleston and all of us.

This is how you name your child so they'll say
"no" only after seeing their face
Restrict your syllables like a haiku
Beware of "black" suffixes like –sha, or –tay, or, –ka
Lest your children become the sluts or thugs
they believe we are so bent on becoming
This is how you hold your tongue so they won't think you're angry
This is how you cloak and bind the curves of your body
so you won't seem like the slut they
think you are so bent on becoming
This is how you walk when you need to
cross the street without looking dangerous
– You don't.

Stay inside if at all possible
but even this will only protect you for so long
This is how you smile benignly to show that
you are not dangerous not too wide
bring the corners of your broad mouth in tight
do not bare your teeth (this is aggressive)
make your eyes soft and friendly, though they are dark
This is how you bow your head when they want to touch your hair
tilt you head forward, eyes to the floor
or just stand and make yourself still
pretend that you are not uncomfortable
because for you to be uncomfortable is dangerous
This is how you wear your hair when it's

time for business, lest you become a distraction
understand that your texture is one of curiosity and
curiosities and fetishes have their designated time and place

This is how you laugh when you don't really want to laugh,
because to not laugh at a joke at your expense
would be rude and dangerous
This is how you hold in a cry that is just building
in the corner of your eye
and the back of your throat like a storm
This is also the same way you swallow
all the words you want to say but can't
This is how you hug a man you love
when he may not come back
From the store
From work
From a walk
From a run (that of course, would be deserved.
under no circumstances run, unless they ask you to)
This is how you pick your words carefully
like fruit before they try to silence you
This is how you pray without getting shot
This is how you bear the entire weight of a
man with his knees upon your naked back
while your face is smashed against the earth
This is how you still the quiver in your belly and
spine when someone else has died once again
– You don't.

This is how you try to remain neutral as to not
seem too anxious or angry which is dangerous
This is how to be "one of the good ones"
This is how to keep the boat steady
This is how to try to play it safe
This is how to pretend to be smiling to not
show that the things they said, denied,
ignored, or questioned hurt you
This is how to shut up and keep your job

so you won't become the freeloading, dependent slut
they think you are so bent on becoming
This is how you make yourself small because
to not do so would be dangerous
This is how to be black, but not too black,
but black within reason
This is how to be that lovable, sitcom,
"I'm comfortable with you filling the
position of my only black friend/teach me
that new dance/phrase you all do/say"
kind of black which is not too dangerous
This is how to smile when that same friend
doesn't come to your defense
This is how you prepare for the worst
when you know that it may just be a matter of time
This is how you place your outrage on repeat
This is how you try to hide your anguish from your elders
to protect any spirit they have left
This is what it's like when no place
Not the street
Not the school
Not the church
Not the country
Not your home
is safe for you
This is how you die
courteously, slowly and elegantly
without a fuss
as they would have you do
But what if they still think I'm dangerous?
if all else fails
when they come for you
This is how you play dead

This poem was previously featured on *For Harriet* at http://soar.forharriet.com/2015/06/
how-to-play-dead.html#axzz4V0ifNA2r

Thelma Zirkelbach

No Seat at the Table

SHE NEVER SAT AT OUR TABLE.
In all the years she worked for my family, Minnie never walked through our front door. In the South, African American maids entered through the back door. They ate their lunches at a table in the kitchen, never with the family. My mother was from integrated Nebraska, but, despite her liberal Jewish upbringing, when she married and moved to Texas, she adopted southern ways. Although our family dearly loved Minnie, we never deviated from our community's accepted pattern.

My childhood in Austin, Texas was a time when blacks and whites did not mix. It was a time of "colored" rest rooms, "colored" waiting rooms at bus and train stations, even "colored" water fountains. On playgrounds "Eeny-meeny-miny-mo, Catch a nigger by his toe," was chanted as mindlessly as "One potato, two potato."

I barely noticed such things. I gave no thought to the lack of black faces in restaurants or swimming pools or movie theaters. That was just the way it always was, barely causing background static in my white privileged life...until the year I turned fifteen.

That summer I was to have an eye operation. I had suffered from strabismus since age three, began wearing glasses at four, and at seven had my first operation to correct my eye muscle weakness. The correction lasted for only a short time, so now I was to have surgery again.

Unlike today, strabismus surgery was an in-patient procedure. After the surgery I had to wear a patch over my eye and rest for at least a week. My ophthalmologist was in San Antonio. We would stay at the St. Anthony hotel, then the nicest hotel in San Antonio. My mother first considered leaving my eight-year-old sister Betty with relatives, but Betty resisted. Daddy was at work all day, and she did not want to stay in his cramped office during his long hours. Finally, with no other options, Mother asked Minnie if she would accompany us, and babysit Betty during our stay. Minnie, who Betty always referred to as her "other mother" said yes. That solved the problem. Mother was delighted.

Not so the St. Anthony hotel. I don't know if Mother contacted the hotel beforehand or if she just walked in with Betty, Minnie and me, but the hotel manager was horrified. Under no circumstances could a colored woman walk across the lobby of his prestigious establishment. Of course she could not occupy a table in the coffee shop or even ride in an elevator with white people. Apparently Mother told him about having one child who needed surgery, and the other too young to stay alone in the hotel. The manager had clearly never been faced with such an outrageous situation. He relented but laid down strict rules: Minnie could not enter the lobby; she would have to use the servants' entry. She could not use a guest elevator; she must use the servants'. He would probably have been happier for her to sleep on the floor rather than contaminate a bed meant to be occupied by white people, but he didn't go that far.

I don't know how Minnie felt about this. Insulted? Angry? Hurt? Maybe relieved not to suffer the scathing looks of the white hotel guests? She never said and no one in the family asked. We returned to Austin after I was discharged, and life went on as usual.

■ ■ ■

IN 1957 I GRADUATED FROM the University of Texas and went to work as a speech therapist for the Houston Independent School District. I provided services in five schools, all white, of course. The district employed twelve speech therapists, two of whom were black and served black schools. That spring, our supervisor suggested we have a workshop on cleft palate. We were thrilled when she invited a prominent plastic surgeon to speak to us. At first she considered asking him to have some of his young patients accompany him so we could learn about cleft palate speech first-hand. Then she changed her mind. "Parents may not want their children to appear before Negroes," she announced, her condescending tone a counterpoint to her cultured southern voice.

And so we had our workshop. We had expected lunch to be provided but it wasn't. At noon we walked across the street to the YWCA to eat. Not all of us went though, only ten. The black therapists could not join us. Even though the Y was known as a welcoming place, there were no seats at the tables for colored folks. The few other choices for food in the area did not allow blacks either. We later learned the two outcasts spent the entire day hungry.

■ ■ ■

THESE INCIDENTS SOUND "so twentieth century." Tables everywhere are open now, from truck stops to posh restaurants. Our president is black. And yet...the echo of racism lingers and all too frequently dominates the headlines. Do black lives matter? If so, how much? As much as white lives?

Is it appropriate for a black quarterback to protest the racial divide in our country by refusing to stand for the national anthem?

Racism reflects our deep-set fear of the "other," whether that other has different skin, different religion or different sexual orientation. It's a fear that traces back through countless millennia, to our times on the savannah when we lived in small tribes that didn't welcome strangers. Can we overcome that innate distrust by community dialoguing, better police training, school choice or no choice? Will the day come when we open our hearts and minds to African Americans just as we have opened our schools, pools and restaurants? ■

Wanda Easter Burch

Neighborhood Youth Corps Volunteer

I N THE SUMMER OF 1967, I volunteered to collect data for the Neighborhood Youth Corps' employment program offered specifically for black youth in downtown Memphis, Tennessee, in the Orange Mound area. Orange Mound was a subdivision built at the turn of the twentieth century on a 5,000 acre plantation owned by John George Deaderick. The old historic marker noted that it was named for the row of mock orange shrubs that lined the side yard of the Deaderick plantation, but the presence of an imposing early Indian mound at the entrance of the area would give reason for another meaning of that name.

This "Negro subdivision," mostly composed of small single family houses, had been devastated by poverty, bad public housing built along the neighborhood boundaries, a lack of jobs, and easy acquisition of drugs and alcohol. Pawn shops, shabby bars, and door-less schools with broken windows lined the streets nearest the neighborhood. These original houses were often filled with multiple children from an assortment of relationships under the guardianship of equally diverse relationships. The reward, for me, would be extra credit in a social studies class at Memphis State University [now The University of Memphis]. The assignment was an overt departure from my comfort zone. I had grown up in a white post-World War II suburb of working class families, primed for prejudice and irrational fear, but I also grew up in a generation seeking change.

My experience, and ultimately my reward, was life-changing. I had picked up an armful of questionnaires designed for teenagers who had expressed interest in summer jobs. The youth corps office sent me out the door to meet a fellow-student partner, and we were advised to travel in pairs and to report any problems. There were no cell phones, and we were expected to use our own cars for transportation. My "partner" never appeared. When I realized she was not coming then – or ever – I made a decision. I would go alone. I chose not to listen to the voice in my head that shouted rules, that recalled stories from the inside boundaries of Orange Mound, that incited fear. But I was afraid. I took a deep breath, pulled out the map, and began winding my way through neighborhoods of broken glass, trashed lawns, collapsed outbuildings, and unpainted houses, here and there a small house with Chinese lettering on a painted mailbox, my first introduction to a prejudice that drove Asian shopkeepers into black neighborhoods where they defended themselves from the hatred of two cultures.

I found the first address and parked my car at the base of a small hill. The single window shotgun house was unpainted but tidy. My hands were shaking and my knees barely held me as I gathered my clipboard, addresses, and surveys into my arms. I looked up and saw an elderly black man standing at the door. My legs were visibly shaking. The man moved back inside a little and pulled a ladder-back chair from a wall, and sat it immediately inside the door. "Sit down," he said with a smile. He asked me to take as much time as I needed to pull myself together while he went out back. He said he would come back in a bit. He did. I smiled back this time, and he pulled another ladder-back chair a little closer, across from me, and told me to ask my questions. His voice was soft and deep, like music. He offered some water, always welcome on a Memphis summer day; and I felt all the stuff that terrified me leave.

For the rest of the summer I visited at least fifty houses, and found myself having to give back a little in order to receive the information I needed. I ironed children's blouses in one house while the mother asked questions and completed the survey. I ran interference between a mom and her teenage daughter who had no intention of working until she realized she had a few choices on the kind of job she would have. Her mom had signed her up. Her boyfriend nodded, a final authority in her decision to say "yes." I braided young girls' hair while another mother completed forms for multiple teenage children. The heavy lard-like pomade covered my hands and stuck to the pages. I stopped at a corner store and bought paper towels. I went shopping for another family, and I was often invited to have a sandwich or biscuits and gravy, occasionally a side of ham and, always, sweet tea. Saying "no" would have been rude. And the stories! The stories came house after house. I began to ask more questions – how long had their families lived in Orange Mound? Where had they been born and did they see a future that was better or even different? Did they still have dreams?

Then the last day came. I had become over confident in my ability to be safe in Orange Mound, and I had never told anyone that my partner had never shown up. There was one more house on the list. But this time the neighborhood was different. There were no complete dwellings. The road was dirt with tall spiky grass growing between the tire ruts. Old mattresses littered the yards, and the stench of urine and sewage and rotting food was overwhelming as I drove carefully down the dead end street. The address was nailed on a board in the yard of a shelter composed of lean-to metal sheets, and, inside was a dirt floor that smelled of urine with a step-height rise of packed dirt used for sitting. No furniture. A stove in the corner. Some dirty food crumbs and dead rats on the floor. The woman was plump and pleasant. She ordered all the children to come closer as she nursed the smallest one. The children stood in an arch around me, some tugging at tattered dresses or shoving their hands into pockets of pants either too big or too small for them. None of them spoke. She shifted the nursing child and looked at each child individually as she called out their names. There were at least fifteen of them. Each had a different last name and she told me the story of each of their fathers, none of whom were part of her life or theirs. I was again drawn into the stories and asked more questions. She matter-of-factly shared her stories of seduction, drugs, alcohol and feelings of passion that wreaked havoc with her life and with her children's lives. Then she stood up and brushed her hands over her dress, brushing away the past like so many crumbs.

The interview was over, and I walked out the door, looking down, gathering my papers, walking the few feet toward my car, when I heard the heavy slam of the makeshift metal door behind me. Startled, I looked up. Between the door, now closed, and my car were maybe five or six teenage boys, one standing near the door, one sitting on the hood and one on the roof of my car, alternately throwing knives on the dirt road, picking them up and retaking their place on the hood or roof. The rest hovered around the edges of the road. I had nowhere to go. I could not turn back. I was on a dead-end street. I would not be afraid, I told myself. Calm took over my head and my body. This time my legs were steady. I walked slowly to the car, staring straight at the young men. I moved around one and slowly opened my car door and slowly got in. I rolled up the window and locked the door – slowly. I started the car, backed up, turned and slowly drove down the dirt road. One by one the boys slid off the car and walked away. Blocks away as I rounded the old Indian mound, I took my first breath.

Less than a year later Martin Luther King Jr. would be shot and killed just on the edge of Orange Mound, just on the edge of change. ∎

Quincy Scott Jones

We Are Assata

We are braces and birthdays
weekend barbeques
commuter traffic
and job interviews

beauty salon barber shops
the doorbell on a first date
healthcare homeless vets
rising murder rate

We are "Killer Wanted"
We are post no bail
come home honey
go directly to jail

We are warning lynchings
and church fire bombs
charred black child
cross in her palm

We are eating at the counter
We are staying in our seat
cracks in our head
burns on our feet

from street protest and bus boycotts
while grandma in the kitchen *don't you stir no pot*
and grandpa in his bottle *it's all for not*
still we march on arms in a lock

or hands on the car hood stopped by law
frisking our skins with a delicate claw
like master on the selling block bearing us all
auctioning out our womb selling off our balls

We are history
economy nickel and dime
We are the blackness of gravity
and the burden of time

We are animals
animus spirit and soul
We are the fossil fuels
 that make things go

the strike that slow the garden hoe
the quiet cry *no means no*

We are the crooked beaker the combative preacher
smart street sweeper and the secret teacher

the car that rolls on the investigation goes on
the Medgars the Emmetts the Seans and the Trayvons

We are Assata Shakur
We are America too
and if you're reading this
we are you

BLACK SPACES / BLACK PLACES

"No man can know where he is going unless he knows exactly where he has been and exactly how he arrived at his present place."

—Maya Angelou, *The New York Times* (April 16, 1972)

Alan Britt

Africa

(For George Nelson Preston)

Hungry, as in haven't eaten for days,
weeks, belly full of scorpions
from insults hurled like grenades.

The League of Nations reincorporated,
but the new League of Nations has a budget
that doesn't include my bursting belly;
the new League of Nations has bigger
fish to fry; meanwhile my belly full
of Aunts, Uncles, Cousins,
& distant birth parents doesn't
qualify me for the neediest continent
on this planet.

Their vision.

Not mine.

Sean C. Harrison

A Far Cry From Home

Far from the place where children played and all of life was worship
We were driven by biting, westbound winds,
The smell of the sea replacing the sacred odours of village life.

The ships' bellies instead of our cots and huts
Bore and caged us roughly like cruel lovers giving no comfort.
One by one we filed from boats to blocks–
A far cry from home;

The sounds of disenchantment at our leaving
Still ringing like tribal warshouts in our ears.
It was the elders and children who mourned us
For they were not strong enough to come.
We were not strong enough to stay
And neither had the strength to pray.

And all day as we worked, we heard in the distance
The gibber of apes, the lions' roar, the drums:
A far cry from home;
Trying to reconcile it to the silence of canepieces and cottonfields
Where whips cracked and no welcome met us
But that of early mornings promising fruitless toil and pain
And deepening fears of never returning again.

There was and it was indeed a far cry, a far, far cry from home.

Vicki L. Ward

Black Lives Have Always Mattered
Imani's Life Mattered

FOR A WHILE, I have been collecting bits of information to include in a book I plan to write about the Middle Passage, of stolen lives that came to rest in North America, South America, the Caribbean and elsewhere. I have long considered the plight of the lives of taken persons; attempting to put names, faces, thoughts and emotions to them from the point of being captured to their journey out of Africa.

It has been difficult to understand; to absorb their terror felt at the moment of capture and for the rest of their lives. I am at times consumed with a flood of emotions, and recurring images, painful thoughts and feelings of loss. That they survived on the hellish, heinous, and treacherous journey known as the Middle Passage was merely the beginning of what was to become a demonic orgy of degradation of black human lives for many years to come!

An entire race of people imbued by the Creator with rich dark melanin in their skin were deemed by those without this coloring as subservient to them. These dark skinned humans whose lives mattered from before their conception are indeed valued. Their reason for living with others who valued their lives, loving, and raising children, and enjoying the prosperity their forefathers built were declared less than human and valued only as property; whose life value became to only serve and prosper their captors, their masters. Were they no longer proud men and women?

Once you experience grief, you know how devastating and paralyzing the loss of a parent, partner or child to death can be. I have long questioned what it must have felt like to have a family member suddenly snatched away from you. There is a death in the family.

Visualize the fear and anguish Sarafina, an African mother felt when she discovered her oldest child Imani was missing. Searching their home, the village and the surrounding bush, she came to the realization that her first born, a beautiful, young, smart girl was missing and was most probably gone forever. It had occurred in this village to other mothers, and in neighboring villages. Their lives were now steeped in caution when going to the river or when straying too far from the village. Yes it had now happened to her baby, her dream; her heart's sake was no longer with her and would never be seen again. The despair she felt could not be soothed. She wailed day and night refusing food and comfort.

Her beautiful young black princess was of her flesh, of her lineage that indeed mattered so much to her and she was to be no more. For weeks, Sarafina's wailing pierced the dawn of the rising sun and accompanied the stillness of night. Medicine women, elders, and others sought to, but could not assuage the pain which pierced her core.

For her father Kunjufu, Imani represented his dreams for a child he was already proud of. To him she was a cherished young woman who he would someday entrust only to the smartest, bravest, and most handsome young man in the village. She was learning to cook as well as her mother, and to sew better than many other women in the village. She would make him a proud grandfather, with grandsons to continue his legacy. Yes, the life of this black girl has always mattered.

For Imani's brother Hakim, she was to be protected. Even as a young boy he was being trained to protect, and to provide for the family. He recalled at the tender age of ten fighting off a large water snake that had begun to encircle his small sister when they went to get water at the river. He entered that fight knowing he had to be victorious, because her young black life mattered.

For her older sister Aria, there was so much to teach Imani. There were skills for which there was no discussion, as she taught her tribal rituals, and lessons all young girls must learn on the path to womanhood. She taught her modesty; to become a woman of respect. She taught her how to cornrow her hair and adorn it with feathers and beads. Aria had begun teaching her the distinctive tribal patterns that were included in their garments. She was eager to have Sarafina by her side as the women prepared food for meals and celebrations. She wanted to help her sister learn which specialties pleased their father, and would indeed someday be favored by her husband. Yes, Imani was a young black woman who indeed mattered to her sister.

As for the youngest girl Amayah she saw Imani becoming the strong woman their mother was. She watched her older sister with awe as that delicate flower of a young woman went about her chores, soaking it all up with all the deliberate fierceness she had. Amayah saw her older sister become a young woman serious about what she was taught. She learned much watching Imani stand strong, yet humble when challenged. Yes, she indeed mattered to her younger and very impressionable sister Amayah.

Never forget their black lives mattered too. Remember the black lives that exist today in the twenty-first century are descendants of the Middle Passage, whose ancestors survived that heinous journey and arrived on the shore of a foreign land. They were considered chattel of bigoted racist businessmen who assigned prices to purchase those who had at one time been free to live, to breathe, and prosper with families, in a land of their own. Never again.

Now, they were viewed as not worth the kindness offered a stray dog. Yes, as arrivals to a foreign land, chained, beaten, starved, degraded, and raped, bartered for and sold on those shores, these black lives mattered then and always have. Why would they not? In the eyes, minds, and souls of these captives, their value as intelligent people, as creative people never wavered. These proud people with dark skin; the men, women, boys, and girls who were necessarily fearful for their lives and their futures have always believed their lives mattered. What was different now, they wondered? Why should their worth change? Who made that decision?

Yes, upon arrival they were shamed; women were forced to bare their breasts, men fondled them, examining their private parts, destroying all modesty. Children were sold away from parents, husbands from their wives. THESE WERE STILL BLACK PEOPLE WHOSE LIVES MATTERED then, and every single day, month, and year from their birth unto their deaths, and beyond.

■ ■ ■

IN 1994 I HAD A PARTICULARLY EMOTIONAL RESPONSE to the question of whether black lives mattered. As a West Coast native, I had lived in California for over thirty years before I traveled to Georgia, and Alabama. I recall clearly, and will never be able to erase the visions, the thoughts, the feelings of sickness and fear I had when I took my son to college. Our flight was bound for Atlanta, Georgia. I was floored looking out of the window of the airplane at the vast foliage that seemingly engulfed the city. Upon landing, we rented a car and headed for Tuskegee University in Alabama. I remember the highways were wide bounded on both sides by enormous growths of trees, and forests. It was initially a beautiful sight, though the density surprised me.

I was completely unprepared for the rush of raw emotions I felt on this journey, as I recalled the stories of slaves escaping never to be seen or heard from again, of lynchings, of lost and missing black individuals and families. These densely populated forests spoke to me first in whispers, and then shouted so loudly, I had to pull off the road to calm the loud chatter in my head, calm my rapidly beating heart and stop the torrent of tears shaking my body, and streaming down my face.

That was an experience I have never been able to erase from my memory. I have shared my experience with others who told me they had heard similar tales both from those who lived in the south and those who visited from other parts of the country. The era of Jim Crow, segregation, lynchings, beatings, murders, marches, cross burnings fights of class, color, culture lasted much too long as black people who have always mattered fought to be recognized as just that. History has recorded over the years those often nameless pioneering men, and women who alone, or with others stood, laid down, sat down, sang out, cried and died to protect the fact that black lives have always mattered.

Racism is an ugly scourge that seemingly allows the arrogance of one group to believe, assume, and dictate that another group of humans should live beneath them. They lack the understanding that the same God who created black men and women who matter, also created them. Now, though God gives humans free will, it is the ego that makes one group believe they should reign superior. These individuals are ignorant to the laws of humanity; and believe they have been chosen to reign terror over another group of people.

What many fail to understand today is that the Black Lives Matter movement is not new. This movement was born the day black lives were hauled malnourished, beaten, whipped, bruised and battered in chains from slave ships onto the shores of America. For so long, the inhumane atrocities African Americans have lived through from 1619 when the first slaves were documented setting foot in this country until today is not new.

The injustices that have been perpetrated on black people are numerous from when they stole the first people from Africa to this very day in 2017. The atrocities include the murders, lynchings, rapes, beheadings, burning homes and churches, bombing churches, killing little girls, and killing leaders in the driveway of their homes only steps away from their wife and children. This includes the assignation of a nationally renowned civil rights figure summoned to the city to fight for a living wage for workers to support their families. How long are people who are black and have always mattered supposed to continue demanding equal treatment?

Think about the masses that fled the South searching for a place to raise a family, free from harassment by those without pigment in their skin? What about ghettos created by racially biased practices in substandard housing, with overcrowding and deplorable living conditions created for poor people. These were places whites did not feel safe, yet blaming those black lives who still mattered for creating these living conditions.

Imagine having a massive fire fighting water hose turned on full blast pointed at you, tossing you down a street and into buildings like a rag doll? Well, black lives who have always mattered had water hoses turned on them for daring to stand tall, so that they can earn enough money to support their families, and not be harassed. They wanted their children to get an education, and have dreams to live, to love, and to prosper.

Some people get the Black Lives Matter movement wrong. It is human nature to want to belong, to nurture, to care for, and to link with those who have similar cultures and life experiences. For the clueless, check out the human condition: There is not one person on earth whose life does not matter. There is not one group of people who believe their life truly should be permanently subjugated to the will of another group. Not all law enforcement officers in this country are racists, it would be ludicrous to believe that, yet the law enforcement community, over the span of 400 years, has not recognized the laws of nature; that at some point when you poke the bear too often, the bear will let you know how much he matters.

Too many mothers and fathers have lost children. Too many wives have lost their husbands due to illegal and immoral profiling supported by police policies that have not included cultural diversity training and understanding. Black men, women and children have been treated as animals, as second class citizens by those who believed they could cover up their bigotry. Yes, these black lives have always mattered.

It seems law enforcement agencies in America have denied the fact that black lives have always mattered, and for too long they continue to murder, maim, arrest, and unlawfully stop individuals. The proliferation of cell phones has become a game changer as incidents of racial profiling are being taped and shown on social media platforms that spread like wildfire. These tapes are forcing police officials to hold their officers to a standard of conduct for all of its constituents, regardless of the color of their skin, language, or culture; to serve and protect all. The American judicial system and law enforcement agencies must change the way they engage African Americans, whether it is through police reform, sensitivity training, better hiring practices, and cultivating better community relations. How can people be governed or protected by those who have no vested interest in learning about the very people they are sworn to serve and protect?

Black lives who always mattered, including the thousands of broken, beaten, burned, and mangled bodies that were hung from trees, buried in shallow graves, discarded into swampy rivers, or riddled with bullets. Their lives have always mattered to their family and friends. Their lives have always mattered to me.

America, don't allow the phrase, "black lives matter," to cause you fear. It does not suggest that black lives matter more than other lives, or that other lives do not matter. It is a call-to-action to change the worldview that black lives matter less. *Remember Imani, her life mattered.* ∎

Lisa Braxton

The World I Didn't Know Existed

WISH ALL THE BLACK PEOPLE would go back to Africa."
With those words, my idyllic world was shattered. My innocence
was lost.

I was a nervous, shy child growing up in New England in the late
1960s. I favored sitting in my mother's lap as she watched her afternoon
soap operas instead of going outside to play. When it was time to enroll
me in Kindergarten, my parents weren't sure public school would be
right for me. They were concerned that because of the large class sizes,
I would retreat further into my cocoon. They decided to enroll me in
a parochial school with grades Kindergarten through eighth.

My mother dressed me in a brand new plaid jumper, folding the
Peter Pan collar of my blouse just so. She pulled up the color-coordi-
nated knee socks, and turned them down to an inch below my knee.
She checked the Buster Brown shoes to make sure they fit perfectly
for that first day. As my mother inspected my appearance her gaze
intensified making sure I looked just right.

She clasped my hand as she led me to the classroom in the little
brick building. I climbed onto my seat and found comfort in the
friendly faces that surrounded me. Because class sizes were small, I
found it easy to make new friends. After a few weeks, I was raising my
hand freely. My classmates began calling me the teacher's pet.

We began each day with prayer and religious study. On Wednesdays, we walked over to the church for chapel.

While in the third grade, my world changed. We made our usual
stop at the water fountain after leaving the church. Over the sound of
chattering, one of my classmates blurted out in a loud voice,

"I wish all the black people would go back to Africa!" Her eyebrows
pinched together like a knotted rope.

All talking stopped. A hush fell over the line of students as her
words lingered in the air. I instinctively searched the faces of the few

classmates who had brown skin and thick, textured hair like mine. Our eyes narrowed as we looked at each other connecting our emotions. Hurt etched across our faces, as our eyes grew wide with feeling. They looked as bewildered as I felt.

It was 1970. I was eight years old. I knew that I had African ancestry, but I didn't know why someone would want me to "go back" to a place I'd never been. I lived here in the United States with mom and dad, just as their parents had, and their parents before them.

When I got home, I told my mom what happened at the water fountain. When Dad got home, my parents sat down with me. They explained that my classmate most likely heard that remark from her parents and simply repeated what they had said. I felt my energy drain from my body as sadness took over. All the children had been around each other's parents at parent/teacher nights. This classmate's parents seemed like such nice people. I couldn't imagine why they would say something like that, or feel that way about black people.

Even though I was hurt by what my classmate said, I'd had enough religious training in my young years to understand the importance of not lashing out or trying to get even with her as children sometimes do. School went on as normal the next day with no mention of her remark by anyone.

Years later, I realized that the incident wasn't isolated. Whole sectors of society were in agreement with the sentiments my classmate had expressed.

As an innocent Kindergarten child, there were many things I hadn't learned or experienced. My parents grew up in the South under segregation laws. They chose to move North in the 1950s. They sought to protect their shy child by choosing the small, private school. By doing this though, they constructed an invisible wall in order to shield me from society's failings. They wanted me to have a carefree childhood like other children. It was their hope that I wouldn't have to learn about the biases and prejudices of the real world until I was mature enough to understand. However, my classmate's outburst crushed that hope.

I never forgot the incident.

I preserved it in my memory as a significant event and didn't tamp it down as just an insensitive remark. Not long after I graduated from college in the 1980s, my heart raced as the driver of another car attempted to run me off the road. That driver intentionally rode my bumper screaming racial slurs at me.

I was a television reporter in the 1990s in a northeastern Pennsylvania community with very little ethnic diversity. I received anonymous messages left on my voice mail account at the TV station from an angry viewer, shouting,

"You're ugly. You're ugly. Why don't you go back to where you came from?" Having once endured my classmate's "go back to Africa" taunt helped to prepare me for these encounters and others to come, but the pain still ripped at my heart.

I shared details about what I had endured with a woman I befriended in an adult Sunday school class. She simply said, "Pray for them."

I thought she'd flipped logic on its head so I asked her to repeat herself. She couldn't have really said what I thought she said.

"They need help," she said. "The best thing you can do is to ask God to work on them."

I dismissed the idea at first. I felt that I was the one who needed to be prayed for. I needed God's protection from such hurtful people. But as I began to think about her words, I realized the truth in them. I realized these were flawed individuals who needed compassion. The burden began to lift from my shoulders.

Ironically, my classmate, who yelled the racial remark at the water fountain, is one of the few people I've run into repeatedly on return trips to my hometown. Typically, we end up at the same restaurant or the same store in the shopping mall. Each time, we reminisce about our school days and trade notes on what's happened in the lives of our classmates and our own. Throughout these conversations, her outburst at the water fountain plays in my mind like a well-orchestrated movie score, evoking just enough tension to make me feel some anxiousness. But, I have never sensed any of the vitriol I felt from her that day so many years ago. I have wondered though, if she remembers what she said on that pivotal day. I doubt that she has any idea the impact it had on me.

I learned many lessons at my elementary school, some taught by the teachers and others by my peers. My classmate taught me that skin color was all the reason a person needed to feel anger and hatred, a reality that has never gotten any easier for me to accept. ■

C. Liegh McInnis

Woe Unto You Judeasippi

Woe to those who enact evil statutes and to those who constantly record unjust decisions, so as to deprive the needy of justice and rob the poor of My people of their rights so that widows may be their spoil and that they may plunder the orphans. Now what will you do in the day of punishment, and in the devastation which will come from afar? To whom will you flee for help? And where will you leave your wealth?

– Isaiah 10:1-3

Those that refuse to plant and water justice
will continue to harvest crops of chaos and destruction.
Them that mis-educate their citizens mangles and misdirects their
own future into a mass of muddy magnolias drowning in deceit.
Confederates who engineer a schoolhouse to jailhouse pipeline
will continue to handcuff and strangle their own development.
State legislators must be shepherds and feet washers
rather than pirates plundering the pantry for their own profit.
They ask us to tighten our belts while their bellies continue to bloat
from the fat of pork deals they hoard while the masses
    remain malnourished.
Our obtuse officials are obese with injustice, and democracy is
    dying from
the diabetes disseminated by these dysfunctional dictatorial demigods.
The cancer of classism continues to eat away the body of Mississippi
as the entire state is a petrified plantation trapped in the past by
fragmented funding and fueled by poverty plowed by
    sharecropper schools
that rarely teach students how to shower themselves with sovereignty;
how long will we continue to give teachers toothpicks and duct tape

and expect them to repair the state's dilapidated engine of education,
especially since it's been the legislators who have dismantled
    the machine
so that they can ensure enough laborers to man their fields
    of inequality?

Governors whose eyes remain clouded by Jim Crow memories
don't have the vision to craft curricula that liberate
children from the state's low-performing policies and enable
its work force to butterfly blossom into a rainbow of skills
that shine like diamonds illuminating a new day.
Yet, due to our constant gloomy forecast,
businesses don't come to Mississippi because
Mississippi keeps giving the business to its people,
and it's difficult to grow your own businesses when you are
fertilizing the soil with the blood of the workers.
Paying people peanuts will only perpetuate a Pandora of
    pandemonium
for it's a "dying wage" when people with jobs can't feed their children.
Forced to choose between paying bills and purchasing medicine,
most people's healthcare plan is a paper-thin prayer not to get sick.

If an apple a day keeps the doctor away,
will not investing in preventive measures keep the
high costs of healthcare from avalanching us into oblivion?
As the mountain of mental health is treated like a speed bump,
students and workers are left to die like discarded road kill
steamrolled by apathetic drivers of the legislative locomotive.
Mississippi is on life support because our lawmakers
    consume the comfort
foods of kickbacks rather than the nutrition of fully funded Obamacare.
Or, is it just that their hearts are made of the same stone as the Pharaoh
and have not the love to create an exodus from their history of hatred?
Yes, "let's go walkin' Mississippi" so that we can trample
the flesh-eating diseases of ignorance, greed, sexism, and racism,
and walk into a new land in which fairness flowers like ripe fruit.

And don't let their twisted tongues fool you—
these artificial aristocrats are an army of arachnid associations:
>   the chamber of commerce is a union of political pit-bulls,
>   the country club is a union of city-slick sheet-wearers
>   the Mississippi Manufacturers Association is a union of arm-twisters
>   the National Business Association is a union of blood-suckers.
It seems the only time the rich are allergic to unions
is when the people unionize against their evil.

Like rivers merging into a mighty ocean
we need many Mississippi Mouths Mobilizing as One Voice.
We need One Voice sounding as a trumpet blasting notes that trample
the brick wall of injustice.
We need One Voice pounding like a sledge hammer breaking
the backs of billionaires who build
their temples on the backs of the poor.
We need One Voice to echo the names of Medgar, Fannie Lou, and
Vernon Dahmer
allowing the power of our ancestors to become tidal wave
of righteousness.

If it is true that we reap what we sow,
then Mississippi will never yield good produce until we learn
to sow seeds of decency rather than casting webs of exploitation.

Kimmika L. H. Williams-Witherspoon

Not Just

Like Katrina –
Without the water –
Watching helpless . . .
Made hapless.
Waiting . . .
Waiting for rescue
Relief –
the *good guys*
To ride in on white horses
(not those with *white hoods*
spewing hatred & grime)
but rather, to those
to "make it right"
just
in the nick of time –
honor
our humanity;
stop
the insanity;
& save the day.

But for those of us
"pathologized,"
Ostracized,
Marginalized and then
Terrorized –
Time and time again –
Institutionalized oppression.
For some,
No relief comes.

Assault
Turned insult,
Just another,
Then another,
& another
in the action frame
or virtual
video game
of living life
all too real—
till the focus is made to shift
& the populace
made to forget,
& we return again
to the usual order of things
discounting
what we feel.
sentient
& intelligent but
born Black
& unequal
in America.

This be
"Slavery's Legacy"
Part II—the sequel.
Grotesque scenes
Played out before us
To control the people—
Gratuitous
Violence
Both, to,
& by us—
With booming bass,
& urban city's
"surround sound"—
From pleading breath
Hands up!

Don't Shoot!
I…Can't…Breath…
To bleeding
Silence –
Please…
Don't kill me…
Here,
The death scenes
Are *real.*
Where *Hate*
Is allowed to surface
Free
& surprisingly P.C. –
political correctness
in this *"Retro-Reconstruction."*

This
Is not just
innocent nostalgia.
Let's be clear…
They
are trying to take *"their*
America back"* –
One
Black
man
shot in the back
At a time!

And the crime –
We're left with
Faux Freedom,
Rehashed racism…
In this novo
Jim Crow/Jane Crow remix,
This is what it
Feels like
Right/Wright

Richard
To slip back
into *white*
noise!
Made
the *Invisible Man*
Woman
Child
Black...
Brown...
Native – colored –
Othered!
Not worthy of respect,
In their eyes
Yet
Warranting, as epitaph,
a #hashtag
After they've come to collect the body
& laid it to rest.

And we can't get mad,
mourn,
grieve,
it seems,
because they just won't
leave
us alone.

I am what I am
But for the grace of God!
I am
Mankind's queen.
The Black man
Is *the King's* king.
And yet,
There are still some
Evil
People who

can do these things –
Full of malice
& hatred
& disrespect.

Awww…
But it ain't over yet!
Harkening back to the parable
Of the tortoise and the hare
If we care…
build *community,*
dare to use our intellect,
"By any means"
Malcolm.
To "the full measure of our devotion"
Abe…
Shades of David Walker,
Denmark Vesey, Nat Turner,
Frederick Douglass.
Remembering
Garvey, Martin, Medgar –
We must struggle on –
We must continue the struggle!
Defy injustice,
Resist
the constraints that bind us,
work
till it's won –
To the last Black man standing
If we must.

I say:
When did *unity*
Get to be
a dirty word?
I say:
When will we reap
What our ancestors *earned?*

I say:
Stand up!
Speak up!
& be heard!
I say:
With justice
There is peace.

NOTES

1. Hurricane Katrina (2005) was one of the costliest natural disasters in the history of the United States ($108 Billion dollars in damages). An estimated 1,833 people died. More than a million people were left homeless in the Gulf Coast and in New Orleans.

2. Abraham Lincoln, "Gettysburg Address." 1863.

Ronnie McGrath

Flatline

We fall with the wounded rain / onto the dead embers of an immolated planet / skin of me blasted by the politics of media manufacturing folk devils / the puppeteers' fingers in many pies / always in many pies/ pulling on string theory/ pulling on lynch ropes / hypnotising drones with a scent of the magnolia trees obsession / its eyes of bullet holes swinging like the maleficent music of some macabre quartet in black face and minstrel mode / history repeats itself / again and again / like a hail of nefarious bullets / heat-seeking melanin / penetrating mela-skin with barcodes and nana satellites entering shakti / entering dark matter/ entering light/ Dendera's zodiac in chaos/ the melon man watered down / the melon man forced underground / the melon man shot / the melon man killed / Malcolm /Martin/ Medgar / MURDERED/ choke hold / choke held in the indefinite detention of servitude / their solar boat minds consumed by a conspicuous consumption / their solar boat lips misrepresented by the crude obesity of augmentation/ intestines of some hyaluronic shim/ a grotesque restyling of Nubian features morphed into dollars signs and thaumaturgical car symbolism / their pharaoh's nose imaged wrong / the black of their blue slanted / burnt sugar skin bleached out of the fold / filtered out of the celluloid night / where screens imitate the flickering shadows of primordial cave paintings/ reality in drag again/the weaved contour follicled/ the false fingering of a dissonant notation blemished/ the holographic universe concealed like our secret knowledge purloined / drapes of the censored eye pulled over the gaze like iron curtains / another man down/ down/ down/another man getting down/ down/ down/ with Gil/with James/ with Mayfield/ with Marvin/ get down black man /onto your knees/ your hands of oppression raised into the air/ where the stars hover as witness to your slaughter/ subaltern speaker of truth you/ civiliser of the people's rights you/ Ra's astrological earth child/ revolutionary mouth of some architectonic geometry/ get down black man/ beneath sunlight and Baobab tree/ beneath ship bowel/ beneath the sea level's reckless eyeballing / beneath Zong/ the dark moon falling with the wounded rain / entombed coffins of the sands sarcophagated floor /where a man overboard is thrown/ among the servitude of women/ the seventh extinction of him / into the iron lungs of dead sea water / O the carnage of Atlantis/ the fall of Kemet/ black Ark drowning in a southern tree/ I can't breathe/ I can't breathe / flat line/ ■

Bernard Keller

Today Might Be a Good Day

Today just might be a good day
to teach a little bit of
history.

Might be a good day
to remind the world
we were the first to die
when America stood against
the rule of one man,
that we fought to reunite
the "house divided,"
and the "war to end all wars,"
the battle at Pearl Harbor,
and on the tiny island of Iwo Jima,
and the "Great War" to "save"
the world.

We served in the Korean Conflict,
and the war in Vietnam,
the Gulf War,
the Persian Gulf,
in Iraq and Iran,
and Afghanistan.

We are buried in graves
from Boston to Gettysburg,
from Flanders Field
to Arlington,
from the jungles of Southeast Asia
to the deserts of Afghanistan.

We built the White House
and laid out the design of this nation's
capitol.
We were the backbone of this nation's
wealth,
we saved the agriculture of the South,
(despite being chained, beaten, raped
and lynched).

We took gold in 1908 in London
with a runner born to slaves,

in '36 in Germany against the
"superior" race,
in '40 at London,
in '60 in Rome,
in '64 in Tokyo
and '68 in Mexico City,
in '84 at Los Angeles
'92 at Barcelona, Atlanta in '96
and '08 in Beijing.

We made blood transfusions possible,
and performed the first
heart surgery,
and invented the traffic light,
the gas mask,
and the Real McCoy,
helped Bell and Edison to make
their inventions work,
and brought America
blues, jazz, r and b,
and hip hop.

Today,
might just be a good day
to teach a little bit of
history.

Go on.
You can look it up.

Ellin Sarot

Atlanta Night

Dogs stop, feet invisible in the shell
over winter earth; their whines, nose to nose,
flaw blank night. Noses lowered, their paws tap
the brittle cover, fret wet mash, heaped twigs,
their breath glows clouds strung in the night air where
paw-thrust leaves are sent flying to the same
trees, mute as gibbets, that lately dropped them.
Scratch, scratch – undoing the pebbled cover
insistent paws ferret what's under, catch
on brightness in dirt, some mother-of-pearl
button, cloth, and, freed, brush these from the pit
in which as they discover it they sink:
buried bone treasure – the skeleton small –
where the well-fed beasts lie down, stretching long
spines, burnishing their ecstatic shoulders
against the grave their rolling bodies warm.

Shuddering, legs luxuriously splayed,
taut backs lapsed on carrion, flanks heaving,
belly up they lie, exhausted, exposed
to the neutral moon glistening on snouts
that snuffle ribbon, torn, once worn in hair.
Suspended light gleams in half-closed eyes. Then
they stand; shake gloriously; sniff; then – run!
The noiseless zigzag of their pock-paw tracks
pricks the fragile shell as if wild nothing
were crossing the point between wood and road,
between adventure and house, beast and dog,
until, out of breath, tongues hanging, they slow

nearing home. From their bright fur an odor
steams, staining the long, wide night, and although
they stop to try, they cannot lick it out:
who waits for them will know where they have been.

Note: Between 1979 and 1981 twenty-four black children, mostly boys, were found murdered. A few girls were also victims. A news account of the discovery of the body of a girl
prompted this poem.

Mark B. Springer

Grade A Stock

ON APRIL 4, 1968, I WAS INSIDE my mother's womb the day when Martin Luther King Jr. was shot dead. Fast forward, I'm now inside the belly of incarceration seeking deliverance, determined not to place my lips on the cup of bitterness and hate. Eyes open to the contempt of others who don't share in my current position in life, nor my complexion.

My naivety deceived me. Born at the height of the push for civil rights by this nation, which was beginning to distance itself from the evils displayed on the world stage by the media against people of color, I only knew about the desegregation of the public school system.

Momma must have known. Every doctors' and dentists' office, and governmental assistance agencies we visited recognized us as black. I had no clue about the dividing lines of the world; I didn't know the struggle personally, but time has revealed a harsh conflicting reality.

The institutions that labeled and counted the races in this country, momma must have known. Was it her maternal instinct that sheltered me from racism and white supremacy? Or, was it her hope that Martin's dream, which seemingly gave new direction to this nation that the tone of our skin no longer mattered?

I was unequipped when I faced the adversarial system of criminal justice as a legal adult. In the classrooms I attended, we weren't taught any of this. Multiple times I've watched and listened to Martin, as the moral leader of our nation at that moment in history, share his dream of equality and unity for humanity. I searched my mind for the whys and in the eyes of, who? I notices that the labeling began way before me, as an American of African descendant, we've always mattered.

Daddy had to know. He had to know about the darkness surrounding Jim Crow laws and Black Codes, with all the visible hatred pouring out of the hearts of those who didn't acknowledge our blackness. He instructed me around the house, spoke riddles about the ways of life, but I couldn't understand his language then, and he never took time to explain.

So I was left to myself to seek answers to the many challenges awaiting me, and ran headstrong out the door of our home into the hills and valleys that called to me, wanting to fulfill my purpose with no direction. Childishly, I walked through the doors of addiction and crime, addicted to the crack cocaine that was pumped into my neighborhood playground. And because of bad choices, I caused the death of another.

As an adult black malefactor, I wasn't treated with equal dignity in the criminal justice quarter of American life. As a people we've been told, slavery is over. Since October 28, 1989, as an inmate and a ward of the state, I am a slave. Yeah, that's what Article 1, Section 6 of The Bill of Rights of The Constitution of Ohio calls me for the punishment of my crime. Yes, all lives matter, and I live my life now trying to make sense of the life I destroyed. And it took time for me to realize that my life also matters.

In President Barack Obama's farewell address to the nation, he spoke briefly on the problems of our criminal justice system, and the Jim Crow laws still operating today. My question is, should black men and women caught in discriminating circumstances such as myself hope we're not forgotten; that people still care, and help is on the way? As recycled blackness, property of the state's Grade A Stock, warehoused, we matter. We are the sons and daughters, fathers and mothers and grandparents of this one nation under God. ∎

Je'Lesia M. Jones

Nightmares

I SKIPPED ALONG ALEXANDER STREET, a slight breeze propelling my tiny feet through the humid Mississippi air. Beginning with the new school year, my parents had granted me the right to walk home alone from Saint Theresa's Catholic School, and I treasured the privilege. The 99 degree September temperature created urgency in my step, although injustice inflicted by the elements was no reason to complain about my newly designated independence. I understood my recent rite of passage offered possibilities. The tinge of anxiety that caused my heart to escalate was a gracious nod to the inherent trepidation that comes with freedom. I was, after all, eleven years old, and a sixth-grader.

The walk home via Alexander Street was a simple route, a straight shot, curving only once at the Interstate intersection, I-82, that ran through the city of Brandon. Mrs. Gibson, a retired St. Theresa's teacher, stood watch for me and the other schoolchildren to arrive at the intersection promptly at 2:50 p.m. She walked us across the congested Street. Southern hospitality included motherly responsibility.

I slowed my bouncy skip to a stroll, despite the sun piercing through the navy blue pima cotton uniform, and the sweat beads forming about my forehead. Somehow, my casual saunter helped garner bravery, and I began to sing loudly the curious Irish song the German nun, Sister Benita, taught the six-grade girls during music class:

In Dublin's fare city where girls are so pretty
I first set my eyes on sweet Molly Malone
As she wheeled her wheel barrow, through streets broad and narrow
Singing cockles and mussels alive, alive-o.

Alive, alive-o, alive, alive-o
Singing cockles and mussels
Alive, alive-o.

What a foolish, silly song, I thought to myself. *Girls selling fish on the street. Disgusting!*

I skipped past the two and three-bedroom wood-frame houses that opened into a progressive working class neighborhood of blacks, sprinkled with Asians, mostly Chinese and a few Japanese. The races coexisted amiably in the Mississippi Delta in 1963, unlike in the hills and backwoods of southern Mississippi, where blacks were brutally murdered, or in northern cities where residents deluded themselves into thinking racial problems did not exist. Brandon, dubbed "Mainstream USA" by the liberal press in the North because of its smooth integration of schools and overall civil race relations, had recorded no incidents like those of Fayette or Philadelphia, Mississippi. Brandon had an award winning daily newspaper that covered the civil rights movement with brazen objectivity, to the chagrin of some white folk who viewed the newspaper as an affront to their so-called "white supremacy."

One month earlier, my family had moved into our brand new four-bedroom, pillared house on Pine Street. Our previous home was a Victorian in a comfortable, black middle-class neighborhood in Brandon, but we were renters there, the new house we owned.

After his mother died when he was five years old, my father, Raymond, a college professor, had picked cotton and worked odd jobs to help pave a decent future for his family. My mother, a writer and an educator, believed that home ownership was a preliminary step to American equality; however, they both understood education was primary. With eyes as wide as budding magnolia blossoms, I had run down the gold carpeted hallway that brilliant morning into the bright room with yellow trim exclaiming: "this is my room."

Our new home was grand, the only house on a plot of land that took in a city block, surrounded by Bermuda grass on either side and a vast field of giant blue flag irises and wildflowers to the back. This garden of wildflowers and various iris species of crocuses, freesia, and gladiolus inspired what would be my lifelong love of flowers.

Looking forward to the Sealtest ice cream sandwich my mother had promised as a treat when I got home from school, I began to skip again. My sheltered world held no reason for anxiety. I approached Delta Street, the dividing line that separated the working class neighborhood from the more prosperous residential section populated by white educators, doctors, lawyers, business owners, and the only other black family, the Smiths. Dr. Smith was a dentist, one of merely three dentists in Brandon. This was my neighborhood.

The cumulus cloud-filled heavens began to darken, giving way to a menacing gray-black sky. My heart felt like one of those large catfish boats swirling into a merciless undertow in the deep of the mighty Mississippi River.

Suddenly, a sky blue Studebaker flickered in my peripheral vision. I glanced quickly in the direction of the sluggishly moving vehicle, slowing my skip with the glimpse. A grubby, balding white man stared directly into my eyes from behind the steering wheel. White men frightened me. Only two weeks earlier, on September 15, my family had gathered around the Magnavox television set, weeping at the news of the bombing deaths of four little black girls in the 16th Street Baptist Church in Birmingham, Alabama. I stared directly into the white man's face, but instead, visualized the face of Denise McNair, the youngest of the four little black girls preparing for Sunday school that hot September morning in Alabama. I had been especially emotional over Denise's death; Denise and I shared the same age: eleven.

Through the open window of the passenger side door the white man asked, "Want a ride?"

My body came to an abrupt stop. My mind flooded with questions: *Did those white men come to Mississippi? Is he one of them? Is Alabama that far away? Does he have a bomb in his car? Why did he pick me?*

"I asked if you want a ride?" the strange man said, his voice louder. He leaned over the seat of the sky blue Studebaker and reached for the passenger side door.

Sweat poured from my body. The white lace socks inside the mandatory saddle oxford shoes clung to my ankles like wet towels. My mind raced, my arms shook like the long spidery limbs of a weeping willow tree, but my gaze remained fixed on the ghastly white man behind the wheel of the sky blue Studebaker threatening to cause me harm.

I did nothing wrong. Neither did Denise. Jesus, help me!

"Yo' mama said it was alright for me to give you a ride. Come on, get in! I'm not going to say it again," the white man said.

I continued to stare, frozen, as I digested the lie. My mother had cautioned me on the evils of some men and their thoughts about young black girls. She had shared tales about her own childhood in the rural hills of Southern Mississippi and had sobbed as she comforted me on the fate befallen Denise McNair and the other little girls in Birmingham.

Mama said that the bombing was the Ku Klux Klan's answer to the March on Washington. She would never grant a white man permission to drive me home from school.

Without warning, the horn of a green Chevrolet Impala blew to the rear of the Studebaker. I practically fainted. I had not noticed the car approach. The driver of the sky blue Studebaker was forced to turn the corner. Seizing the opportunity, I leapt, then ran across Delta Street like a sprinter in the 100-meter dash and quickly conquered Colorado, the final street before my house.

I ran down Colorado when suddenly, in bold horror, the sky blue Studebaker appeared to my left side.

"Get in, dammit," the white man yelled as he stretched his body across the front seat and opened the passenger side car door with his right hand. His voice was fierce and firm.

I abruptly stopped running, and in a determined display of anger fueled by fear, swung my body around and hurled a large jagged brick I had grabbed from the curb through the open window.

You will not kill me! You will not! You will not do to me what you did to Denise McNair! You will not!

My thoughts spoke to my courage.

The rock landed in the middle of the white man's forehead. Blood gushed over his eyes, temporarily obstructing his view. He screamed and his right foot awkwardly hit the accelerator. The car jerked, then skidded as he blindly hit the brakes. He threw his hands to his face.

My feet propelled me around the front of the Studebaker and into the grassy lot in the back of my house across the street. I tripped on a shiny object protruding from the Bermuda grass, fell forward and landed with a thump, the wind knocked out of me. After a few seconds, I recovered and lay still, outstretched on my stomach, peering between the bearded irises and black-eyed Susans, praying the white man in the sky blue Studebaker could not see me.

My grandmother's favorite spiritual came to my mind:

The wind and the waves shall obey thy will
Peace be still, Peace be still ...

No water can swallow the ship where lies
The Master of ocean and earth and skies ...
Peace, Peace be still.

I breathed with my mouth open until my heart began to calm, saliva collecting into a cool puddle beneath my face on the soft Bermuda grass. Suddenly, a loud screeching sound rang in my ears, and I saw the Studebaker speed off down Colorado Street.

I turned onto my back and exhaled. Puffy cumulus clouds appeared in the crystal blue heavens, and the sun broke through the clouds like brilliant streaks of golden ribbon.

Denise McNair smiled down at me.

I smiled back. ■

Janel Cloyd

Our Names Remain Stuck in America's Throat

Our Names Remain Stuck in America's Throat
Or
America, You Call Me What You Call Yourself
Or
America, You Call Me What You Are

America,
Every name you ever called me
is tattooed on my skin.

*Nigger*Bitch *Slut*Slave*Chattel*Peon*Serf
*Vassal*Mammy*Workhorse*Victim*Captive
*Wench*Gal*Servant*Property*Lackey*Subservient
*Bondservant*Wretch*

I am running out of epidermis.
Running out of space on my flesh for your
white tears.
white angst.
white whiteness.

America,
You have left an indelible mark on my womanself.
Filleted me into an unrecognizable fish.
My once feet now flippers.
My once hands now gills.

Desperately trying to navigate the waters
you tried to drown me in.

America,
By now you should know,
My unanswered prayers
line the bottom of the ocean.
Peopled by my kin who dove
into indigo blue waves for salvation.
Populated by those of us you thought
were ushered into expiry.

America,
We will never die.
We will chant and whisper our calls
for freedom into the rapture.

Amelia Simone Herbert

Black Exodus

Everybody knows
all the Black families in Conshy
came through Caldwell Lane House,
first stop on Alien Soil
after making it out the Black Belt alive.

Grandpa saw his cousin strung up
on a cottonwood in Saluda, South Carolina.
Only his landlord's last minute plea,
"Horace is a good nigra,"
saved him from becoming poplar fruit.
He decided then
his progeny would learn to run.
Having a dream was a far-off luxury.
Anna-Mae didn't have no daddy
to chase him with a shotgun,
her mama was raped by an Irishman.
So they joined the sharecropper's flight
and never looked back.

They weren't the first runaways
to seek shelter on Lenape land
and they kept Conshohocken doors open
for migrants on the way to Philly.
They traded cotton field days
for labor on the river banks.
Horace cleaned the paper mill,
Anna Mae scavenged freight rails
for loose coal to burn in the stove.

3rd grade educated brains of the house,
she minded the bills while he made stew
with parsnips from the garden.
Their children never stopped running.
James joined the navy and set sail
to anywhere but here.
Ogilee traded 5 baby boys for Brotherly Love.

Daddy learned to swim in the Schuylkill River.
Like other men in my family, his life story
is a series of escapes from death.
Clarence felt the undertow coming
and knew he had to sink or fight.
Fought the currents all the way to a college degree
only to find out
scrappy boys don't dominate on Wall St.
This survivor from the home of Smokin' Joe,
who had running in his blood
and fighting in his bones,
worked the paper route at the crack of dawn
then roped a tie around his neck
and crossed a tunnel to One Liberty Plaza—
all so his kids could have freedom dreams.
Horace never told him about dreaming,
said Dr. King and all the others were troublemakers.
How does one dream
when nightmares reverberate through the bloodline?
When terror-induced fight and flight is the family inheritance?
When Clarence's progeny speak of Exodus,
he tells us, "This is ours cus we built it!
We got more claim than anyone.
We ain't going nowhere."

After mommy left him, daddy returned to Philly,
rented the 3rd story of an old stonehouse in Germantown.
Along the Schuylkill, all the mills are gone,
replaced by French bistros with rustic settings
and "converted farmhouse charm."

Only breweries still have a place
amongst Spring Mill Cafés and
Manayunk Watermill Condominiums.
Horace and Anna Mae's home is property of the state
since Uncle Edward couldn't pay the taxes.
But daddy still reminds us—

All the Black folks in Conshy
came through Caldwell Lane House
on the way to Philadelphia Freedom.

Fikisha Lois Cumbo

Seven Slices
Brookshire, Texas

IT'S 5:30 A.M. IN THE BROOKSHIRE BOTTOM. Uncle Ootnin'
(Hiriam), holds my tiny four-year-old hand gently in his as we walk
through the dew soaked grass field, its wetness kissing my legs, on
our way to milk the cows. *Carrw, carrw, carrw,* echoes black crows
sitting on moss-draped tree branches looking down on us, their necks
moving from one side to the other as we walk pass. The morning fresh-
ness that hangs in my nostrils exhilarates. Pecans from Biggie Bone, the
name we children call a huge pecan tree, lay all over the ground. Biggie
Bone is just one of the many pecan trees on my grandparents' property.
We hand pumped water from our well near our grandparents' home.

Papa Hiriam and Grandma Chaney bought over forty-five acres of
land at the turn of the century in the Bottom and more on the Prairie.
In the Bottom, Aunt Bobbi and Uncle Ootnin' lived on a part of it
near the Bayou, part of the Brazos River. Aunt Bobbi would bathe me
and then wash my hair in the same grey, oily water. The soap she used
made the water grey and oily because it was made from hog fat and
lye. I couldn't stand being in that nasty looking water in a big round
grey aluminum tub. I guess I was pretty dirty after running and playing in dirt all day. Aunt Bobbie and Uncle Ootnin presently had two
children, Roy and Eddie, who were older than me. Their three sons,
Hiriam, Bennie and Jack had yet to be born.

My brothers Perry, Sam and I would come to the country, Brookshire, every summer from Houston, to spend time with our aunts:
Sanka, whom I lived with, Mama Mandy and Aunt Hait' (Harriet)
where Perry and Sam stayed. Although we thought Aunt Hait' was
kind'a mean, Sam and I played at her house much of the time.

Sanka was a sweetheart. She and I would ride early in the mornings in her ole rickety horse drawn wagon to the Bottom. When we

crossed a dangerous high bridge full of gaps and missing planks which allowed a view of the rushing water some fifty feet below, she would say, "Thank God-Jesus Sis' Rete" and I would reply in my tiny voice, "Thank God-Jesus Bro' Pete." We remembered her late beloved husband, Veek Pierce, daily with these little names.

She lived on what was called "the Prairie" as did our other aunts. Sanka's house had a big kitchen, two bedrooms and a living room. In my room lots of stuff was stored overhead. Those hot, fluffy biscuits, maple syrup, and bacon or sausages always made the mornings smile. In my desire to get back to Houston, one time I wrote a letter to Ma'Dear asking to come home because all I was eating was "syrup and bread." Sanka found that letter and was deeply hurt that I would want to leave her. It was pretty sad because our aunts Sanka and Mama Mandy always gave us children the biggest hugs and kisses, which we never got from our aunts on Ma'Dear's side of the family.

Sanka had chickens in the backyard and a heavy fruit laden pomegranate tree that hung lazily over her front porch. She'd ring a chicken's head off. From the doorway I watched that headless chicken running all about until it fell dead. That poor chicken fed us at dinner.

I would walk through the Prairie to Mama Mandy's or Aunt Hait's house to play alone or with my brother Sam. I built my doctor's office on the side of Mama Mandy's house, and installed a telephone and an operating table. I found castor oil or what ever liquid available in the containers in the nearby trash pile, then caught big yellow grasshoppers and "operated" on them using the liquid in my procedures. At Aunt Hait's, sometimes Sam and I would catch bumble bees or wasps, then trap them inside match boxes. We'd then catch big grasshoppers, tie them to the buzzing match boxes and watch them race across the floor. Sometimes we caught fire flies (lightening bugs) too, and on sneaky occasions we'd climb up on the unfinished ceiling in her home and watch her oldest son, Boo Boo and his wife fight like cats and dogs, then make mad, crazy mind-wrecking, tear-the-house-down love. Hiding from them we'd giggle, all the while thinking how strangely they acted.

My daddy and other male family members dug out a pond some small distance behind Mama Mandy's house where snakes, leeches, turtles and frogs lived. We could see their heads bob up and down on the water's surface. One day my cousin, Orndoff just picked Sam and me up and threw us into the water. It was sink or swim! That was a terrible way to learn how to tread water, but we did it and got out safely. I'm sure at some point during those summer visits we got back in that brown water pond but at that moment we were plenty angry at Orndoff who was more than twice our size and age. We swam with the snakes and turtles and nobody ever got bitten. Leave animals alone and they will leave you alone.

Papa Hiriam and Grandma Chaney had fifteen children. My daddy, Emanuel "Bud" (1908-1983) was the last born when Grandma Chaney was forty years old. He grew up spoiled and selfish.

They lived in a house in the Brookshire Bottom that stood three feet off the ground, built that way to withstand the high water floods and hurricanes. My brothers Sam and Perry remembered that memorable flood when Papa Hiriam died. They said the water was high but the body had really become fetid and had to be removed from the homestead. The water was so high the casket holding the body had to be floated out on a wagon while my brothers rode out on horseback. Even the horses had to swim out of the Bottom. Perry and Sam were around six or seven years old. Grandma Chaney had long since passed away when my oldest sister, Agnes was around three years old.

Papa Hiriam and his two brothers each bought over forty-five acres of the low land in the Brookshire Bottom. The sellers probably figured it was not worth much since it bordered the bayou and flooded easily.

Papa Hiriam's brothers were hard living men who gambled, drank and chased women, and in the process lost their land. Little did anyone figure in their wildest imagination that that same ole low land, where a few dinosaurs probably perished, would bring windfall profits when oil was discovered in later years. The land that once was my great uncle's now looks like an oil refinery with so many wells and huge trucks hauling crude oil several times a day from the oil field. It sits at the apex of the oil fields. Our family, next door, only has eight active wells. What family feuding and crooked business went on before the business of the oil, with the lawyers aid, was finally settled. My first cousins actually tried to push daddy's children totally out of the inheritance. One cousin, Cheryl, had her portion totally stolen by the other unethical cousins who made phony wills for her grandmother, Mama Mandy and our Aunt Mother Illergert. Aunt Illergert lived to be around ninety-nine years old. She said her name was "Illergert Touch-Me-Not-On-The-Beauty Spot." But our aunts were dead and we could not prove the false wills. All those thieves are dead and gone now, but their descendants still get the benefits of their misdeeds.

Papa Hiriam was a short dark skinned, bald man with a patch over one eye. I only remember his dark bedroom where he lay in bed suffering from "sugar" diabetes. Sam, two years older than me, said he used to get in his bed with him and smoke on his pipe. The fire place burned continuously while his daughters moved busily in and out of his room tending to his every wish and need. He had been a farmer in his day. Ma'Dear tells us back in the day, they used to amuse themselves by telling ghost stories on the veranda at night when she lived with daddy and the family in the Bottom big house. She recalls telling the family how she saw a man pull off his work clothes, enter the bed by climbing over the end of it and going to sleep. To her horror she almost lost it when they all laughed saying, "Oh that was just ole' Charlie Dick" who had been dead for years. That scared her out of her wits and she fought off seeing spirits from then on.

Mother Illergert, Mama Mandy and Sanka told us when we, as adults, visited them in Brookshire as we always did when we had the Evans (Ma'Dear's side of the family) reunions in Houston, that their grandmother's name was Mariah. She was born in Guinea, West Africa and taught them words in her native language. To my chagrin, I did not record those words. Mariah was the cook on the plantation in the big house and her husband, Charlie, refusing to live as a slave, ran off spending the rest of slavery days as a maroon, living in the woods and in hollow logs. Somehow she managed to get food to him and three sons were born from that union. We heard the stories of an ancestor who the slavers tied a ball and chain on to keep him from running. Cousin Jack ,Uncle Ootnin' and Aunt Bobbi's youngest who still lives on the land, presently keeps the ball.

Papa Hiriam, the youngest of Miriah and Charlie's boys was born in 1864, a year before slavery "officially" ended in Texas. It was June 19,1865 when captured Africans, in a statement read in Galveston,-Texas, found out they were freed by Federal decree. This was over two years after the official Emancipation Proclamation. Black soldiers in the Union Army were in Texas to enforce this law. This is how Juneteenth became a celebration for black people in Texas.

Our aunts told us further, that Great Grandpa Charlie had Seminole Indian blood and that his father probably came from Jamaica,

West Indies since the Caribbean was the area in which African captives were "broken" before being sold in the United States. This is probably why he decided to live as a maroon, totally rejecting enslavement. We learned that Grandma Chaney's mother Amanda Baines, the cook for the big house was a mulatto imported from Florida. She and the Commanche horseman, She'sna, who worked on the plantation fell in love and had two children, Uncle Charlie, and Grandma Chaney (1868). I don't know how Chaney and Hiram met.

On the Prairie, downtown Brookshire only had two of three stores all on one side of the street. The railroad track ran across the street. We used to walk there with our aunt along what seemed like an eternity of heavily laden beige sandy road, the sand so thick it covered my ankles. But my most vivid memory was of a hurricane that happened while Perry, Sam and I were staying at Sanka's. She told us how to get out if the house blew down. We survived. But I'll always treasure my sweet days on the Prairie and in the Bottom of Brookshire, Texas with our loves, Sanka, Mama Mandy, Aunt Bobbi and Uncle Ootnin'.

My sister Chaney had godparents, the Moores. I always wanted some too, so I'd hang out at their home with Chaney whenever I could. Old Mr. Johnson lived in the house with them but he was kind'a creepy and strange. One day we sneaked into his room and rummaged through his cedar chest where he hid eggs he'd taken from the Moores. He had chewing gum and lots of stuff in that chest. The warm comforting smell of the cedar still lingers. Luckily we didn't get caught.

Her godparents were deeply religious and would take her to the Church of God in Christ, which we always called "sanctified" because of the manner in which members would sing, shout, dance and fall out. They had a testimonial bench called "the moaners' bench" and little Chaney and her friend Ruthie would sit up there and watch the moaners testify. That kerosene lit gathering with its haunting mystique saved many a soul. Sam swore that he also sat up there on the moaners' bench. Chaney didn't believe him. I know I wasn't on that bench but I do recall the ethereal, other worldly ambiance.

When her godparents brought Chaney home, Daddy would open the door for her because she wanted to come home and not spend the night at the Moores although they lived just up the road. One night after too many of those late night drop offs and waking him up to open the door too many times, Daddy told them to keep her over night next time. Chaney was small and fragile, like most of us siblings, except Perry, whose birth name is Carlos. I can only imagine her big eyes and tiny face then. Maybe, thinking of her tiny innocent face, we started calling her Chaney-baby.

Mother Dear, Daddy with all seven of us children lived in a one room house that my father built. Mother's parents built our kitchen addition. Ma'Dear partitioned the room by making a "croker sac" (burlap) wall then plastering it with newspaper to add strength. So now we had two rooms and a kitchen. Mother made cabinets out of boxes to hold the dishes.

Chaney tells of the "chinches" (bed bugs) that hid in the seams of our mattress and bit us while we slept. She would squeeze and pop them while running her hand down the mattress seam watching the little buggers burst and splatter blood they had stolen from us.

My oldest sister Agnes, and Sam, my brother next to me were born in Rosenburg, Texas at my maternal grandparents' home. Buck (Newell), Jean, Chaney, Perry and Lois were born in this little house on the Prairie in Brookshire, usually with a midwife assisting, but some of us were already born by the time she arrived. Ma'Dear was an amazingly strong, resilient and brave woman. She planted a garden and raised chickens. She knew how to shoot a rifle too, shooting swooping chicken hawks "smack dab" right out of the sky causing them to drop her chickens.

Buck and Jean were buddies who created all kinds of games. They built stilts from tall sticks and tin cans, then they climbed a fence, to mount the stilts. They had big fun walking around high in the air. They caught black birds with BB guns and sling shots; picked off the feathers and washed the birds in the pond. Buck turned the sling shots upside down, added a stick to make a cooking rack while Jean sneaked into the kitchen and took salt when Agnes wasn't looking. They fire-roasted the birds and feasted.

In Brookshire, the Baptist Church held yearly 'Sociations (Associations) at a big building with large surrounding grounds blanketed with food vendors like Ma'Dear. She sold fat hot link sausages. The women dressed in all white. People busied themselves tasting and feasting on all the goodies the lady merchants had for sale while much preaching and wailing carried on inside the building.

But times were hard and it paid a toll on Mother Dear and Daddy's relationship. He was gone much of the time working in Houston so they decided to separate. Buck, Jean and Chaney went to live with Daddy, his cousin Arthur and sister Aunt Babe (Cleopatra) in Houston while Agnes, Perry, Sam and I went to live in Rosenburg at Mama PG and Papa Allen's, Ma'Dear's mother and father. I was not yet two years old, so I do not recall the year we lived there before Ma'Dear and Daddy decided to try their relationship again because he kept encouraging her to move to Houston, so she yielded. I do remember riding at night in the dark in the back of my Uncle 'Watha's (Hiawatha) truck, filled with furniture and other goods when Mother moved us to a house on Elgin Street reuniting with Daddy, Buck, Jean and Chaney. We were so happy to see each other again.■

Adam Szetela

My Country, 'Tis of Thee

"The whole problem is really the blacks. The key is to devise a system that recognizes this while not appearing to."

–H.R. Haldeman, Chief of Staff to Richard Nixon, 1969

"There are more African Americans under correctional control today–in prison or jail,on probation or parole–than were enslaved in 1850."

– Michelle Alexander, 2010

My country, 'tis of thee
Built by bodies chained in slavery
For thee I mourn.

Land where black families cried
Land where runaways died
Broken land of black genocide
Let us never forget.

My country, 'tis of thee
Where white-hooded politicians
Manufacture criminality
To rechain those who Lincoln freed.

Nixon.
Reagan.
Clinton.
The war on drugs.

In this new Jim Crow
Black bodies harvest crops in a row

Or their prison labor stitches tags for white CEOs
Whose shareholders only care for what is profitable.

Steel chains.
Steel bars.
Black sweat.

In this land of the free
Our textbooks and TVs whitewash history
And conceal the lived conditions of reality
Where so many of my brothers and sisters
          still do not hear the bell of liberty.

Our struggle for democracy will fall
If we don't turn freedom for some into *freedom for all.*
And open our eyes to an incarcerated nation
that is the new guise of slavery and subjugation.

Cynthia Leann Jones

Will the Freedom Bird Sing?

Rusty chains clanging soul crushing sounds
Shivers down my spine
Walls surrounding like possessed trees choking faith.
Trapped with the gunshot illusion of
freedom staggering in my mind.
I am a prisoner of war can you see?
Ready for my freedom bird to sail me to liberty.

Oh freedom bird, oh freedom bird where are you?
Sing to me a cherry sweet sounding melody.
One that can pour in me the strength to
believe the sun is always shining behind a nightfall cloud.

Or the freedom that will allow me to sing at the top of my lungs
angels of heaven will shower down like
golden harmonies to stand with me.

Oh freedom bird, oh freedom where are you?
The chains are restricting me like carrying a
box of poverty filled with disparity; I need you freedom bird!
I am sinking and the hope inside me burned to my core.

Can you show me God's soothing silk love;
give knowledge that will overflow.
Lost in a world of forsaken wisdom and slicing words.
Chasing a dream without a vision.

Will you sing for me freedom bird? Will you?
In the midst of the gloomy clouds,

a bird appears soaring through the sky
her glossy feathers glistening like a smooth orange unfolded.

She begins to sing a song so gracefully
the chains around me slowly unraveled.
The mellow-richness sounds of her voice
dives into my soul and I was hearing a
church choir on an early Sunday morning.

My soul rises from spiritual darkness and
sees freedom's shimmering gift.
I listen to her while she sings my freedom song.
A mother who quilted comfort, courage, and respect.
A farmer who harvested the soil of justice and integrity.
A teacher who nurtured the culture, language, and wealth.
A land that was churned with firm and mighty hands.

Gold, silver, monuments, temples, towers and
farms unveil the greatness of their world.
Shoulder to shoulder they danced in high spirits,
sang lovely praises, and believed in each other.
And out of nowhere a powerful storm came.
The gray clouds hovered all day until the
sky opened and the rain fell in daggers of waves.

Trees shook like rags as the wind tore the city.
The sound of the thunder echoed in explosion.
Rain poured down the silent street,
lightning raping the land, and transformed citizens into slaves.
Deceived with blackberry wine seductive lies and a gleaming smile.
Rebirthed in a place called Captivity.

Families were shattered like glass
leaving them restless and reeling.
The sweat trickled down their backs and faces.
The blood of death and despair stream down
their hands from harsh and bitter cotton.

Bruises and scars line their bodies so deeply.
Hijacked their steel strong and courageous identities.
The tears of agony flowed down their faces
searching for freedom in high and low places.

Freedom, freedom where are you?
Freedom abandons them like a motherless child.
A wound freedom refusing to heal.
In their spirits and minds the truth of their freedom was crucified.
In their wrenching hearts silent and sacred prayers froze in fear.

The road to freedom seemed a mirage.
Roaring bells of the passionate voice
flooded the dirt roads of segregation.
Carrying the laws of Jim Crow on their rigid backbones.
The chanting and pleading were
packed in their suitcases to freedom.

Still, lost in the clanging uproar of the world,
it was a tumultuous hurricane who destroyed their humanity.

It was a constant torture like
fire burning across their chests – suffocated
with the angry wave of oppression.

Freedom, freedom they sang
Freedom continued to knife their
hearts over and over until it could no longer feel magical beats.
And they marched rimy mornings, days, and nights
It was a system constructed in cannibalism.
Still, they continued to prize-fight for equality in flourishing hopes
to save the new generation.

Education breathed freedom into a new treasure
It was an orchestra firing the mind
with a tirade of notes on a spring day.
Education provided the sand at the beach and
liberation against the waves.
To feel the glorious universe who gives brightness to the stars.

The graveling road of fear was behind and
the sweet strawberry taste of success was at the doorstep.
They said to reach the golden mountain and
a hardworking picture has to be maintained.
Education will lead to rich jewels and sweet honey praises.
Instead it came with the price of imprisonment with
the twisted and rewritten lies of history.

Tempted to trash the community told that is
the real enemy and deny the elegance in one's truth.
Drape ourselves in the wolves' rags and speak in their sleek speech.
Was this education worth saving? Or freedom worth treasuring?

Freedom bird swoops down and sings her last tune.

She trumpets: Freedom is enjoying
the rainbow in the somber sky
Freedom is having a kiss at the crack of dawn
on the face of the walking earth.

Now sing your freedom song.
Listen to the colorful melodies of
the world and have your voice become
blossoming dandelions on a summer day.
On weary days you are still fighting a
war in a world that is always
shouting and screaming,
"Hands up don't shoot, or black lives matter"
to bind in the soil of those who lost their freedom.

Unwind your chains, gather the hands of your people,
and walk on the freedom bridge.
Sow the knowledge, produce fortune,
and you have flowered into a freedom bird.
The truth of your freedom is within you;
it has always been brimming in your bloodstream.
Soar, the freedom is you.

Samantha McCrory

America

Police slamming Black girls to the ground,
Slaying Black boys with toy guns on the playground,
Choking out Black men in front of stores,
Suffocating Black women on police car floors,
Shooting Black men with the right to carry...
America the beautiful,
Praised for its opportunities, is quite scary.
Scary for Black and Brown girls and boys
Who shouldn't fear going to the pool or playing with toys
But should enjoy being young and carefree
Rather than witnessing beatings and lynchings
recorded for the world to see,
Wondering, "Will that be me?"
Scary for Black and Brown women and men
When death by police is justified by Black-on-Black
crime and gang killings,
Whose skin is pitted against blue suits chosen to be worn,
or the "vanishing majority, privilege born.
Oh say can you see,
America, we just want to be free.
Free to walk to stores in our parents' neighborhoods,
To be disassociated with from Crips and Bloods,
To receive educations without discrimination,
To be realized as true citizens of this nation,
To eradicate the groups of THEs,
To be treated with mercy, grace, and love.
These truths we hold to be self-evident,
THE Blacks, THE gays, THE Muslims, THE Mexicans
were phrases used by the new president.
As he ran for rule of this country, of which he now reigns,

He promised to turn back time and make her "great again."
Great again for the KKK, nationalists, white men,
Not for the Native, Immigrant, Latino/a, Muslim,
Gay, and Black American.
What about all of us "others,"
Those not seen as American sisters and brothers,
Those here since before the buffaloes roamed,
Those brought in chains against their will—far from home,
Those lured by the promise of pursuing "the American Dream,"
Those who aren't "batting for the right team"
Or those seeking religious freedom,
An entire religion blamed for the actions of some.
My country 'tis of thee
Our request: May we experience sweet liberty?
Lady Liberty towers with busted chains,
Overlooking lands where racism reigns.

BLACK LIVES
REMEMBERED / RECLAIMED

"A people without the knowledge of their past history, origin and culture is like a tree without roots."

—Marcus Garvey

Stephanie Freeman

Celebrate the Leaves

Round and round go the seasons' changes
One is in and then out
Like rain on a cloud-soaked day
all around sits change
but it is predictable
and ever present
so no one should be surprised
and yet when the winds blow fierce
and the leaves sail across the road
we close our eyes and try not to let the dust come in
but we are too late
the dust permeates
just a few specks
but just enough to cause pain
the bitter, unrelenting cold of winter
white and pure
the browns and reds of fall
bright and brittle
the vibrant hues of spring
fragrant smells mixed with annoying pollen
and who can forget the yellow heat of summer
with its sweat and play
to everything a time
and this time we celebrate the leaves
that change and fall and leave trees bare
when we see that all is the same

Shanna L. Smith

Close Quarters

In close quarters, a blood-battered history looms
casket weary and refusing to stay underground.
It was never quite buried, this *knowing*
this long-stinking lie—
a grown woman lying on a boy to her husband—
a believable lie that masculine brown beings, no matter their age,
desire the supple whiteness of certain women.
She was this certain woman on a steaming Mississippi morning,
who, targeting a boy, a throw-away out-of-town Negro,
sidled to her husband suggesting the boy assaulted her
     with a leering whistle;
that her creaming sensibilities were contaminated by a lustfully
     blackened soul.
Two men lynched Mamie Till's boy, bludgeoning and beating,
shooting and sinking him with chains to the throat
into an already lynch-dirtied river—before church.
Murdered in Money, Mississippi's murky Tallahatchie depths;
murdered again in the courthouse of Sumner, Mississippi,
     his killers surfaced free.
And, the lie also rose, a shroud unraveled, from a fifty-year-long
     fetid grave
perhaps pushed forth in the contemptuous air of newly elected bigotry.
We are in close quarters again
sharing public space with unrepentant hate, unpunished white crime.
This woman—her name—will be blotted, shamed among
     the dis-remembered;
yet Emmett Till, and his mother, Mamie, bear the memorial of
     the recalled—
their names a banner, their memory a disinfecting fragrance
in this ten acres, our quarter of American ground.

Marcia L. McNair

The Incident Revisited

Once riding in old Baltimore,
Heart-filled, head-filled with glee,
I saw a Baltimorean
Keep looking straight at me.

Now I was eight and very small,
And he was no whit bigger,
And so I smiled, but he poked out
His tongue, and called me, 'Nigger.'

I saw the whole of Baltimore
From May until December;
Of all the things that happened there
That's all that I remember.

"The Incident" by Countee Cullen (1925)

I STUDIED THE WORK OF COUNTEE CULLEN as part of my Black Literature class at Dartmouth back in the 1970s. The use of the word "black" was considered radical since there were still people who felt Negro or colored were kinder, gentler terms (as if blackness was a blow to the ego that had to be softened), but soon the term "black" fell out of favor. Afro-American was the new name until someone figured out there was no such country as Afro, and we were really Africans in America, that is, African American. We've been called many names, but there's one name that's always outlasted, outwitted and outplayed all of the others – nigger! When one of my white male students referred to me as "my nigga," in writing no less, I was offended, but not surprised. I had a very different reaction when I was about the same age as Countee Cullen.

Cullen wrote his poem in 1925. I experienced my first incident in 1965. What's brilliant about Cullen's poem is that he articulates with profound simplicity the destructive power of the word as it symbolizes the loss of innocence. There is a natural propensity, on the part of children, to express goodwill toward others. Suspicion, mistrust, and hate—these things are learned, and children are unwilling students.

After school let out, I often lingered on the school playground since my hardworking, single mom wouldn't be home until much later. Instead of feeling sad about Mama not being home to greet me after school like most of the white kids, I took advantage of it: I had the playground all to myself! No scrambling to stake a claim to the monkey bars or waiting in line for the swings. All of my competition had either been picked up by their moms or walked home. While they were doing homework, I was on the swings, working on my back kick—the one that would take me so high that I'd be parallel with the top beam. I never saw anyone get that high, and I was going to be first!

Here's how you do it: lean forward as far as you can, then push both legs back and then lean backwards lifting your legs as high as you can, same level as your hips, then repeat to build the speed that would take you up and up and up. And you gotta close your eyes, of course, so it feels like flying. I drifted higher than I had ever been. The wind swept away the perspiration on my forehead before it was born. I felt lighter, yet stronger than ever before, like I could achieve anything if I could do this, and I was about to until I heard the word, leveling me like a sucker punch: "nigger."

Immediately, my eyes flew open. Who said that and who was he talking to? Mama taught me to "mind your business," so I didn't bother to look around, especially since whoever it was couldn't possibly be talking to me. See, not only was I not a nigger, I never knew any. I only heard the word once in my household and that was when I was told, "You are not a nigger. You are a Negro, and don't you forget it."

On the upswing again, I felt my excitement rising too. I gripped the rusty chain links tightly and leaned back as far as I could. "Nigger." The word broke my concentration, cut into my mission to rise. Who was saying that? And what if, what if he was talking to me? I glanced sideways on the downswing to see Snotty-Nose a.k.a. Michael G. who had the reputation of always teasing or picking fights for no reason. He was poor like me, but worst off. His folks couldn't even afford tissues, so his nose was perpetually caked in snot, hence the nickname "Snotty-Nose." Our eyes locked briefly before my ascent, but just long enough for me to know there was no mistake—that word, that dirty word, was meant for me.

Surprise turned to anger. Why was he calling me that? I am not a nigger! Niggers are dumb. Me? I'm smart. Niggers are lazy! Me? I always do my chores. Niggers are ugly. Me? I'm beautiful! Niggers are losers. Me? I'm a winner! I am a Negro, and my people are Negroes, and there's even some folks who call us black. Grandpa doesn't like that word black, but Mama is down with it! I am a black butterfly flying high in the sky!

"Nigger." I stopped myself from jumping off of the swing and into his face with balled fists. Mama wanted me to stop fighting. It wasn't ladylike, she said. I repeated my promise to Mama silently—no more fighting, no more fighting, but Michael G.'s incessant repetition of the word was like a thousand paper cuts: a single one a mere sting, a simple annoyance, but more than one, in the same tender spot, driving deeper and deeper, it becomes a life threatening wound.

"Nigger." What? He said it again? I let the soles of my loafers drag across the blacktop until I came to a full stop. Mama always wondered why my shoes didn't last. Michael G. ruined my high hopes, literally. I felt special, was going to set a playground record, until this mean-spirited, little boy made me feel like I was lower than low, like he was better than me no matter how high I got. And he could drag me down with that fact always, until not only would my feet stay stuck to the ground, my entire body would sink into it, for racism is like quicksand that suffocates your true identity.

I looked Michael G. dead in his face. He grinned like the fight he had been goading me for was already won. I felt my throat tighten up, and my lips poked out like they always did when I tried not to cry, as the recognition dawned on me, something I could never articulate as an eight-year-old, but nonetheless flickered in my budding consciousness that no matter how icky and stinky a white kid was, he was still considered better than me, a nigger. I decided to call him a name back. I hadn't made any promises about name calling to Mama, and it was going to be something really bad, worse than nigger, a word that would hurt him because it had the ring of truth in it, a word that would freeze him into silence. It was then that hot tears of frustration welled up in my eyes. I realized there was no name to call him as bad as the one he called me. That's the thing about the word nigger. No other group has a racial slur that equals it. Whitey and cracker just seem weak in comparison; perhaps because they have no history of oppression, subjugation and shame.

In the late 1970s we so-called Afro-Americans, took back the word nigger, planting the seeds of what would eventually become a fully grown re-appropriation, in order to defuse its power over us. It became a private joke of sorts. We laughed at the irony of calling each other the word pronounced with an "a" at the end to distinguish our usage from the pejorative. Yet, in the 1990s, despite its new disguise as a term of endearment, the African American intelligentsia stopped using it; though we didn't necessarily condemn its usage by our less enlightened brothers and sisters in da hood who had taken the fight for racial and economic justice to the music, infusing the entire culture with a newfound radicalism that we thought ended with the civil rights movement. Their public use of the word declawed it. Referring to yourself, your friends, and your family as niggas became a pre-emptive strike. Hell yeah, I'm a nigga, so what else you got? You got *nada!* This word no longer had the power to hurt or destroy or control us.

It was a bad word *gone good* until—white people starting using it, *again.* They questioned if African Americans used the word freely, why not them? Why are there any taboo words? Women call each other bitches now, and gay people call each other queer, so why can't a white person use the word nigger?

Here's the issue: anyone can be a bitch, and anyone can be queer, but only a black person can be a nigger. It's a word reserved just for one race and not even an entire race, but that race of people who live in America. Many people claim we've come a long way in race relations in America, but is that due to progress or adaptation? Schools are more segregated now than in 1968 when President Johnson signed the Civil Rights Act. When the white male student referred to me as "my nigga," it was not meant in the same way as Michael G's use of the word. The student used the possessive my, just like African Americans use it to greet each other: "What's up, my nigga?" "What's the word, my nigger?" "What's poppin', my nigga?" Yet, I question why I've never heard any other race or ethnic group greet each other with a racial slur. I've never heard: "what's up, redneck!"

The student did not mean to degrade or dehumanize me directly. He simply established his privilege as a white man to say or do anything he wants, to never be excluded from any place, any word. Equality would mean I could refer to him as my cracker, knowing he would not be offended, secure that I would be protected, even if he did think it offensive. When I read the words "my nigga," they had an eerily familiar ring to them, evoking memories from the collective consciousness perhaps, of the days when my people did belong to whites who used the possessive to denote ownership.

When Michael G. called me a nigger on the playground, my budding sense of dignity was insulted. My parents, grandparents and great grandparents taught me that if we Negroes behaved perfectly and did everything right, we could prove to whites that they were wrong about us. Ultimately, they would see we were just like them, deserving of the same human rights. They believed what Dr. King said. They believed that not only would we overcome, but they would overcome, too.

I'm no longer a believer. My loss of belief has been a slow burn off. A white classmate came to my rescue that day on the playground over fifty years ago. Things have changed. I've adapted as has everyone around me it seems. When I reported the incident, the administration and colleagues assumed it was an African American student, which spoke volumes about what all races think about African American young people. Initially, only one person expressed outrage and, ironically, she was white. I realized that if adults don't recognize the problem, how can we expect our young people to?

Ultimately, I channeled the character of the African American teacher Mr. Sweeney in one of my favorite films, *American History X*. Mr. Sweeney uses a vicious hate crime as a teachable moment by assigning his student a research paper, which eventually leads to his redemption. I decided to do the same. I gave the student the choice of dropping the class or doing a research paper on the history of the word "nigger." He still failed the English class, because he did not do anything else that semester, but we both succeeded in *Life Lessons 101*. Unfortunately, this imaginary class never runs due to low enrollment.

Cullen the boy was brutalized by the fact that his open hearted, small sign of brotherly love, his smile, could be met with contempt simply because of the color of his skin, and that his identity would never be based on his words or deeds, but by this one cruel word alone. It was a hurt he never forgot, but one I did in the heady and steady race for equality that left me in denial about the cold, hard truth in an old joke: "What do you call a nigger with a PhD? Nigger!" ■

Bob McNeil

Text to Resurrect Revolution

Countee Cullen
and I are of this consensus:
Prejudice drafts psychopaths.
Their warpaths
transfix our people to many a crucifix.
There resides the reason why
my protest must never relax
from typing its attacks.

Addressed to your psyche,
my compositions are microphones for
Emmett Till, Michael Griffith,
Yusef Hawkins, Amadou Diallo,
Sean Bell, Ramarley Graham,
Trayvon Martin, Darius Simmons,
Jordan Davis, Renisha McBride,
Eric Garner, et cetera,
et cetera, et cetera.

Addressed to your psyche,
you can hear the murdered entreat:
"Don't allow another name to join
a homicide report sheet.
Don't allow another name to join
a homicide report sheet."

Addressed to your psyche,
the compositions
I've written are parts of a bulletin,

the passages transmit
to our terra firma's retina.

Addressed to your psyche,
my protest wants life
to evict the combustive
and discriminative.
If armed with you,
Lawfulness will live.

Abiodun Oyewole

Amy Spain

In 1865
the spirit of Amy Spain came alive.
She was only seventeen when
the confederates took her life
but they couldn't kill her dream.
She knew when she was hung
it was her call to glory
so this is the saga
Of a black woman's story.

Many of our young sisters will identify
with this brave young woman
who wanted to testify.
After hearing that freedom was near
she showed no fear
and proclaimed her right
to be somebody right here.

She celebrated a victory
she had prayed for would come
but the celebration was premature
the war had not been won.
The confederates arrested her
for crimes so they say
they put her in jail
and said with her life she would pay.

She stood tall on the auction block
where slaves had once been sold
now she was going to hang

because she acted a little too bold.
There was a big mob of white folks waiting to see
the hanging of this black girl
who cherished being free.

They thought she would wither
and die like a weed
but she stood tall under the noose
like a sunflower sprouting seeds.
According to all accounts
she didn't holler moan or scream
she knew they could kill her
but they couldn't kill her dream.

So when you think of this sister
who went against the grain
who would rather die like a warrior
than to live in shame,
think of this sister
and remember her name,
she's someone to keep you strong
and her name was Amy Spain.

NOTE: Amy Spain was a seventeen-year-old slave in Darlington, South Carolina who, mistakenly thinking that Union troops had liberated her, looted her master's house, taking some household goods and clothing. Her master, Major A. C. Spain, defended her in court, but she was hung anyway on March 10, 1865.

Anna Christian

The Man Behind The Mask

DADDY WAS A CHAUFFEUR for a family in Bronxville, New York; Mama was a stock clerk for a big department store in downtown Manhattan. We lived in a three-bedroom railroad flat in Harlem. There were six of us, Daddy, Mama, my two brothers, my sister and me. As soon as he came of age, my oldest brother left home to join the Air Force. A large extended family, at times our aunts, uncle, my grandmother and even cousins stayed with us when they came up from down south; my uncle when he returned from the army. Even though his sisters were older, Daddy was the decision-maker, the one to come to whenever there was a family problem. Our home was the gathering place, the place where if you needed somewhere to stay, you came to our small apartment and stayed as long as you needed.

Whether going to work, taking Mama for a night out, or going to church, Daddy was a sharp dresser. He wore a dark double-breasted pinstripe suit, white shirt, polished shoes and a hat cocked to one side. He was outgoing, gregarious, a smooth dancer and when he talked, he gestured with his hands that reminded me of an Italian. He had style. Everybody in our block knew Daddy.

Every evening when he came home from driving Mr. Bernstein, he'd park his employer's big blue Packard in front of our apartment building, climb the stairs to our apartment and knock his special knock. We would run to the door to let him in. No matter how late he came home, Mama would fix his meal and sit at the table while he ate. On the windowsill behind their bed, Daddy kept a bottle of gin and a bottle of ginger ale. Though he drank regularly, he was always in control. My mother and father were very much in love. Every Friday he brought her a pair of nylon stockings.

When he wasn't working, Daddy would lecture us on all sorts of topics, mainly how to conduct ourselves through life, and how to deal with the racism we would inevitably encounter. He lectured my sister when she began dating and when she wanted to take a summer job as a maid, he discouraged her from taking the job. "Don't want you working in nobody's kitchen." He lectured my baby brother on how to be a man. When a boy who lived near us gave me a cheap bracelet, he made me give it back. "When a boy gives a girl presents, he expects something in return." We girls were reluctant to bring boys home because we knew Daddy would lecture them on proper behavior. He taught his children to be proud. He told us never to say, "yes sir" and "no sir" "yes ma'am" or "no ma'am," and to always look everyone in the eye. To this day, his maxims have been ingrained in me. Though he had little schooling, he urged us to get a good education and a good job. My brother and I thought our father knew everything.

The title "chauffeur," is a misnomer. Daddy was much more than that. He practically raised his employers' children. Their family relied on him. He was on call twenty-four hours. Sometimes he would get home late and have to go right back out if they called. We couldn't make plans because we never knew when he would be called to attend to the Bernsteins. They were an integral part of our lives. Mr. Bernstein paid our telephone bills so he could always reach my daddy. For years, I didn't realize how much they intruded upon our lives though I knew from time to time, Daddy would bring home a large box inside of which were their discarded clothes. We looked forward to them; Mrs. Bernstein's shoes and dresses, their children's clothes—skirts, pants, shoes, shirts, and coats. They were in good condition and of good quality. Inside the blouses and shirts, the children's names were stitched. I wore mine proudly as they were unique from the other poor kids in my school. Working for the Bernsteins, Daddy faced many demeaning incidents. He told Mama how Mr. Bernstein invited him to a party. When Daddy walked in, he was handed a tray and told to serve the guests.

A close-knit family, we went on trips together, visiting relatives, or going to the park or to the beach. It was a happy time. Then came the day when for the first time in a long while, Daddy decided to take us to Jones Beach. It was one of his rare days off. Daddy sat behind the wheel of the Packard; I sat between him and Mama. In the backseat were my sister and her beau, and my younger brother. We were passing through a small town in the suburbs. We came upon a long line of cars. Traffic had slowed to a crawl. The police were stopping cars for some reason; however, when the cop told Daddy to stop, he didn't. Maybe he didn't hear him. Daddy drove slowly through the intersection to the next block and stopped. The young white cop came up to the car, yelled at my daddy as if he were a child, made him get out of the car, and put his hands up. Inside the automobile we sat, trembling. We were in an all white community and this was the 1950s. I don't know if they gave him a ticket. All I remember is that the day was spoiled. When he got back in the car, Daddy turned it around and we rode home in silence, feeling his humiliation. Soon after that, I began to notice my father who could always handle his liquor, began to lose control, not a lot just enough so that I was aware of a change. When he was at home, he seemed to lose his temper more frequently and he drank even more heavily.

There was a terrific snowstorm that year. Earlier in the day, though he wasn't feeling well, Daddy went out to shovel snow along our street. He died the next morning. He was 41. No one knew he was being treated for a bad heart, not even my mother. Paul Laurence Dunbar's poem, "We Wear the Mask" always reminds me of my Daddy and how much he struggled to maintain his dignity, and instill pride in his children while living in a society that didn't think black lives mattered. ■

Christine E. Eber

When a Man Loves a Woman

In memory of Percy Sledge (1940-2015)

They didn't let him within a mile of their sisters, let him
even think about sliding a leg over a lunch counter stool.

They made sure he never saw the front of a bus,
ate his popcorn in the balcony, reeking of sweat and urine.

But when it was time for a slow dance they couldn't wait
to hear Percy's voice. They'd grab their girl by the waist,
pull her close and rock to his music
'til they thought they'd never love another.

He unlocked that lovin' feelin' in them night after night
wherever they danced to his song, be they black, white,
young, old.

Slow dancing to his music, they didn't think about
who belonged where, or who had the right to what.
They just thought about who they had in their arms
and how to do her no wrong.

J. Kates

Leroy and I

I N 1956, FOUR OF US SAT at a table made by our desks pushed together in a sixth-grade classroom of the brand-new North Street School in White Plains, New York. There was Brenda Philbrick, the daughter of an FBI celebrity who churned wonderful home-made ice cream in their shady suburban house in a neighborhood called Prospect Park. There was Rocky Magnotta, the only friend of mine who lived not in a house of his own, but in an apartment in a square red-brick building at the foot of Longview Avenue. I was fascinated by that, and by the intimacy of his family's life. And there was Leroy Johnson. I never visited Leroy at home. I didn't even know where he lived exactly, but likely in the "Projects," a large apartment complex downtown, which had recently been built in a sweep of what was then called urban renewal. We were friends in school, but not beyond. In White Plains, this was as much a matter of class as it was of race.

Starting in seventh grade, I went off to private school, returning to a brand-new White Plains High School as a tenth grader in 1960. Brenda and her family had long since moved to New Hampshire. Rocky and I hardly spoke to each other during our high school years. We moved in different circles and it was a very big school. It wasn't until our twentieth high-school reunion that we renewed a friendship that still endures. Leroy's path did not cross mine again, except when, as the editor of the yearbook, I monitored the senior pictures. In his, he's wearing glasses (something even those of us who normally wore glasses didn't always do in formal photographs), smiling with a wide, gap-toothed smile. He graduated with our class in 1963, the same year I registered with the local Selective Service Board for the draft into the United States Armed Services, as every male of my generation after World War II and Korea did when he turned eighteen.

In fall 1968, I applied for status as a conscientious objector from the White Plains draft board. Hometown boards retained jurisdiction over those who had registered there, even after they moved away, and those were the days before a random lottery system. Local boards had total discretion over whom they picked to be conscripted, and whom they left alone. My board was not unusual for its kind, made up of very old, very white men, probably volunteers from veterans' groups. After an interview with them, I wrote up a memorandum, which reads, in part:

One board member asked me where I lived. I replied, "Rochester, New York."

"No," he said. "Where did you live in White Plains?"

The board chairman and I replied simultaneously, "Ogden Avenue."

"Where's that?" one member asked.

Another replied, "In the Highlands. Right near where I live..."

The chairman then said, "We got your marks from your school anyhow, and you are a very good student. Your marks were very good."

The chairman then said, "It looks like we can give him his I-0. Are you willing to do alternate service?"

I said yes again, and asked if I would be permitted to choose my alternate service.

The chairman said, "Yes, as long as it's outside your area; that is, as long as it's not in White Plains."

I asked to see a list of available alternate services, and the chairman called a female assistant or secretary who was outside the room. She stated that she had such a list, but that the ruling of the Selective Service only allowed a 1-0 classification on religious grounds.

The chairman then asked to see the new regulations, and the secretary brought them and read the relevant passage (which she pointed out) to the board. The passage concerned the non-eligibility of applicants on political, sociological or personal moral grounds.

The chairman said, "Then the new law only allows Quakers and Seventh Day Adventists?"

The chairman of the board then told me that I would have to be classified 1-A, but that I ought to appeal. I asked him the procedures of appeal. He told me, once again advising me to appeal my case.

I was then dismissed, and one of the board members called after me, "Good luck!"

In Rochester at that time, nominally in graduate school, I was actively working with draft counseling, coaching others how to stay out of the army, out of the growing catastrophe of Vietnam. We were trained by the American Friends Service Committee in legal and political maneuvers. We knew all too well how race and class were used to classify young men, what the Selective Service itself called "channeling" poor and minority men into service while richer white men were encouraged to stay in school or volunteer for officer training. Although we began from positions of principle, we encouraged almost anything that kept a young man out of the military machinery. Each local Selective Service board had a quota of manpower to fill, and back in White Plains a large pool of eligible poor people of color supplied the draft. I refused a student deferment and pursued my appeal on the grounds of personal conscientious objection. With a bus load of others, I went through an all-day pre-induction physical examination in Buffalo.

A year went by. I moved to Massachusetts, and, having been refused my conscientious-objection status, was notified by the board in White Plains that I was scheduled for induction into the armed forces on a certain date. I wrote a letter to the board informing them that I would refuse induction if called, and I never showed up for the date. Another year went by, and the board did not test my will. They did not call me again. My lawyer through all these years, Joan Goldberg, asked me if I wanted to pursue the case actively or just let it drop. My ambiguous reply was to send her my draft card in a bouquet of flowers. In 1971, I aged out of the system, and went on with the rest of my life.

Leroy Johnson was not so lucky. He went to Vietnam.

He died there.

I learned that simple fact long before visiting the Memorial Wall in Washington, DC, where the exact date of his death, February 1, 1968, is listed, probably having heard the news at a high school reunion. The information available at the Wall is eloquent. The records reveal that Leroy had actually been a couple of years older than the rest of us at the sixth-grade table, that he had since moved to New York City, and that he had indeed been drafted. His tour of duty began on January 12 – he survived less than three weeks in country.

Okay, okay. Leroy was dead even before I went before my draft board in the fall. That's chronology. And tens of thousands of other young men died in Vietnam. But Leroy Johnson has always stood symbolically for the unknown man who went to Vietnam in my place. Knowing his fate, I would not have changed any of my anti-war activities at all – in fact, I might have intensified them – but that does not make me less conscious of the cost of the freedom to make my own decisions, the trade-off of my privilege. After half a century, I have a name and a face. It is only right that the person who filled my number in the quota should also have a name and a face. ∎

Gil Fagiani

Miss Johnson is Dead

For 43 years
Miss Johnson worked
for the New York State
Office of Mental Health,
in one asylum or another,
double-shifts
double the delirium,
her front teeth lost
to a patient's knuckles in '53,
half a thumb lost
to a seclusion room door in '73,
otherwise back sprains, bites,
scratches, occasional kicks.

She wore a wide smile
and a round black wig
above her round brown body,
in her purse she carried a skinny pistol
the legacy of a payday robbery.

Once when a coworker
said he preferred to work
with a younger woman,
she called him a dog-faced motherfucker
in front of the ward psychiatrist
who chastised her for her language.

Miss Johnson ate the same lunch every day,
fried chicken with collard greens
fried in bacon fat,

she played the same number every day,
triple deuces for a fiver,
and she let a drunken janitor
stay at her place everyday
if he wasn't too pissy.

Recently, she bought
a royal-blue Cadillac
twice the size of the psychiatrist's Toyota,
and was set to retire
to Noccalulu Falls, Alabama,
where her 96-year-old mother lived.

Instead they found her dead
in her sixth floor walk-up apartment
her stroke-stiffened head
purple as an eggplant.

Inside a travel trunk
was a framed certificate of appreciation
signed by the Governor,
a large-print bible,
an electric broiler,
two auburn hair extensions,
a wig cleaning kit,
a chrome cocktail shaker,
two packs of Gypsy Good Time
playing cards,
and a book on how to interpret dreams
for love and money.

Bettye Kearse

Mammy Warriors: An Homage to Black Maids

TWO BLACK WOMEN IN LUMPY, threadbare coats stood silently near the intersection. The wall shielding the private tennis club behind them seemed, through the window of my car, a barrier not only to the club but to the wealth of its surrounding community. These "foreigners" stared into the street, ignoring the dry leaves swirling about their ankles. The taller woman, probably in her forties, wore sneakers and a brown knit cap pulled down over her ears. The other, a few inches shorter, and at least a generation older, wore ankle-high boots and thick socks. Wisps of gray hair poking out from under her frayed scarf wafted in the chilly air.

I had just pulled up to the traffic light a few blocks from a mass transit stop where I had often seen black maids trudge toward nearby affluent homes or climb into upscale cars driven by white women. On those previous occasions, I paid little attention to their faces, but the look of determination on the countenance of these two women captured me. The younger's had vigilant eyes and a firm-set mouth; the elder's, though flaccid and wrinkled, was lifted upward. In them, I saw dignity and self-esteem.

Though it was early morning, their drooped shoulders suggested they were already tired, the younger woman lightly supporting the older at the elbow. Their resolution notwithstanding, I sensed they would have preferred not to be at that corner in a neighborhood both miles and worlds away from their own, waiting to clean someone else's house, cook meals for someone else's family, change diapers soiled by someone else's baby, launder and iron someone else's clothing. They stood there, I believed, not only to survive, but to do whatever they could to make real a vision of what the future could hold for their children and grandchildren. For me, these two women were testimonies to the generations of black maids whose manual labor had not only fed and clothed their own families but had also pushed open doors to better education and better jobs for all who followed.

I felt a kinship, both historical and personal, with these two women. In another time and place, they could have been my great-grandmothers. When my mother's maternal grandmother, Betty, was liberated from bondage, she turned her back on her master's cotton fields and went in search of some measure of independence and security. She took in laundry so that her ten children could attend college. My mother's paternal grandmother, Martha, also a former slave, scrubbed floors so that her daughters and granddaughters would not have to get down on their knees to do the same. Though illiterate, my great-grandmothers – with each tub of somebody else's dirty clothes and each scrubbed floor in somebody else's house – made it possible for their children and their children's children to stride across college thresholds.

My grandmother, and then, my mother, became teachers. I was taking pre-med courses in college when the civil rights movement swept our country. The movement – born in the degradations of slavery, the failures of Reconstruction, the terrorism of Jim Crow, and the disillusionments of the Great Migration – demanded that the ideals of the Declaration of Independence and the promises of the Fourteenth and Fifteenth Amendments to the Constitution be made reality for all Americans. One outcome of the nonviolent freedom marches, boycotts, and sit-ins – often answered with violent billy-club beatings, fire-hose water lashings, arrests, and murders – was that more black women could begin to consider a broadened array of careers. Yet, too many black women were not able to elude the life of a domestic servant and its associated cultural assumptions, in part because of the pervasive appeal and conjecture that the proper role for a black woman is that of the "Mammy."

An image beginning in the antebellum era, Mammy remains one of the most persistent and popular totems of America's black women. In response to the social, political, and psychological pressures of slavery and its aftermath, believers in southern mythology recall a middle-aged or elderly, overweight, dark-skinned, sexually unappealing house slave who pampers the mistress and is so loyal that she loves the master's family more than her own. This prototype for Aunt Jemima and other long-lived fictional Mammies wears a white pinafore over a long-sleeved cotton dress that covers her from the base of her neck to the top of her feet. A bandana tied at her forehead accentuates Mammy's grinning face.

This stereotype is a distorted caricature. The historical Mammy comprises individuals of varied ages – including adolescents. In historical reports, she is seldom obese—food rations for slaves were not generous. She is rarely dark-skinned—light-skinned slaves (often the product of a master's sexual indiscretions) were favored as house servants. The real Mammy would not have displayed a constant grin. Her life—restricted and precarious—was daunting.

Among slaves, positions in The Big House held prestige and were coveted because they were far less physically demanding than field work. House slaves received better food and clothing, partly in order for the master to impress southern visitors with his wealth and to show northern visitors proof that slavery was a good and kind institution, consistent with his view of the correct order of things. Tours of work fields and slave quarters were rare.

There were downsides, however, for maidservants working in close proximity to their owners. The master's wife was often oblivious to the personal needs and responsibilities of the women who served her. The mistress's constant scrutiny and demand for total subservience were often oppressive and dehumanizing.

The most far-reaching and complicated myth of all is that Mammy was not sexually appealing to white men. In fact, it was quasi-acceptable for a master to violate a female slave. She was, after all, his property, to be used according to his liking. She was expected to look after his household, and, all too often, regardless of her age or marital status, she was expected to satisfy his lust. If Mammy refused any of these "duties," she risked being banished to the fields, beaten, whipped, starved, or, worst fate of all: sold away from her own family and slave community.

Antebellum southern whites were conflicted about the master's dealings with Mammy. Their notion of her as an aging, dusky, plump woman with a clownish face was antithetical to the European standard of feminine beauty and sexuality. Along with her prim attire, this mis-representation served to reassure the mistress that she had no reason to feel threatened by Mammy's presence.

But while white southerners believed that the master would not be tempted into the bed of someone they found so physically unappealing, they also believed that any white man, no matter how scrupulous, could fall prey to an imagined lure of the sexual advances and carnal skills of black women. Mammy grinned, many southern whites subconsciously feared, because she knew she was a threat to the purity of the master's bed. Mammy grinned, the nightmarish delusion conjured, because she was about to have her way with a white man. Some southern whites insisted that a black woman, compelled by such passions, could not be raped.

■ ■ ■

FOR CENTURIES, BLACK WOMEN have served as domestic servants. Before the Civil War, because few white families could afford slaves whose labor did not bring in money, most house servants lived on wealthy plantations. During Reconstruction and the Jim Crow era, black labor was so inexpensive that even lower middle-class white families hired their own "mammies." Many white women, not just the wealthy, could be the "mistress," while many of America's black women continued to serve in the "master's" house.

Since the feminist movement of the 1960s and 1970s, domestic jobs have swung away from white working-class homes and back toward those of the elite. The black woman's long history of servitude has etched her role in "The Big House" into the American psyche, despite an influx of poor women from around the world seeking to take her place. According to this imposed legacy, the black maid, heading for the other side of town, meets Mammy at the bus stop. Mammy climbs on board with her, and en route, settles in.

But when I see these black women early in the morning, they bring to mind the resolve of my great-grandmothers to keep their daughters and granddaughters off their knees, out of the fields, away from the white woman's kitchen and laundry basin, and beyond the "master's" reach. Out of gratitude and respect, I call these maids "Mammy Warriors."

■ ■ ■

THE TRAFFIC LIGHT CHANGED. I took one last look at the two women waiting with resolute dignity. Having left their own homes for "The Big House," they could be misconstrued to be modern-day versions of Mammy. Perhaps their interactions with the "mistress" were in keeping with the antebellum tradition, but I prayed their interactions with the "master" were not. Whatever their dreams, whatever their experiences, on either side of town, these Mammy Warriors—one wearing a faded cap, the other a tattered scarf—were not grinning. ■

Esther Whitman Johnson

On Kissing Her Husband Goodbye

—dedicated to a young couple in North Carolina

Be careful, my love, on your long drive home,
don't speed, go five miles under, please.

Put your signal on at every turn, reach
for nothing on the floor. Drop anything,

leave it where it falls. Stay to the right
when traffic crawls, although you want

to pass. Hang back, be inconspicuous.
Nothing's worth taking chances with a cop.

If he pulls you to the side, don't ask what for,
don't say you've done nothing wrong.

Keep your license on the dash, say it's there
before you move your hand. Keep a smile

frozen on your face, indignation locked
inside. *Wear the mask that grins and lies.*

Kiss the children when you arrive, dignity
shaken, but alive. Say Mommy misses them,

she'll be back soon, but all's fine now.
Daddy's home.

Poetry fragment in italics, Paul Laurence Dunbar, "We Wear the Mask."

Jeffrey A. Scott

Dignity

I T WAS SUMMERTIME 1963. From our home in St. Louis, my mother took me and my brother to visit her mother way down in Muskogee, Oklahoma—a small town dusty and slow-slow-really-slow-paced, and scary, feeling like my worst nightmares of the deepest South. And hot so hot, like being a dripping sizzling piece of meat roasting in an oven. Greg, my younger brother and I leave the house looking for any place with air conditioning.

I'm fourteen, feeling bad, feeling ashamed that I'm not in Washington, D.C. taking part in the huge Civil Rights March happening right in that moment on August 28, 1963. I really wanted to be there. I had been following the drama of the Movement for the last few years—the lunch counter sit-ins, the Freedom Rides, marches, beatings and arrests. Feeling the beckoning call of the protest movements and the mounting heavy burden of being young and black in a world, felt like it was relentlessly squeezing the life out of my very soul. But I was also feeling deeply shy and terrified of any act of self-assertion, especially in the company of a bunch of adults. "I'm just a kid, I can't do something like be marching in a demonstration." So I didn't even try to go with the bus loads of Civil Rights activists from my city.

So here I was feeling bad about myself wandering the streets, searing as a cast iron skillet. We found an ice cool drugstore with an inviting soda fountain. The only customers in the store, we sat down at the counter. A long time passed while we were ignored by the young boy working behind the counter. Why this was happening hit me with sudden shock. Greg wanted to leave quickly. I hissed "We ain't going nowhere. We're staying here until we get served." I told the kid, "I want an ice cream soda!" I was very angry, determined that here and now I was claiming a dignity from the abyss of a humiliation I felt my parents and my grandparents had been borne into. It was my first protest demonstration, a real sit-in demonstration. And we got served our ice cream sodas.

I learned a lot in that drugstore. My anger was abated when I realized that this kid about my age didn't really believe in segregation. He had quickly fixed our sodas, and nervously kept looking at the store entrance terrified that white adults would appear to discover what he had just done. A sick society forces everybody to submerge their true selves.

As we cleared the front door of grandma's cottage, I was surprised to see Mom and Grandma watching the March and rally. It was a live reporting of thousands and thousands of people – the reporter excitedly shouting that there were at least a quarter of a million people gathered in front of the huge statue of Abraham Lincoln. And then Martin Luther King Jr. began the most amazing speech I had ever heard. The whole scene was so mesmerizing – all kinds of folks there. Black people, white people, young folks, really old folks, college students, union members – a mass of humanity colored every flesh hue imaginable there in D.C. for civil rights, for human rights. And I had just come from initiating my first sit-in demonstration. My spirit was fully in my body and with the marchers in Washington. I had claimed something precious and unconquerable in my soul, and felt I had, indeed, embarked on a strong hearted road of emancipation. ∎

Gabrielle David

Epitaph of a Poet

Upon the assassination of Malcolm X
February 21, 1965

"It is a time for martyrs now, and if I am to be one, it will be for the cause of brotherhood. That's the only thing that can save this country."

—Malcolm X, February 19, 1965
(Two days before he was murdered by Nation of Islam followers).

you smelled death from around the corner
instead of fleeing you stood ground
with the gift of the griot, your
prophecy was thrust into martyrdom
for inclusion in the american pantheon.

w/intense single-mindedness, you rose
rose above oppression & emerged
a freedom fighter, a rebel god
a rebel god of the inner city exploding
the gospel according to the nation &
with bittersweet eloquence, you
challenged our beloved king's vision
both terrifying & electrifying us
with incandescent language
that opened wounds, & with
finger-searing racial judgment you
cut down the enemy w/your tongue—
forcing us to reexamine racial pride
the emasculation of black manhood
connecting us to the motherland—
betrayal never entered your mind.

brilliant & funny, you—
a pent-up volcano became the
controversial fruit that tasted
oh so sweet & when your
ties w/the nation soured &
you made pilgrimage to mecca
your struggle for truths
became our truths
you struggled—
not knowing how to
recreate yourself on the run &
in your struggle
evolution pointed towards revolution & you—
you became more powerfully potent
more dangerous—
a clear threat to powerful forces, yet you
continued along the path of self-discovery &
in your final gesture
    blasted backwards
        in a bedlam of gunfire
    blasted backwards
        again as you laid in your own pool of blood
    blasted backwards
        by the hands of black men manipulated
        by white men into yellow hands you fell.

& when you blasted backwards
we fell backwards too
while your imminent death hearken a
call for revolutionary upheaval &
militant uprisings
they were never quite fulfilled.

years later your presence still hangs
palpably among us
in the fevered anticipation of your cinematic second coming
your words of indigestible fury wld be deciphered into
    slogans   clichés   sound bites

mired in conflicting interpretations that
enticed a new generation of
dispossessed descendants.

once again holding us spellbound
your words & images became fashionably consumed
X marked the spot on
     buttons   t-shirts   posters   baseball caps
a stinging rebuke for what you really stood for
successfully shielding the reality of
your life & death.

in all these years, the arrested
revolution's chains have rot
the rage of your children have billowed
    we struggle
    we struggle w/our daily lives
    we struggle w/your memory
we continue to struggle & as we
look to the grave for leadership we ask
how do we begin, Brother Malcolm,
how do we truly begin?

Michelle Mann

Just a Few More Dreams

A FEW MONTHS AGO I was driving from Toledo, Ohio back home to the suburbs of Chicago. Before I left I found a CD box set of Martin Luther King Jr.'s speeches in the back corner of a used record shop, and I thought they would make for a good companion on my five-hour journey. After listening to the first few disks I was in awe of the brilliance of this man. Throughout his work as a civil rights leader, he maintained a vision and a rhetoric that inspired hope and dedication for millions of people and future generations. I was so moved that about halfway through the drive I had to pull over because I was weeping. This was in part because I was inspired and touched by his words but also because I was heartbroken – for some reason I couldn't shake the feeling like there was so much more that I wished he could have said and done.

The mix of inspiration and sorrow set in the most when I was listening to Dr. King's memorialized, famous address, "I Have A Dream." He eloquently reminds us of America's founding promises, and how they were remorselessly withheld from African Americans over the course of this country's history. He advised us to consider the "fierce urgency of now." One of my favorite points in that speech is when he explains that black people in America were given a "bad check" from the "bank of justice," but that he refuses to believe it is bankrupt. What Dr. King did not have the opportunity to mention was what happened when your bank account is emptied because someone else had taken your funds, and placed them in their own interest-bearing account. See, there was great power in the concept of Dr. King declaring that it was time for black America's check to be written, but I do not believe that the check he requested was enough. The check Dr. King described urges white America to grant the funds of justice and prosperity that were being taken from black people, so that we could be equal under the law, but that check did not say anything about the interest that had been swelling inside white America's bank account. There was no memo about white privilege, and America's enduring racial order.

Let us take a step back to explain. See, from 1619 when the first slaves arrived until 1865 when slavery was officially abolished, the relationship between white and black people was that of master and slave, superior and inferior, owner and property. Slaves were raped and murdered, their families ripped apart, and that was this land's reality for two hundred and forty-six years which, from 1619 until present day, is over half the time that both groups have been here.

To rationalize the blatant injustices committed against blacks, white people used things like science and religion to defend the obvious horrors that accompanied slavery. For example, *Crania Americana* by Samuel Morton in 1839 argued that skull sizes separated the races, making blacks unintelligent and passive, thus fit to be enslaved. Carl Linnaeus, who established the modern technique for categorizing life forms into domains and kingdoms, suggested that blacks and whites were different species. In 1851, Dr. Samuel Cartwright used his "science" to explain why all blacks are crazy and dangerous. The list of scientists, politicians, and religious leaders who used their work to justify the practice of slavery is frighteningly long.

Even beloved President Abraham Lincoln acknowledged his feelings of white supremacy despite arguing against slavery. In an 1858 debate with Stephen Douglas, Lincoln argued that there are physical differences between blacks and whites that prevent them from having complete equality. He goes on to state, "There must be the position of superior and inferior, and I as much as any other man am in favor of having the superior position assigned to the white race… I have never seen to my knowledge a man, woman or child who was in favor of producing a perfect equality… between Negroes and white men." President Lincoln's words foreshadowed what would continue to happen between races in America—blacks would be given rights but would never truly be equal because of that interest of privilege and superiority swelling in the bank account of white America. Changed laws may have granted some freedom to black people, but when you work for two centuries to build a hierarchy and way of thinking, when it is a part of the foundation of a culture that you learn and then teach it to your children and your children's children, it is quite difficult to let that interest and power, go. It is hard to admit that principal paid generations ago has continued to pay dividends.

Over the course of multiple generations, multiple centuries, the seeds of difference, hierarchy and privilege were sown deep within the consciousness of a young nation so much so that no matter how many seasons it would go through, the fibers of injustice would always be woven into old roots and in the new leaves of each era. By the time Dr. King spoke about his dream in 1963, so many seasons had passed. Slavery had been abolished but started to take new forms from 1865-1877 during the Reconstruction era, when laws referred to as "black codes" were instituted to continue control over blacks. Though a few pennies of justice did start to trickle into the lives of black America, the changing status quo led to violence and terror, and from it the Jim Crow era emerged as a legal form of discrimination and segregation, with society continuing to debate the humanity and equality of African Americans. From 1877 onwards the legacy of injustice continued until we hit the modern freedom and resistance eras of the early 1900s. This is where we find our beloved Dr. King alongside countless civil rights leaders. He encouraged us not to wallow in the valley of despair and provided hope that all of God's children would one day be free. He had a dream.

After hours of listening to so many of his passionate sermons, I pulled over on the side of I-80, weeping and heartbroken. I knew of just how often we call on Dr. King's legacy as a sign that racism is over, how much we want to celebrate him for his dreams, but felt in my heart they had not yet been fulfilled.

I thought of the widely discussed scientific and political reports that resurrected the pseudo-science of the 1850s to declare that black people fell on the lower end of the intelligence bell curve because of genetic inferiority, or that they lacked the family structures and motivation to make it out of poverty. I thought of how Dr. King's request for freedom and justice was responded to with a "war on drugs," criminalizing poor blacks' drug use one hundred times more than the same drug use in white communities, leading to an exploding and lopsided prison population of nonviolent or innocent black citizens. I wept knowing that an entire generation of African Americans had been ripped from their communities, and put behind bars, capitalized on, for the creation of a multi-billion-dollar private prison industry.

I thought of Dr. King's dream that black people would no longer be the victims of police brutality, and wept thinking of Sandra Bland, a woman who went from sitting next to my family at church to being pulled over for failing to signal a lane change; thrown to the ground with a knee shoved in her back, and then died in a jail cell that she never deserved to be inside of in the first place. I thought of Dr. King's dream that his black children would not be judged by the color of their skin, and wept because of twelve-year-old Tamir Rice, who was gunned down for playing in a park. I wept remembering a decade before Tamir was killed when my mother quickly grabbed a toy gun out of my hands and with fear buried somewhere behind her eyes told me that it was dangerous for me to play with toys like that.

I also thought of the many daily interactions and situations, the microaggressions, that, alone, would just be a little frustrating but in unity point towards a larger problem. For example, I thought of when my white neighbors let me know that it was surprising to see me attending such a prestigious university; how I often heard my white peers on campus discuss that a table full of students of one racial or ethnic minority group is "exclusive" or "self-segregating" without seeing the sea of all-white tables that are also filled with students who simply have similar lives and interests; and how my white acquaintances still refer to my hair as "unique" or "exotic" without acknowledging that it could inhibit my success in a job interview.

I thought about the statistically proven tendencies for qualified African Americans to be hired at lower rates than less qualified white peers, and the higher frequency with which qualified black loan applicants are denied. I thought about many families where actual monetary interest has been passed down from generation to generation until present day. I thought of many of my white friends, the descendants of more recent immigrant grandparents who had their own stories of struggle, but were able to assimilate and gain access to opportunities while my family, here for far more generations than this country itself, has always had to fight to gain access to those same opportunities. I thought about how it is apparently my responsibility to explain my oppression over and over again but, at the same time, be considered whiny and ungrateful when I call out the ways in which my life is still affected by structural racism.

I am grateful for Dr. King and his dreams. I share many of them myself. His hope persists today and is visible in the resilience of the black community, the continued quest for justice, the beauty of the art, technology, music, scholarship, and culture that we create. I am inspired knowing that it was through hope, and the hard work of multiple generations that many a freedom check has been cashed into black America's bank account but, my friends, there is still the interest. America teaches that racism is overtly expressed hatred or bias, but it doesn't discuss how it takes larger structural forms, or is a part of subconsciously learned privilege and superiority. Either way, there are still differences in the daily lives of black and white Americans because of their race. Dr. King's dreams have seemingly not quite come true yet.

So yes, after thinking about all of this at once, I was just overwhelmed and I wept for my people as I have done so many times before, but as I wiped my tears away and continued my trip home, I tried to think of a few more dreams that we could work on.

I have a dream that one day I can drive my car without fear of being killed for changing lanes or reaching for my wallet, and that I won't have to fear my children's safety if I buy them certain toys. I have a dream that our government will not jeopardize sacred Native American burial grounds or permit militarized attacks on people who are trying to protect the land and water that has truly always been theirs. I have a dream that one day clean water in Flint Michigan will be an assumption.

I have a dream that my white brothers and sisters will focus not only on how explicit, overt acts constitute as racism, but on how things that they say or do are from the descendants of racism created so long ago, and how certain daily encounters or lifelong stressors that they do not experience because of their race reinforce our enduring racial hierarchy. I have a dream that they will take me at my word when I discuss the oppression that I have faced.

My friends, my dreams may sound vast but they boil down quite simply, and my request is rather small. I dream that we will not subscribe to the dangerous narrative of color blindness and will instead recognize how our past has shaped our present. I dream that we will examine the ways in which we are ignorant of our own privileges, see how they interact with our daily lives, and adjust our actions accordingly. I want us to be able to confidently say that the United States of America has yet to become great, but that we as a nation will do the work necessary to take one more step closer to the day when we are great, the day when we follow through on the pledge of liberty and justice for all.

Today, we, the burgeoning generation, had no part in the goings on of 1619 or 1865 or 1963...but we are the leaves that grew from those same troubled roots, and the fibers of injustice are still pulsing through the core of our nation, infused into every one of us whether we like it or not. So for good and for bad, it is our responsibility to make more informed decisions as we pursue the great potential we have. Sisters and brothers, these are the American dreams that I have. I hope that you will pursue them with me as we move together into the future. ∎

Victorio Reyes Asili

Insufficient

For Oscar Grant

If I could
resurrect you
with my imagery
what would I say?

I'm sorry you're dead?

I'm sorry that all of the marches,
and petitions,
and sit ins,
and grassroots organizing,
and meetings,
and flyers,
and eloquent poems,
couldn't keep you alive?

I know now
that there is no
flowery way to say
that Tatiana can't hug
you because
America is racist,
always has been.

I left the movie
theater this evening,
    as I watched you on the big screen,
    your life taken by the poison from
    a cop's gun, your body

handcuffed to the cold
concrete of the train
platform, your life
stolen from
little Tatiana,
your girlfriend,
your mom,
your grandma,
speechless.

I wanted to scream:
OSCAR GRANT IS DEAD!

And no metaphor
can go back in time,
cover you in a bullet
proof shield
and protect you
from our failings,
from the completely
fucked up criminal justice
system that sentenced
you before you got
off that train
at Fruitvale Station,
before you were born.

But Oscar, you deserve that type of metaphor.
Tatiana deserves that type of metaphor.
The kind that can re-write the wrong.

And no, I don't expect these words to bring your soul comfort.
And I wouldn't pretend these inscriptions could capture
the feeling Tatiana must have when she thinks
of never hugging you again.

In fact, if I've learned
anything this evening,

it's that

these lines of poetry
(if you wish to call them that)
can only be categorized
       as
thoroughly
       and
painfully

                insufficient.

Debra R. Riley

Black Lives Have Always Mattered

Coming across the Atlantic in ships
packed like sardines,
we mattered

Being separated from our loved ones
while sold on the auction blocks
we mattered

While being taught Christianity
in order to further our confusion
we mattered

While being hung on trees
Whipped until we bled, or dead
we mattered

While picking cotton
serving the oppressor
and could not read
we mattered

While our men were desecrated
tied to animals,
tarred and feathered
we mattered

While our sisters were raped
giving suck to Massa's chil'ren
denying her own
we mattered

While being denied basic human rights
we mattered

While Jim Crow kept us segregated
we mattered

While building this country up for free
we mattered

While Abraham Lincoln supposedly
out of the goodness of his heart
set us free
we mattered

While we pleaded
to be a part of this sick society
we mattered

While Martin Luther King Jr.
who once had a dream
turned into a nightmare
integrated us into a burning building
we mattered

While Malcolm X
said by any means necessary
we mattered

While President Johnson
signed Civil Rights into law
we mattered

While the laws put into place were design
to annihilate our race
yeah, we mattered

While drugs were placed into our communities
destroying a generation
we mattered

While the devastation in our hoods took hold
and there wasn't any good
we mattered

While we fought
to vote and be educated
in their schools
we mattered

While our music our culture was stolen and
sold to the highest bidder
we mattered

While we gave up right for wrong
smiling, dancing, and singing our song
"We Shall Overcome Someday"
we mattered

We are a people who have survived horrendous conditions
yet we still fight racism on every front. We are the catalyst
for hope and change, but we must first acknowledge the self-
hatred that has been programmed into our psyche

BLACK LIVES HAVE ALWAYS MATTERED!

THE LEGACY OF
BLACK PROTEST CONTINUES

"I am America. I am the part you won't recognize. But get used to me. Black, confident, cocky; my name, not yours; my religion, not yours; my goals, my own; get used to me."

—Muhammad Ali

Ran Walker

Legions: A Kwansaba

I beat my fists against a sky
filled with legions of our black angels,
praying you see a man, not a
monster, whose talons scrape at your idea
of the American dream. You move, gun
drawn, ready to fire your hate into
my soul, but I refuse to die.

William Harris

From Montgomery to Ferguson
The Civil Rights Movement and
Black Lives Matter

From Montgomery to Ferguson
The echoing cry of a movement against racism and police brutality; a rising slogan spread across the U.S. in its radiant simplicity.

Behind this slogan, lies activism symbolizing a generation of awoken, engaged, and involved millennials of color.

Yes, color.

The same color that has been a target for hate and discrimination is becoming a catalyst for freedom in a new generation.

On the one hand, it is a demand and need for equal rights for African Americans, but there's a lot more to this issue and we're not looking for just a settlement.

It's not just about police brutality; it's about outdated systems purposefully designed to oppress black lives in different aspects.

For example: the prison industrial complex, economic and voting rights, food supply, limited opportunities leave us less likely to survive.

It's an explosion of frustrations, built up from many years of segregation.

Activism that stands proudly on the shoulders of movements that came before us, to make our voices loud and clear, so they can no longer ignore us.

Black Lives Matter is an Epideictic Genre,

evocative words and images used to ignite a revolution.

Through social media we connected with the world, and inspired a global movement.

Palestinian activists protested for cooperation between the Israeli state and the U.S. urban police department.

Inspired by Ferguson, another movement protesting violence against indigenous people in the U.S. known as Native Lives Matter became prominent.

The movement not only emphasizes the need for Black Liberation, but the need for equality for both genders and all races.

From a symbolic perspective, we agree to the visions of ourselves created by those before us who paved the way.

Leaders like Dr. King, Rosa Parks, Malcolm X, Nelson Mandela and the list goes on even to this day.

From Mike Brown to Travyon Martin, from two hundred thousand to the Million Man March in Washington.

But there are those who counter the slogan, misunderstanding the message.

It's true that All Lives Matter, but take a look at it from a different perspective.

According to the justice system, blacks are more likely to be killed by police, and twice as likely as whites to be killed while unarmed.

Blacks are more likely to be stopped and frisked for drug use and marijuana, and even serve a longer sentence than whites for the use of drugs.

So it's not that all lives don't matter, it's that black lives don't matter as much, but they should.

So in conclusion, to obtain racial justice in this generation necessitates a New Civil Rights.

What began in the 1960s is the same reason why we continue to fight.

Whereas the Civil Rights Movement carried out its political victories,

We now confront the role of neoliberalism in our economic and political policies.

Being devalued to a permanent marginalization as an African American majority.

Seen not as members of this economy, but more so as surplus humanity.

So then, Black Lives Matter and the fight for freedom have become necessary.

A transformative social movement rooted in history.

Being devalued to a permanent marginalization as an African American majority, seen not as members of this economy, but more so as surplus humanity.

So then, Black Lives Matter and the fight for freedom have become necessary, a transformative social movement rooted in history.

Deva R. Woodly

Black Lives Matter: The Politics of Race and Movement in the 21st Century

Understanding the movement and what it represents.

WHERE SHOULD WE BEGIN in accounting for the rise of the movement for black lives?

The tragedy of twenty-first century America is that there are innumerable places one could begin. The grievances that have sparked the cry, "Black Lives Matter," might be rooted in the killing of black bodies at the hands of police, or the exploitation of black citizens in the extortion schemes of local governments that seek to keep their taxes low amidst the hegemony of austere politics. Or, it might be rooted in the lack of safety that black people feel in a polity that still regards them, as W. E. B. Du Bois pointed out over one hundred years ago, as "a problem." In this way, the new century is not much different from before – the state sanctioned and, often, state-implemented exploitation of black and brown bodies is, wretchedly, as American as apple pie.

So, this story, like most political stories, is one that is always already in medias res. However, the makers of Black Lives Matter (BLM) began the current iteration of the black liberation movement in a moment of painful politicization on the morning of July 15, 2013 when vigilante George Zimmerman was acquitted for the killing of seventeen-year-old Trayvon Martin, a Florida teen deemed so suspicious and scary for walking, hoodie-clad in his Dad's suburban neighborhood, that he could reasonably be stalked, attacked, and murdered on sight.

So sure were Florida authorities that the death of young Trayvon required no accounting that it took forty-five days of protest for the admitted killer to be arrested. The trial that followed the arrest was watched with interest by the nation, but, as in most things American, a distinct racial divide in perceptions of the proceedings – specifically what, if any, political issues were at stake and whether justice was likely to be done – characterized the country's attention.

According to a Pew Research Center survey taken in early July 2013, 78 percent of African Americans believed that the case raised important issues about race that needed to be discussed, as opposed to 28 percent of white Americans. Additionally, nearly six in ten African Americans reported following the trial "very closely" compared to only 34 percent of whites, with 63 percent of blacks claiming that the trial was a focus of conversation when talking with friends compared to 42 percent of whites. Given the racial divide in both the attention to the trial and the assessment of the key issues at play, it is not surprising that upon the verdict of acquittal, 86 percent of African Americans declared themselves "unsatisfied," compared to 30 percent of whites.

But these statistics only give a pencil-sketch outline of the political tumult that the killing of Trayvon Martin, and the subsequent sanctioning of that death by the U.S. legal system, produced. They cannot convey what those 86 percent of African American respondents felt on that day. For that, observers, like those who found themselves shocked (if not altogether surprised), must turn to the virtual sphere that provided a place to express the nuance and intensity of people's reactions and make them public: social media. That day, the virtual public sphere was awash in conversations, dissections of the trial and evidence, and polemical rants, but more prominent than all of these were outcries of pain. And fear.

Like many African Americans, I took to my Facebook page with an emotional post:

> I have been struggling with what to say. I'm a political scientist. And a political junkie. I ought to say something politically productive. But my predominant response to this verdict is this thought running through my head – 'I am the mother of a black boy. The wife of a black man. They are not safe. They are not safe. They are not safe.'

And indeed, empirically, they are not. A recent study of racial bias in police killings (compiled from data from the U.S. Police-Shooting Database, the FBI's Supplementary Homicide Report, the CDC's National Vital Statistics System, The National Lawyer's Guild's Stolen Lives

Project, the Fatal Encounters Database, the Killed By Police database, and the Mapping Police Violence project, as well as additional data compiled by *The Washington Post* and *The Guardian*), finds that "the probability of being black, unarmed, and shot by police is about 3.49 times the probability of being white, unarmed, and shot by police, on average."

I did not know these statistics at the time of my Facebook post, but I knew like many other black Americans what I felt and feared and, in the tradition of the black feminist epistemology of Patricia Hill Collins, Audre Lorde, and bell hooks among many others, I recognized those powerful sensations as a kind of knowledge, an indicator of political urgency. And so I wrote my personal dread in a public forum, because I knew it to be political:

> I cannot keep them safe from eyes that have no capacity to consider their humanity and no notion that they might be ordinary men, innocent of any crime but walking around in their skin. My loves, my whole life, everything we have built together, may be snuffed out by any armed coward who takes it upon themselves to exercise their prejudice at any time, in any place. And there may be no recourse. And there will certainly be no justice. Because all my pictures here are of my beautiful, brilliant boy. Of my talented and dedicated and hardworking husband. They mean nothing to a stranger with a gun. I am overcome with sadness that this is my America.

I would remember to fear for my daughter—who, at the start of this iteration of black democratic insurgency in 2013, was not yet born—and for myself, as I shared in the pain of the fates of Tanisha Anderson. Rekia Boyd. Miriam Carey. Michelle Cusseaux. Shelly Frey. Kayla Moore. Sandra Bland. I witnessed the catastrophe of their killing through the collective mourning and political demand of #sayhername, another politically galvanizing twitter campaign by the Black Lives Matter movement, which emerged in May 2015 as a reminder and exhortation to acknowledge and publicize the stories of black women killed by police. Stories that too often went unmentioned, as the gendered burdens of women often do.

Listen. This is personal. And political. And empirical. And philosophical. This is about justice. And technique. And innovation. Which is to say, this is about the making and sustenance and vision of a mass movement in the twenty-first century.

What we know about movements is that they emerge from more than grievance. Grievances are ever-present: resources are scarce, inequality is a fact, and systems of governance, including democracies, lean towards oligarchy and bureaucratization. Instead, movements emerge when people (1) come to understand their grievances as being caused by the status quo arrangement of power while simultaneously (2) coming to believe that protesting that arrangement of power is both urgent and efficacious. This understanding of grievance as a public problem that has the potential to be solved through the political effort of ordinary people is what social movement scholars call insurgent consciousness, which often coalesces and is amplified through injustice frames that activists create.

In twenty-first century social movements, hashtags can become injustice frames. Alicia Garza relates the genesis of #blacklivesmatter, writing:

> I created #BlackLivesMatter with Patrisse Cullors and Opal Tometi, [...] as a call to action for Black people after 17-year-old Trayvon Martin was post-humously placed on trial for his own murder and the killer, George Zimmerman, was not held accountable for the crime he committed. It was a response to the anti-Black racism that permeates our society...

For many African American millennials, this was the moment of their political discovery of what Franz Fanon calls "the fact of blackness," or the social and political fact that as a black person, one will always "experience his being through others," having to move through life not only aware of how she will be viewed as an individual, but also as an example of blackness as it is constructed by the ideology and historiography of white supremacy.

I should pause here to make an important point. White supremacy, properly understood and as deployed by the movement for black lives, is not a prejudiced feeling about the superiority of white people. Instead, it is the name of the current state of social relations structured by and operating through institutions and social mores that shapes all of our subjectivities, arranges power, compounds inequality, and distributes privilege based on the historical legacy and continuing daily impact of racial categorization. In other words, white supremacy is a social and political fact (which exists amidst other politically relevant social facts) that structures – that is, organizes, the consequences of being in the world.

The moment of political awakening to the effects of white supremacy that many experienced on the acquittal of Martin's killer might have subsided, without blossoming from grievance into movement, if not for three factors. The first is the mind-boggling and heart-rending regularity of the trauma of black deaths at the hands of either vigilantes or law enforcement. The second, the availability of social media to announce, discuss, mourn, analyze, and demand acknowledgment, accountability, and justice in the face of the endlessly repeated collective ordeal of loss. The third is the skillful and dedicated efforts of individuals and organizations across the country (indeed, worldwide) to turn these moments of trauma and rage into a sustained and sustainable political insurgency.

The heat and light of insurgency

THE AUGUST KILLING OF MICHAEL BROWN in Ferguson, Missouri proved to be the tipping point for the mobilization of a movement that had been percolating for at least two years. DeRay McKesson, a prominent activist in the movement for black lives and co-founder of one of its prominent organizations, Campaign Zero, recounts that he was initially drawn to Ferguson by curiosity. "When Trayvon died," he reflects, "I just had no clue what the news was, I just didn't know what it was, and I didn't want that to be the story in St. Louis." The demonstrations that erupted on the night following Brown's execution in the street, where his body lay uncovered all day as people gawked and gathered in grief and outrage, were large and grew by the hour. Even so, activist Johnetta Elzie remembers that the sentiment that kept repeating on her social media timelines was one of resignation: "It's just another dead black boy. No one's gonna care." But, she reports, "I just didn't believe it. All I had was my twitter, and my Facebook and my Tumblr and my Instagram [...] and I felt that someone, somewhere would care about what I was seeing."

And, indeed, people did care. The coverage of the national cable networks was uneasy, yet attentive, with both CNN and Fox News reporting upticks in their ratings over the two weeks that followed the initial uprising on August 9. The coverage, though extensive, followed the format of most media coverage of protest, less focused on exploring the reasons for the uprising and more on the spectacle of disorder. McKesson observed, "CNN was sort-of painting this picture about chaos. And Twitter and Instagram were painting a picture about pain and it was that that was a call to action." Though he was originally in Ferguson as an observer, a kind of citizen reporter, McKesson recalls, "The second night, I got tear gassed–it was the first night of the curfew–it was in that moment that I became a protester." In this transformation from a curious and attentive bystander to avowed political challenger, he was not alone. The police response, with law enforcement officers outfitted in military-gear pointing war weapons at American citizens as they sat atop armored tanks (the Missouri Guard went so far as to refer to protesters as "enemy forces" in their internal communications), was shocking to many. Photos of young people approaching human walls of police in riot gear and videos of officers threatening to "fucking kill" unarmed Americans exercising their First Amendment rights went viral and caused people of many races to ask themselves and each other: "Is this our America?"

As is often the case, especially in democracies, the vividly repressive response of the state turned public pain, which activists had made coherent in an injustice frame, and communal trauma, which had been forged into shared affect on social media, into collective action and political demand.

In Ferguson, people remained in the streets for two weeks and two days, and, just as the nightly demonstrations began to die down, a coalition of activists, including one of the founding-women of the movement, Patrice Cullors, and prominent Brooklyn-based queer activist Darnell Moore, planned the "Black Lives Matter Rides" to Ferguson, Missouri. This action, modeled after the Freedom Rides of the 1960s, brought over 500 people from Boston, Philadelphia, Chicago, Detroit, Houston, Los Angeles, Portland, and Tuscon, among other cities, to "support the people of Ferguson and help turn a local moment into a national movement."

Those who ventured to Ferguson, most having raised funds to cover the cost of their travel on crowd-sourcing website Go Fund Me, went not only to protest alongside the still-shell-shocked residents, but also to strategize. Several small, local organizations including

OBS: Organization for Black Struggle, Hands Up United, and Missourians Organizing for Reform and Empowerment, met, often in local Churches, but also at community barbeques and other civic, community-building forums, with those who had come from afar. During these dialogues, they talked together about how to connect the dots – politically, rhetorically, organizationally – between the particular institutional abuse that led to Michael Brown's death and the systemic vulnerability of black lives across America and throughout the world.

Accounts of the Black Lives Matter Riders' experiences in Ferguson emerged on personal blogs as well as on popular websites like Feminist Wire and in the columns of major news magazines such as *Salon, Ebony,* and *The Guardian.* Participants reported that they were moved by the experience of standing in the place where Brown's body had lain. That they were made more determined than they had been because they witnessed the pain and fear of the people who lived in the town. That they were impressed by the commitment of all those who gathered – a commitment that was made concrete by the promise activists made to each other to take what they had learned and discussed during the Rides back with them as they planned actions tailor-made in and for the cities from which they hailed. A BLM rider and writer for *Colorlines* magazine, Akiba Solomon, related the aftermath of the rides this way:

> On Facebook I friend everyone I recognize from the trip [...]. Throughout the week, tag-filled testimonies begin to appear. Several people (including me) say they can't find the right words to describe our journey. One rider describes a change within: "I felt something shift in me and more importantly, I bore witness to an emergent Black political consciousness and a movement led by our youth.

The moment of mass insurgency that caused the whole world to watch in the early weeks of August 2014 was remarkable enough, but activists working for different organizations, on different coasts, and in locales in between, showed an impressive savvy. The Freedom Rides forged the popular injustice frame "#blacklivesmatter" into an insurgency with a collective identity. This is a rare accomplishment for a movement that is neither single-issue, nor located in any one organization or the charismatic presence of any one person. Instead, the movement for black lives re-purposed a successful tactic of the 20th century's racial justice movement. In this way, activists were able to build relationships upon face-to-face encounters which gave participants the selective emotional incentives that Fancesca Polletta and James Jasper note are necessary for the formation of collective identities that are meant to endure during sustained political challenges. These relationships were later able to be maintained and deepened online. This style of organizing, one rooted in real-life, but bolstered by a vibrant and variegated virtual civic space housed on Facebook, Twitter, Instagram, Vine, WhatsApp, GroupMe, and other platforms, adopted as needed by participants, gave the collective action a frame and a slogan to the movement, and additional meaning for the leaders and residents who converged in Ferguson that fall. Not only did black lives matter in the abstract, as an aspirational political goal, but their politicized and mobilized black selves, very clearly and concretely, mattered to each other.

Almost a year later, in July 2015, many of the riders and an additional thousand people, representing dozens of organizations based in cities around the nation including Blackbird, Ferguson Action, BYP100, Million Hoodies, and Project South, came together again. This gathering, held in Cleveland, Ohio, was called the Movement for Black Lives Convening, and was designed as a conference on the activity, strategies, tactics, vision, and trajectory of an insurgency that has proved itself to be much more than a momentary outcry.

BLM as a 21st century social movement

THE MOVEMENT FOR BLACK LIVES shares many of the formal characteristics that have so far dominated social movements in the late twentieth and early twenty-first centuries. BLM is avowedly collaborative, networked, and non-hierarchal. It also utilizes a social media/on-the-ground hybrid model of organization. In addition, the multiple tactics that have emerged in the protest and organizing repertoire of the movement are a mix between traditional forms of protest, like marches, street blockades, and die-ins, and innovative actions like #blackbrunch. BLM has learned the tactics of predecessor movements, but is not limited to them or bound by them.

In terms of what's new about the way BLM and other twenty-first century social movements organize, social media cannot be ignored.

The various platforms that make private thoughts instantly public have become key elements of all contemporary social movements' repertoires. These platforms allow movement participants to communicate with each other, mobilize people in the streets, tell their own stories, frame international and domestic debates, and perform agenda-setting functions that were previously the exclusive purview of trained journalists in established professional media organizations.

However, while social media have transformed the way that contemporary movements organize, it is important that we do not become confused about the nature of the tool. Social media is a technology of protest, but it is not a stand-in or substitute for the long-standing processes of personal engagement, face-to-face organizing, and movement infrastructure-building in the form of regularizing channels of communication, creating relationships of trust, and designing resonant framings and clear collective goals. Unlike some other movements that have emerged this century, BLM has proved itself particularly skilled at not confusing the technology for the movement itself.

The movement for black lives is anchored by IRL (in-real-life) mass action – the movement was catalyzed in the streets. It is reported and reflected upon online. This convergence of traditional, offline organizing with the instantaneous frame diffusion of social media multiplies and magnifies the visible sites of the movement's resistance while nurturing and expanding a vital sense of community and clearly broadcasting the preferred frames of the movement – frames which are often taken-up and amplified by traditional media, which report social media phenomena as news.

Still, the use of social media is not all up-side. In addition to enabling the instantaneous transmission of information, Facebook, Twitter, and Instagram among other sharing sites, also makes the surveillance by officials and abuse from random, often anonymous detractors (known as "trolls") much easier. In addition, social media is not a good tool for accomplishing several essential tasks of movements. The Facebook and Twitter universes are not particularly good venues for developing trenchant analysis, deliberative engagement about purposes and goals, or building the infrastructure required for sustained collaboration and/or organization-building. These activities must be undertaken face-to-face or in private discussion groups that may be virtually hosted, but include only lead activists.

Beyond BLM's savvy with the technologies of protest, old and new, that have become a part of their repertoire, it is important to note that BLM also has its own epistemology of movement. It stands out among twenty-first century social movements because it is self-consciously intersectional, avowedly intellectual, habitually reflexive, and doggedly planning for the long term.

BLM is changing politics

LIKE ANY SOCIAL MOVEMENT, the success of the movement for black lives must be measured by whether or not it is shifting mainstream understandings of the political problem that it highlights. In this dimension, too, BLM is exceptional. Since the emergence of the hashtag-cum-mass movement, the mainstream American conversation has been shifting. Questions about the relationship between citizens and police have been raised repeatedly and in resonant terms by activists and the media, politicians, and ordinary people are thinking about the violence of what social scientists call the "carceral state" in myriad ways. There has been a revival in the discussion of "police brutality" in the national media; elected officials from both parties are calling for "prison reform;" and more members of the polity are now identifying police violence and racial strife as major problems facing the nation. These forms of acknowledgment are not, by themselves, a solution, as many of the proposals for "reform" do not fully address the critiques of activists. However, they are a part of what makes it possible to sustain a movement's relevance and increase its influence, supplying the movement for black lives with the grounds to keep making political claims and challenging the status quo arrangement of power and privilege.

These discourses about racialized police violence, and the need to scrutinize and change the carceral state, allow the polity as a whole to question the "post-racial" and "tough-on-crime" ethos that has reigned hegemonic since the early 1980s. This includes, most powerfully, the question that the hashtag of the movement begs: do black lives matter to the polity? If they don't, what does that mean to us? What is the American polity willing to avow in the face of the dual challenge and charge to prove that they do?

In addition, activists have introduced questions about whether or not the police are "heroes;" whether they are accountable enough, or at all, for transgressing their authority; what causes them to be unaccountable; and whether policing as it is currently constructed (or at all) is serving the needs and expectations of society. In short, BLM has framed the problem of the vulnerability of black lives as systematic and, setting aside the ways that different sectors of the polity are thinking and talking about solutions, the movement seems to be persuading the public that this might indeed be so. That's an incredible feat in itself. And, given the conduct of the movement so far, it seems only the beginning of the change to come. ■

Jalayna Walton

Famous

I never thought of my neighborhood
as a ghetto.
Until it was plastered across CNN
until it was falling out of the mouths of thousands
who had never seen W. Florissant Road
or heard of the (regular) McCluer Comets
who didn't know about beauty supplies that weren't named Sally's
who couldn't fathom a community doing just fine
without a Starbucks
I mean
I love Starbucks
but three new stores haven't replaced the work
of the YMCA on Pershall.
And now an activist is dead
and people around the nation rush to his name
as if a sound bite replaces a conversation
as if Ferguson the hashtag
the moment in time
the memory
is the same thing as Ferguson the people
with their feelings
and their futures.

F.I. Goldhaber

Where Have You Been?

Millions of white women took to the streets
wearing pink pussy hats, carrying signs,
proudly posting their clever slogans on
Facebook, Twitter, YouTube, and Instagram.

The police waved as they went by. No one
arrested; no riot gear in sight; not
a whiff of tear gas or pepper spray; no
flash bangs, rubber bullets, kettling.

Women gathered by hundreds of thousands
in cities around the world, on seven
continents, to protest installation
of white supremacists in Washington.

But, Women of Color, Indigenous,
Queer, Trans, and Immigrant activists could
only ask, "Where've you been all these years while
they beat, shot, arrested, deported us?"

"Where were you while white patriarchy stole
our lives, lands, freedoms, civil rights; murdered
Trans women, assaulted Queers, raped Native
women, shipped Latinas far from their homes?"

More than half of the white women in the
U.S. voted to put xenophobic,
racist, homo hating, misogynists
in the White House. But now they demonstrate?

Those who've been marching, resisting; getting
gassed; shot with "non-lethal" rounds and water
cannons; bleeding and dying; wasting time
in jail; watched in anger at the contrast.

They might allow newcomers to join their
resistance because the danger is so
much greater than white women perceive. The
battle weary don't have time to explain.

Allies are needed. Action's required. But
neophytes must be willing to do more
than march with punny signs and knitted caps.
They must respect and learn from the vanguard.

This fight isn't just about equal pay,
workplace harassment, reproductive health
care, school athletics. It's an ongoing
horrific, bloody, life and death struggle.

For people of other colors, genders,
physical abilities, religions,
sexuality; for immigrants and
refugees this isn't just a parade.

Police don't pose for selfies with them when
they take to the streets after another
unarmed black man is slaughtered, their access
to clean water destroyed, their land stolen.

So many white women come late to the
challenge. They never had police pull their
hair, sit on them, bash in their heads. They've not
been harassed, orphaned, raped, widowed by cops.

White women ignored racism, hatred,
bigotry, slaughter. To move forward, they
must suppress their fragile white egos, step
up, do more, or they just wasted their time.

They must heed those who've
spent centuries fighting for life, freedom;
who've watched their loved ones bleed out in the streets;
suffered cold steel biting into their wrists.

Set pride aside, recognize privilege,
understand how much more other women
endure. Advancing straight white women's lives
won't help queer or trans women of color.

But restraining police, working to end
systemic racism, forcing Congress
to enshrine civil rights for all peoples,
will improve the welfare of everyone.

If this poem offends, if you question
its message, if the election results
surprised you, then open your eyes to the
suffering you're privileged to ignore.

Kimberly Marie Ashby | Christina Marie Douyon
Ammy Sena | Kiara Manosalvas

Demanding a Seat at the Table:
Personal Narratives from Four Women of Color

Positionality: Kimberly identifies as a queer, African American, cis-gender, woman from Philadelphia. Kiara identifies as a straight, Ecuadorian-Puerto Rican, cis-gender, woman. Ammy identifies as a straight, Dominican immigrant, cis-gender, woman. Christina identifies as a Black Haitian-American, cis-gender, woman.

Introduction

AS FOUR WOMEN RESEARCHERS OF COLOR at a predominantly white institution, we are invisible. Invisibility is defined as the lack of, or false representation of, oppressed groups and/or individuals. We are invisible because our intersectionally oppressed racial and gender identities force us to struggle for consideration and validation amongst the bustle of largely homogeneous, white undergraduates that rush through our building. This is mirrored by the fact that, in our scholarship, we have also become intensely involved in uncovering invisibility among black women and girls. We are in an era in which many of the realities of black life are gaining visibility: the crimes of police violence against black people that have gone unrecorded and unregarded when lynching was routine, are now getting air-time on primetime television; gymnast Simone Biles won four gold Olympic medals in Rio but despite her success, her body was publicly dissected; HBO has premiered a new show about the social discomfort afforded to black women (Insecure), and Solange Knowles has privileged the world by giving it *A Seat at the Table*.

It is this zeitgeist, in addition to the many ways we are made invisible, that has positioned us to feel so nourished by *A Seat at the Table*. Solange's lyrics, "You're leaving not a trace in the world," speak to our invisibility. Solange offered us a seat, handed us a plate, and proceeded to speak of the invisible experiences and realities of people of color, of black people, and specifically, of black women.

Music and the arts have always been an important means by which people of color have survived their circumstances. From jazz, to blues, to rock n' roll, to graffiti, to hip hop, artistic expression is how we have endured and how we have made space for ourselves publicly. Within this tradition, Solange has created an album that invites listeners to both grieve our heartaches and also build power around black identity.

For these four brown, women researchers, *A Seat at the Table* has acted as a mirror, allowing us to see parts of ourselves so often neglected, stereotyped, and made invisible. Solange's album made such an impact on us, and as is evidenced by its commercial success on the world, that we wanted to share the ways in which we each personally connect to *A Seat at the Table.*

Kimberly

BLACK WOMEN ARE NOT MONOLITHIC. However, we have long been stereotyped, suggesting that all of us are some form of Jezebel, Sapphire, or Mammy. Just as Solange's album demonstrates that black women are capable of being and expressing themselves in multiple ways, I am not what one would call a "typical" black girl. That is to say, I'm quirky. I listen to indie, neo-soul music. The word "emo" has been used to describe my demeanor. I have tattoos and although I've adopted a gregarious, "fuck-it-all," bad girl attitude, I have spent a good portion of my life being tall and socially awkward. I bring racial diversity to what is otherwise white hipsterdom.

Solange has never been a "typical" black girl either. Since her single "I Decided," in 2009 when she incorporated photos from the civil rights movement in the track's music video, it has been clear that Solange is not afraid to be different. With *A Seat at the Table,* she continues this path by beautifully, unapologetically, and intimately letting the world into her skin as a member of the black community.

Solange is also unique in her authenticity and transparency about mental health. My favorite song on the album, "Cranes in the Sky," speaks not only to the unrelenting presence of racism in the lives of black people but also to the personal and collective experience of trauma and mental illness.

Growing up depressed in a black family has taught me that mental illness is a topic black people tend to avoid. Research suggests that black people tend to be less likely to engage in mental health treatment and more likely to discontinue treatment prematurely. While this is likely due to multiple factors, stigma may be a contributor. Black people are chronically exposed to racial trauma, but lack culturally acceptable means of coping with its symptoms, constituting a health crisis that deserves more than the scant attention it is given.

Solange's repeated phrase, "Away, away, away, away, away," illuminates the personal and political journeys black people have taken to see themselves as valuable in their own eyes and in the eyes of others, honoring the many who have tried to push it "away." Cranes in the sky reach for greatness but are covered by dark "metal" clouds that obscure them in their glory—just as oppression obscures the beauty of black life.

Solange reminds us that sometimes daring to be different in displaying one's authentic self is not only a form of healing but also, in the context of black women's chronic invisibility, a radical political act.

Kiara

IN SOLANGE'S SONG "MAD," an unnamed woman tells Solange, "Where'd your love go?" This struck me as condescending, as if this woman is asking Solange to appreciate what she has and suck it up, suggesting that Solange shouldn't complain for fear of confirming the stereotype of black and Latina women as being hostile and angry. Solange may come from a famous family, but that does not devoid her of the realities of being a black woman. Similarly, just because I identify as a highly-educated, successful, Hispanic woman, does not mean that I cannot identify with parts of my identity that are oppressed. Nonetheless, this is how I have been made to feel by people who refuse to fully listen to my experience as a woman of color.

Growing up, I was ashamed of being Hispanic. I didn't want anything to do with it, so I never embraced that part of myself, nor did I talk about it in the predominately white environments I inhabited. Since I have started initiating conversations on race, some people have told me, "You didn't talk about this before; why do you care now?" Similar to Solange's assertion that it is alright to be angry, I have always harbored anger about the micro and macro-aggressions I have experienced as a Hispanic woman. It was just a matter of time before I felt comfortable enough to speak my truth. Solange and I should not be told to "Stop complaining" and to "stop talking shit" just because we have decided to speak up about our experiences.

My emotions associated with racial injustice are real and should be validated. Unfortunately, as Solange bravely sings, this is not often the case when talking with people who just don't seem to "get it." However, anger and hatred of omni-present institutionalized racism is sometimes what inspires people to gets things done; it is what has driven many to engage in activism, to release albums that may make some people uncomfortable, and to stand up for what we believe in. Unlike my less developed self, if someone degrades my existence as a woman of color, I take no issue in "talking shit."

Ammy

AT ONE POINT, I loved having people touch my hair. I have had to learn to be okay with people not touching my hair. I contemplate this in the context of my Dominican socialization as I hear Solange's song "Don't touch my hair." Solange's smooth voice but assertive and repetitive "don't touch" verses make loud historically silenced and overlooked voices. Solange reinstates the importance of not touching, not involving, not interfering, not appropriating, not judging, not oppressing our hair, or what our hair has come to represent.

Scholars have documented European influence on hair, stating, "the first things the slave traders did to their new cargo was shave their heads." This marks one of the first disrespectful and oppressive actions taken against hair amongst the African diaspora. In her book, *Hair Raising: Beauty, Culture and African American Women*, Rooks states,

> Hair in 1976 spoke to racial identity politics as well as bonding between African American women. Its style could lead to acceptance or rejection from certain groups and social classes, and its styling could provide the possibility of a career, (p. 6).

When Solange says "Don't touch my pride," she refers to all of this and more. She speaks to the role hair plays in sociopolitical identity, to white supremacy's annotation of black hair, to the individual impact on people -mostly, black women and girls.

Growing up, I felt at odds with the phrase "Don't touch my hair" because I wanted nothing more than for people to touch my hair.

Well, not my *pajón* (puffy, natural hair) but my straight, soft, hella processed, deep conditioned, two and a half hours heat-treated mane. Ain't nothing wrong with that, as Solange says "You know this hair is my shit, rode the ride, I gave it time, But this here is mine." What was wrong, however, was my intent behind my hair straightening. I wanted to show people that my straight hair is open to the touch of human hands and the positive judgment of human minds. At the root, I wanted acceptance into the dominant culture; I wanted to exude eurocentric beauty. And if touching my mane did that for people, then touch it.

Dominicans have an interesting relationship with hair, not only influenced by the slave trade but also by colonization and Trujillo's dictatorship, which instilled anti-black/Haitian/dark skin sentiments. The Dominican hair salons, in line with this thought (consciously or unconsciously), create the finest of hair practices to tame the kinkiest of hair into what is *pelo bueno* (good hair). Us Dominicans know a good hair salon, by the heat placed on our heads, and the length of time our hair stays *bueno*. And when I listened to "Don't touch my hair" it brought me back to Dominican hair salons as well as that girl who craved the acceptance of the dominant culture, that girl that needed to prove whiteness through good hair. Through years of racial identity development, years of reading works by Julia Alvarez and Frantz Fanon, talking to my loved ones, engaging in anti-racist spaces; and by feeding my spiritual life and listening to classics such as Billie Holiday, Celia Cruz, and Lauryn Hill, my feelings about my hair changed. My perceptions of myself has changed. I have come to realize that people don't have to touch my hair, and in fact, I don't want them to. It perpetuates oppression and white supremacy. I have untouchable hair—straight, curly, braided, or in a *Tubi* (Dominican hair wrap). I let my hair be curly to further assert my untouchability. "Don't touch my hair." I'm okay with that. But are the white people who have always asked to touch it or who have historically altered it—are they okay with that? What does it force them to lose?

Christina

TWO MONTHS INTO THE FIRST YEAR of my PhD program, a white boy looked at me and asked "Why are you so angry?" His question made me mad, but I wasn't allowed to express that emotion because my anger would be relegated to the intersection of my race and gender, rather than a warranted reaction to my lived experiences. Three years later, Solange called me to have *A Seat At The Table* and told me, "I got a lot to be mad about." In that one song, I was seen, heard, and healed from that microaggression.

Music has always been a platform in which black people, across the diaspora, have told their stories. This is particularly true for black women whose pain is often (made) invisible. As members of multiple-subordinate groups, black women experience "intersectional invisibility." Making it less likely to have our voices heard and more likely to be differentially marginalized as compared to our black male or white female counterparts.

Therefore, it has been of the utmost necessity for black women to affirm themselves as present, and deserving of recognition in the world (i.e., Black Girl Magic). *A Seat At The Table* insists upon the visibility of black womanhood, in all of its numerous and compounding facets by inspiring black women to simply "be," and not permit the oppressive nature of the world to penetrate our personhood and consequence our mental health.

As the mules of society, black women are neither taught that we have needs, nor are we taught to recognize them and meet them. Our perpetual experience of invalidation can often call us to lash out at ourselves, and those who love us, either with an outward expression of rage, or inward, calling us to assume the responsibility for the discomfort and fears of others. Minimizing ourselves in response, so that others may continue to feel big. In "Mad," Solange declares, "I'm tired of explaining/Man, this is so draining/But I'm not really allowed to be mad." Even in her effort to validate our experiences, and give us permission to express ourselves, she too grows tired and weary.

The invisibility and weariness that black women experience and suffer from in silence contribute to our mental illness and subsequent lack of mental health treatment. It's not surprising that black women report higher rates of depression and are also among the most untreated groups for depression in America. James Baldwin noted, "Not everything that is faced can be changed, but nothing can be changed until it is faced." Until we as a country, face the invisibility, the pain and the trauma of black womanhood, nothing can be changed, and the onus for our validation cannot remain solely upon us. ∎

Heather Siegel

Teaching Racism

N O ONE IS BORN RACIST. It's an obvious statement, but one that had crystallized for me last year as my daughter and I scoured the gymnasium looking for her new cheerleading coach.

"She has black hair and is wearing a red shirt," my third grader said, exasperated, summoning all the detail she could as I pressed her to describe the woman she'd practiced with for the last hour.

I scanned the room, rife with prepubescent sweat and pulled off my scarf, the heat getting to me. Black hair and red shirts – the color of the sports shirts given by the Boys and Girls Club – blurred past. Children screeched by. Adults bounded after them. Outside was dark and raining. I'd been up since 6:00 a.m., had an unmanned pot of split pea soup cooking on the stove, and just wanted to get home.

"There!" My daughter pointed. A woman in a red shirt with black hair was fast disappearing through the crowd. I called after her, wielding a permission slip. Coach Tammy turned and waited.

I saw that she was young and African American – two identifying characteristics I, a middle-aged, Caucasian woman, might have used to describe someone I was looking for in a crowd, but my white daughter thought irrelevant to mention.

With a swell in my heart, I knew then what I'd known for the last eight years: that my kid saw people the way she saw flowers, or cookies. Matter-of-factly, they came in different colors, forms, ages and sizes – and she certainly had no feelings of superiority or inferiority about where she might fall in the spectrum of differences, save maybe for being pro-child.

It's true that we've maintained her bubble of innocence in our home-- one I like to think balances art and science, emphasizes education, and considers people through their kindness and contributions to the world. Still, the outside world has found a way to pierce through, if not when traveling outside our bubble, then through *The Nightly News,* or school.

"Mom," she exclaimed last October, heralding a Martin Luther King Jr. reading packet, "did you know that people with dark skin used to be slaves?"

She looked at me astounded, waiting for an explanation. And I looked at her, endeared. Dark skin. That's how she saw us—in various shades—which made way more sense than black and white.

The sick and twisted time in American history she wanted to know about, not so much.

I gave it my best shot—as best as I could in elementary terms—and was taken aback when she asked me what the N-word was, something a friend at school said existed. This, I refused to tell her—no good could come of knowing the word, I told her. But she pressed on. "Was it 'nosy?' 'Nutty?'"

"It's not something to joke about," I admonished. The hairs went up on her arms at my tone, and I knew there was no way out but through the truth.

"It's a word white people have used over black people since slavery times to try to make them feel bad about themselves, and you can never use the word."

And then I told her the word.

"That's it?" She looked at me confused.

"It's a series of sounds to you, but it means something really hurtful to others. Imagine someone called you a name on purpose, knowing it would really bother you."

I couldn't think of an example.

"The bottom line is," my husband chimed in, "it's a terrible, terrible word."

"Worse than the F-word?"

"A thousand times worse," he continued, "And if you ever hear one of your friends use that word, you can't be friends with that person anymore."

"But what if they just say it?"

"There's never a reason to just say it," he said.

Of course, we had more expounding to do after she overheard Dave Chapelle use the word liberally as part of his routine on *SNL*.

Maybe we are bad parents for letting her play Legos while we watch adult television, but as she moves through middle childhood, the dome of innocence is becoming more of a Lite Brite box with holes of light pocking through. Better to filter the topics through us, I'd decided at some point. That said, while I explained that black people are the only ones entitled to use that word, I'm not sure I gave her an age-appropriate, enlightened answer as to why.

"They rightfully took back the word," I said, "to take away its power, the way women took back the word bitch."

No dice. Still, she tried to keep up – soaking in what she could make of events in the weeks leading up to, and following, the election, including the notion of white supremacy and hate crimes.

"But why would someone think they were better because of their skin color?"

The question of the last two centuries, and of the moment.

I talked about ego and ignorance and indoctrination, but I could make no logical sense to her – and for good reason. Not even when she understands that our skin is happenstance.

Thinking about this, I was reminded of an ethics course in college, where I learned about the political philosopher John Rawl's concepts of the "original position" and *The Veil of Ignorance.* Rawls argued that for a just society, people should approach racial, social and political issues from this original position by trying to suspend their knowledge of their own race, gender, religious beliefs, position of wealth, abilities and preferences.

"Racism," I told my daughter, "ultimately comes from selfishness."

People want their agenda pursued, I tried to explain. In some cases that agenda is pure hatred and destruction, in others it's more benign – but ultimately people want more for themselves. White people enslaved black people for free labor, justifying their insanity with the Bible, and somehow passing this into law. Today, 151 years since the official stop to that insanity, some white people are still defending their decisions.

Understandably, I wasn't making much sense to her. For one, this all sounded way too mean to comprehend. If she knew, for example, that her friend would suffer at the expense of a decision she wanted to make, she would have a hard time following through with that decision. For another, I was probably being unclear – as it hasn't been making much sense to me either lately.

I know the right has accused the left of not opening its collective mind and seeing their points of view – it's what supposedly lost the left the election. But I have to say, it's still tough to comprehend how 56 percent of white voters (according to a graphic by Matthew Weber at Reuters) could usher into the white house a person the KKK deems their poster child, with zero regard—or perhaps some regard, but ultimate indifference—for the message it sends to people of color.

Honestly, it's not the white supremacist who has been indoctrinated since birth that has me puzzled—obviously, he's thrilled. Nor is it the newly propagandized xenophobe, whose own gripping fear of being held hostage by ISIS usurps rationality. I wouldn't even say it's the rural farmer or factory worker whose desperation to hold down a job supersedes concern for others that has me perplexed. It's the white, middle class, middle-aged, suburban voter—my contemporary—who, for the most part, is doing okay in this country, that has me scratching my head.

I know some of these people from my own neighborhood. I know them on Facebook. People who won't—or can't—put on that veil of ignorance. People who won't or can't access empathy for others' basic fears and concerns because their own personal agendas are in the way. People who won't or can't see their indifference as a racist act.

At the same time I puzzle over my contemporaries, when I think about my daughter's innocence, and her childhood in relation to mine, maybe it doesn't seem that hard to wrap my mind around.

Like many of those voters, I grew up in the 1970s, one mere decade since the Civil Rights Act was passed, when racism was alive and well, even in the so-called liberal New York suburbs. For a number of reasons—some so preposterous, I would need to write a book about the experience—my family had broken apart; and from the age of six to twelve, I was sent to live under the foster care of an Italian woman who thought nothing of calling black people the Italian word for eggplant, or using the N-word, or warning us, as we pulled into the Pathmark parking lot and saw black faces, to lock the doors.

Spewing this racism was as natural to this grandmother-aged white woman as making meatballs—both learned from her own bigoted parents who'd grown up being taught their own superiority, just four decades shy of the Emancipation.

At school, the bigotry and hate trickled down—my white classmates parroting back what they heard in front of the evening news in their own homes. Unfortunately, my foster mother was not alone in her thinking. The mindset of that little neighborhood, populated mainly by white, blue-collar families, commiserated with her as they mowed their lawns, bitching over their dissatisfaction with President Carter, and anyone else they could blame for their own lot in life. (Little did they know, she blamed them, too; as a middle school lunch lady, she cursed their rotten kids, white notwithstanding, who made her day that much more intolerable).

There were two black students in my class, one of them I'll call Matthew. One day, at lunch, as we pushed our plastic trays forward, I overheard a conversation between the two white boys next to me.

"If you touch him," the first white boy said to the other, nodding in Matthew's direction, "he'll wipe off on you."

"Do you think that's true?" my white friend Karen asked, elbowing me.

"No!" I looked at her. Could my best friend be *that* stupid?

"Try it," the boys taunted each other while poor Matthew kept his head down.

I'd like to say that I stood up for Matthew and whacked my tray against the teeth of those white boys – and that Matthew, who hopefully never again experienced exposure to hate and bigotry, could remember that white-trash, foster girl with frazzled short hair, weird clothes and spaces between her teeth, breaking some white kid's jaw for him. But I did no such thing.

It wasn't because I lacked the courage or grit to do so – I'd been sent home for my share of fist fights, as I worked through the emotional letdown of my parents. It was because I failed to see that the crisis at hand was not first and foremost about the stupidity of those white boys and my friend Karen, but Matthew! Matthew's feelings, and the future repercussions on his soul and personality as a result of this act of racism – even if it was the first and last time he ever experienced it. And I don't believe it was, not then, and not when in 2015, Ta-Nehisi Coates wrote about the fear of being in a black body.

What I did manage to do was belittle the boys for their idiocy; and while it didn't reverse that moment, or reset their minds, it did make them shut up. What I was fortunate enough to have over those other white kids, the one saving grace to act as a counterbalance to the mentality of that white neighborhood I lived in, was my father's passion for women.

My father had a lot of faults, but being prejudiced was not one of them, and when it came to women, following the disappearance of my mother, he dated across the spectrum of color. I'm sure there was some objectification going on – but no more so than there'd been with my white mother. I also think his make-love-not-war sentiments, his love for Motown and 1970s disco, and his endless stash of marijuana, gave him a unique set of glasses from which to view the world – and to rebel against his own bigoted upbringing with his parents in the Jewish tenements of New York, where hurling racial epithets, among other forms of racism, was a way of life.

Can you have a black soul if you are white? If you can, my father has one. Even today, he may look like Al Pacino, but inside he is pure Barry White. No one grooves harder to "Can't Get Enough of Your Love Baby."

There was also his sensitivity toward animals, underdogs, people with disabilities, disfigurements and weight issues that I absorbed. Once, during an every other weekend, as my brother, sister and I waited on the bench seat of my father's Vista Cruiser for him to exit a store, a heavy-set woman waddled by in a duck-like fashion, and we snickered and pointed at what we essentially saw as a human cartoon. As my father approached the car, carrying a bag of black plums, he narrowed his eyes behind his John Lennon glasses. He got in and slammed the door, his voice rising higher-pitched than we'd ever heard.

"Don't you EVER make fun of someone for the way they look. Do you hear me? You should be ashamed of yourselves. Some people can't help the way they look."

He was, in part, talking about himself and his lifelong battle with psoriasis – those baseball-sized patches of silvery-scaled skin that pawed along his whole body and tormented him. Part of the reason, I believe, he fell so hard for my mother – and subsequent women – was that they didn't see *his* skin.

My father's women – during my years in foster care and thereafter – gave me a counterbalance, too, by way of just being themselves. In my eyes, black and brown were not only beautiful, but enviable. I will leave the analysis to the psychoanalyst – though I can guess the Oedipus concept would come up in session – but eventually I wanted to be these women. Ani with her cinnamon skin and mesmerizing Cuban accent that, when no one was looking, I would pretend was mine while reading my Judy Blume books aloud. Bernice with her perfect mahogany brown skin and taut physique that seemed right out of an anatomy textbook, each muscle so perfect and defined – hers was a body I could never have, no matter how long I tanned or how many sit ups I did while listening to KISS FM. I paled in comparison to these women – my own translucent skin with ugly purple veins showing through.

By the time I was eleven or twelve, I would return from an every-other-weekend to my foster mother and defy her comments, openly challenging her, albeit with, "You know, that's really not nice." By the time I was thirteen, and my father had taken us back – taken us to live with Ani – I'd all but dismissed my foster mother's nonsense parking lot comments.

But it would take seven to ten more years to find words to articulate any real thoughts, and to go deeper into the perspective of another. And it would take even longer to realize that a lot of kids I'd grown up with never had any negation to the racism they absorbed.

They came of age and turned not only into voters, but parents.

Following the election, I started thinking – wishing really – that there was a technology that existed to wipe a person's slate clean. Imagine there was a technology that, seconds before ballots were casted, could momentarily erase in a person's mind who she is and where she stands in life. One that would filter out the knowledge of being female, male, rich, poor, gay, trans, straight, black, brown, white, young, old, healthy, dying, married, single, pregnant, a parent, a grandparent, a teenager...

And as I sat hoping and wishing for the impossible, it occurred to me that such a technology does exist – what I've come to call the education of stories.

It's not just research that tells me that reading stories helps elicit empathy and influence people socially, but my own personal experience.

I had my father, and I had his girlfriends. But really, it was stories that worked to further negate the racism I was exposed to, and to see how skewed the world in which I grew up had been – stories in all forms, from literary fiction to commercial fiction to movies to graphic novels, and most especially, for me, stories in narrative non-fiction.

It began with my stumbling upon Frederick Douglass in my teens. Still in a dormant emotional crisis over the quasi-abandonment of my parents, I'd taken up hardcore reading to find some answers. From there it was Richard Wright, James Baldwin, Malcom X – somehow, haphazardly, in my self-study, I found these essential works, as well as others in women's literature and Jewish literature, exploring oppression, marginalization and disenfranchisement.

Sometimes much of the reading was over my head. Years later, sitting in a college lit course, I still wasn't sure I fully grasped Maxine Hong Kingston's *Woman Warrior*. Other times, I'd close a book, my whole body vibrating—Ralph Ellison's *Invisible Man,* Elie Wiesel's *Night.* Lines haunted me long afterward. I still remember the admonition in Sammy Davis Jr.'s autobiography, telling young black men who were reading his story not to be fooled into thinking that they too could rise up from the ghetto; that his tale was an anomaly of rare luck and circumstance.

With each book, and with each voice and story, I came closer to returning to that original position. And at the same time, I felt shame for the wrongs committed by white people, knowing there was little I could do about it. Or was there?

By the time I approached my twenties I saw there were endless ways, really. Small ways that mattered perhaps not in the grand scheme but in the small, criss-cross patterns of life. One of these moments came while on a date with a guy I'd met at a nightclub. I don't remember much about him, other than that he was young and white, and wore gold chains and a sweat-suit, the rage at the time. We saw the movie *Jungle Fever* together and afterward, as we pulled up to my house, he voiced his disapproval over interracial dating.

"No, I would never date a black girl," he said.

"Well, you just did, since I'm half-black," I blurted, everything welling up—the stories, my foster mother's smug look, the unearned superiority complex of a white person, haphazardly born to white parents. The conceit was ridiculous! This from a nothing who had zero to boast of in his own small life from Queens, and who would probably never make any meaningful contributions to society, but still blame the government for his shortcomings—and who would, most upsettingly, teach his kids that associating with people of color was wrong.

His face twisted in apology; I stormed off, leaving him with the zinger, "And I would never date someone ignorant."

Racism, I'd started to understand, was an insidious problem, and the way I could resist spreading it, was not by dropping a big bomb over its spread, but by inserting my own insidious fibers into offenders' minds.

I've made conscious attempts to nurture and guide my daughter not to see color as a defining feature on people. But writing this now, I realize the opposite is actually true as well. I have also tried to steer her eye toward beauty and achievements in diversity.

"He's ridiculously handsome," I will purposely say of Idris Elba—although who wouldn't? "God, she is stunning; her face is literally perfect," I will say of Lupita Nyong'o—again, obvious. "Isn't Michelle an incredible orator?" "Isn't Obama so smart and articulate?"

Maybe it is false of me, or somehow racist, to not do the same for the white people I admire. But if it is, I don't care—they seem to be doing fine rooting for themselves.

Now, as my daughter approaches ten, especially in these strange, and seemingly backwards times, I need to make further adjustments. Fielding her questions no longer seems like enough.

I need to sit beside her, pressing computer keys together as we make donations to important organizations tackling racism and hate crimes with legal bombs from above.

I need to keep exposing her to more stories I wish had been available to me and Matthew when we were growing up, narratives yet to be written like *Brown Girl Dreaming* and *The Thing About Luck;* movies that still hadn't been made, like *Remember the Titans, Woodlawn,* and *Sounder.*

I need go down to her school with other white women from my neighborhood who somehow found their own negation, and are as incensed as me at the chanting of "build a wall" in our middle school, or the school bus remark "orange is the new black."

I need to explain to my daughter that some of her friends, though they may not talk about it, go home scared, which is why we have met with her superintendent—a white woman who has found her negation, too—and has promised to further educate her faculty not to be spectators, but active educators and rule enforcers who remind students of the school's bullying policies. "Some students, unfortunately, only respond to fear of consequences," she told the group of us.

But mostly, I need to prepare my daughter to make her own small moves as they feel right to her— to strengthen her language and quip, so she can offer negation to her own contemporaries, one fibrous comment at a time. ∎

Herbert M. Ricks Jr.

How To Make A Black Russian

Tell me, how do you make a black russian?
two parts Amen Corner, etched with the scrawl
of unchained slave hands exchanging tar heels
for concrete tongues, inheriting hoof and mouth
disease like subordinated status,
spastic migrations constructing Harlem...
one pew at a time; from Sunday wood shaved,
sanded by swarthy belly grumbling,
stained by Saturday night whiskey, drizzling
from communion cups made of Styrofoam...
God in a bottle, capped, holding in the
sins of poverty's refrain; time-released
at dawn; just enough time to separate
the Sun from the holy ghost;

Please tell, how do you make a black russian?
One part Lenin; holding down the Amen
Corner with pulpits splashed in deep crimson;
Marx meets Mao meets Malcolm at the stoplight
dashing between cars on the red scare's heels
stepping up tongue-tied curbs on patented
Seven days, unable to avoid the
puddles, tracking the color of whiskey down
125th and St. Nick; Marx meets Mao meets
Detroit Red in piss-scented tenement
Crystal staircases, blunting and blurring
Langston's Hues down the creaky box of a
hallway, past apartment 7; home to this
scapegoated welfare mom named Karenina
brandished with a scarlet letter; "A" for

anarchist; Asaata! Marx meets Mao meets
Detroit red book, worshipped like a bible;
quoted in secret socials with Ellison's
invisible men, exactly why this
poem was written in blank verse on Juneteenth
while eavesdropping on a conversation
between Richard Wright and Doestoyevski

How do you make a black Russian? Combine
Smirnoff, coffee liqueur, Greenwich Village
and ice in an uptown powder keg. Drink
like it's 1929, and if we
must Claude McKay die, May we all dialectic!!

Vagabond

Blue Supremacy is the New White Supremacy

"It became necessary to destroy the town in order to save it."

— A U.S. Major on the bombing of Ben Tré in South Vietnam,
Associate Press, February 2, 1968

WE SEEM TO BE IN THE MIDST of a huge paradigm shift here in the U.S. It feels as if the country is finally catching up to the hell that black and brown women and children, and even some poor white folks have experienced when it comes to police brutality. It represents everything that is wrong with race relations and classism in America in the twenty-first century.

Police brutality, unwarranted and excessive force due to racial profiling, and other forms of mistreatment of America's citizens is not uncommon, and has been around for centuries. In fact, the Slave Patrols and Night Watches, which were both designed to control the behaviors of African Americans evolved, in part, into the modern police organization as we know it today. The Slave Patrol was a vigilante-style organization that was a means of controlling freed slaves who were now laborers working in an agricultural caste system, which also enforced Jim Crow segregation laws designed to deny freed slaves equal rights and access to the political system.[1] It is this racial terrorism that gave birth to America, so it should come as no surprise that the state's law enforcement agents have routinely engaged in the terrorism of its black and brown citizenry. And contrary to popular belief, even after slavery, Jim Crow and segregation were forced off the books, the rocky relationship with black and brown people and law enforcement have persisted into the modern day lynchings we now witness on viral videos today. The only difference is that for the first time, people are actually talking about it.[2]

When one thinks of the murders of Mike Brown, John Crawford, Eric Garner, Akai Gurley, Tamir Rice, Freddie Gray, Sandra Bland,

Alton Sterling, Philandro Castile and countless others, you would think a reasonable person would recognize their plight as a result of racism and police brutality. In fact, the brutality we witness in law enforcement reflects how the U.S. deals with racism and the military industrial complex both here and abroad. For example, the very same tear gas used by U.S. military forces against protesters in Ferguson is the same tear gas used by the Israeli military against the Palestinians. The harassment and humiliation at checkpoints in Gaza and Iraq is equivalent to "stop and frisk" in New York City. And then there are CIA contractors who are not legally held responsible for illegally detaining and torturing terrorists, or grand juries in Ferguson and New York unwilling to prosecute police for killing alleged suspects shirking an accountability of their actions. How about when the NYPD used a choke hold on Eric Garner that was banned in 1994 as three police officers held him down? The police now act as an occupying force who see themselves in hostile territory that is surrounded by a populace they must profile in order to survive in their tour of duty. Or consider CIA tactics in the form of frivolous arrests, beatings and even killings in community policing that has simply gone too far. Just look at the Chicago Police Department. If they wanted you to disappear, they took you to Homan Square, which operated as a CIA black site. [3] From Guantanamo to Homan Square, the police are using the same militarized tactics that are being used overseas.

What puts police brutality on the map is that our post 9/11 heroic reverence for law enforcement elevated the police from community policing to boldly treating the citizenry as terrorists. This is because the government expanded policing powers to accommodate perceived terrorist threats. Coupled with the politics of xenophobia and jingoism of post 9/11, this perception has often been at the expense of civil liberties (check out the Patriot Act). [4] As a result, the police have become emboldened and at the same time, insulated from taking responsibility for their actions and in particular, the brutality it has imposed.

Many police forces have taken to wearing paramilitary uniforms that includes helmets, gas masks, goggles, body armor and riot shields that are now standard-issue for officers on the job and are often worn at peaceful protests. It is this militarization of the police that has eroded an already fragile relationship between the police and its black and brown citizenry, not only because the gear signals violence, but it increases the likelihood that officers will react more aggressively – an effect that has become more profound than imagined. We are dressing our police officers for war "by any means necessary."

When law enforcement is faced with accountability, it is like telling the emperor he has no clothes, and the emperor tells you "So what?" An example of this kind of naked hubris reared its ugly head during the Trayvon Martin case when President Obama stated that Trayvon could be his son. Although Trayvon was not killed by law enforcement, it was still a shot at law enforcement because of the way the case was handled from the eventual arrest, prosecution and acquittal of George Zimmerman. It is for this reason that white people and in particular, the police, didn't like how President Obama addressed the Trayvon Martin shooting. I believe, in part, that many white people have fed into a stereotype either consciously or unconsciously that black men are dangerous. Questions of why he was in that neighborhood, or that he was wearing a hoodie prevailed and in many ways, was not only very telling, it helped justify Zimmerman killing an unarmed human being. However, in the president's view, the case reflected the racial profiling and risk of violence that young black men face every day in America, and it is this reality that left white people uncomfortable. Because think about it, how many other cases of murder by law enforcement fit the profile of what happened to Trayvon?

In another direct indictment of law enforcement by a politician, the mayor of New York City, Bill de Blasio, whose son is black, has been placed in the unenviable position of having to choose between his role as a politician (who have historically supported the idea that police don't need to be held accountable for their actions) and being a father who can get a call in the middle of the night about his own black son. When Mayor de Blasio expressed how troubled he was over the grand jury's decision to not prosecute officers in the choking death of Eric Garner, he immediately called the Justice Department and asked for an investigation. He also talked about having to talk to his son about how to deal with the police. The NYPD Patrolmen's Benevolent Association's President, Pat Lynch, who refuses to recognize police misconduct, held a press conference and said Mayor de Blasio "threw cops under the bus."[5]

Two New York City police officers Rafael Ramos and Wenjian Lui were murdered by Ismaaiyl Brinsley[6] a mentally ill man from Brooklyn who had an extensive history with the police (having been arrested twenty times, mainly for petty offenses), and shot the officers ostensibly as revenge for the death of Eric Garner and the shooting of Michael Brown. As Mayor de Blasio and his entourage walked through the third-floor corridor of Woodhull Hospital, where the two police officers had been pronounced dead hours earlier, dozens of NYPD police silently turned their backs on the mayor. It was a protest against Mayor de Blasio's criticism against the NYPD.

The impunity that law enforcement operates under in the U.S. has reached absurd new heights. Who do the police think they work for? When faced with criticism from the very people they are sworn to protect and serve, the attitude of the police escapes me. It's this very attitude that has fallen on deaf ears due in large part to the political establishment, which automatically takes the side of law enforcement. For years, the media and the majority of white Americans were convinced that the police could do no wrong, but the daily protests in Ferguson that went on for months dragged the issues of police brutality and the killing of unarmed black men by police onto a national stage. From the massive protests in New York City over Eric Garner to the recent unrest in Baltimore over Freddie Gray, the police brutality show is on a national tour. And if you think you're immune just wait until the national show pulls into your town. That's not to say that there isn't a local or regional horror show of political theater of so-called "justifiable" police killings happening all across the country, it's just that some shows rise to the level of national attention while others do not.

There's a wave building, and the nation as a whole is beginning to really see and feel the injustice that black people have had to deal with on a daily basis for hundreds of years. It's gotten to the point where even politicians who have historically and blindly defended law enforcement are questioning police tactics. You would think that the police would be somewhat nervous and worried about the sudden erosion of their most ardent supporters, but many remain inoculated against any criticism. Instead, they seem emboldened and are digging in for the long haul to defend the indefensible.

The other part of that unrepentant and emboldened attitude that informs the police comes from the history of racism in the U.S. The

U.S. was founded on genocide and enslavement and so it follows that our institutions have been built on that very same foundation. The front line of white supremacy in America has always been law enforcement, and the hiring of black and brown officers has meant little to nothing when those officers are forced to reconcile the intersection of race and policing that demands they stop being black and brown and be "blue." The racial integration of law enforcement doesn't negate white supremacy because what was once white supremacy has now become "blue supremacy."

Currently, there is a lawsuit in New York City by eleven officers of color who are in a class action lawsuit against the NYPD, alleging the department continues to use numbers-driven police tactics, and stunt the careers of officers who have spoken out against this policy. [7] The officers claim that they must make at least one arrest a day and write at least twenty summonses where the majority are people of color. If they do not meet arrest and summons quotas, they will face reprimands and their careers will be placed in jeopardy. Why is this such a big deal? Writing out summonses is an incentivized practice. Because when you don't show up for a court date, the court can issue an arrest warrant and you can spend time in jail, and still owe the court even more money. The whole practice is incentivized. Court fees and added fines for not appearing in court or paying the original ticket often supplement city budgets, not to mention these warrants make it really hard to get a job in order to pay the fines you weren't able to pay in the first place because you had no job, and hence no money. All of this is geared towards the black and brown communities. See the pattern?

One of the police officers involved in the lawsuit, native Brooklynite Edwin Raymond[8], is an active NYPD officer who was denied promotion because he refused to zero in on "black perps" for no other reason then to slap them with summonses he knew could cause potential harm. Raymond's story is one of many. People of color wanting to give back to their communities to protect and serve, yet the lines have been drawn in the sand: If a person of color wants to join the police force to "do some good" or "change it from the inside" they are thwarted by a system that often forces them to continue a long tradition of white supremacy in U.S. policing. This not only applies to the blacks and browns who want to make a difference, it also encompasses the many white police officers who fear retaliation from the blue supremacy. Where does it end?

Meanwhile, in the face of a broad nationwide movement to take stock of how law enforcement deals with this epidemic of killing the very citizens its sworn to protect, the Fraternal Order of Police has asked the U.S. Congress that police be included in hate crimes legislation. "Right now, it's a hate crime if you attack someone solely because of the color of their skin, but it ought to be a hate crime if you attack someone solely because of the color of their uniform as well," said Jim Pasco, the executive director of the National Fraternal Order of Police. [9] Even legal experts have expressed skepticism about whether the proposal would prove effective – or is needed. Under current federal law, police officers already enjoy additional protections: Killing a police officer is a first-degree murder charge, carrying with it the prospect of the death penalty. Citing the color of one's uniform as the reason for treating them differently completely sends the wrong message. When police officers responsible for the murder of black and brown citizens are not indicted, it reinforces a growing sense among many Americans that the police already enjoy institutional protections that an average citizen does not, so the idea that some lives are worth more than others under the law is unacceptable. Yet Pasco wants to put a law on the books at the Federal level that makes hating the police a hate crime.

While the bill is still being reviewed in the U.S. Congress, the "Blue Lives Matter" bill went into law in Louisiana, making it the first state in the nation where public safety workers are considered a protected class under the hate-crime law. [10] Instead of law enforcement trying to investigate their procedures, they are looking to defend them under the cover of blue supremacy in order to nullify any leveling of the playing field.

Finally, outgoing New York Police Commissioner Bill Bratton is asking lawmakers in New York to consider making resisting arrest a felony instead of a misdemeanor. Currently, resisting arrests carries a maximum penalty of one year in prison. If the charge were to become a felony, people could face anything from four years of probation to life in prison. This would further solidify the current thinking by police and their supporters that if you resist arrest then you must be guilty. As far as I'm concerned, resisting arrest opens you up to police brutality, and in some cases, a justified killing by police. [11] So instead of law enforcement seeing if their policing tactics are too aggressive, they are doubling down by defending those tactics with legislation that will protect police in cases of misconduct. We now live in a Kafkaesque world of Orwellian double-speak where you can be charged with resisting arrest without being charged for a crime.

Over 5,000 people have been killed by police in America since 9/11. That's more people than soldiers killed in the Iraq War.[12] The chances of being killed by law enforcement in America are twenty-nine times greater than being killed by a terrorist. If you're a black male you are twenty-one times more likely to be shot and killed by police than if you are a white male.[13] When you think about how worried people are about the threat of terrorism and the amount of time, money and energy spent on combating it, and you look at the actual terror of police brutality and killings, you wonder how priorities can be so misplaced. Or maybe you should have a more cynical view of it and realize that the priorities of terrorism and policing are historically in keeping with American racism.

The protests in Ferguson went viral thanks to the protesters' savvy use of social media, and because of that, the world began sending messages of support and solidarity. It was this global support that helped open the door for the parents of Mike Brown to go before the United Nations to speak about police brutality and the killings of unarmed black men in the U.S. It seems to have made an impact. Following their appearance, the United Nations began pressuring the U.S. to review its record and make substantial changes in the way it polices its citizens. This strategy of going before the United Nations is not a new idea. It was Malcolm X who made the argument that the race issue in America should go before the United Nations and not before the U.S. government. Malcolm X argued that the race problem in the U.S. was a problem of human rights not of second class citizenry. He knew that exposing the race problem in the U.S. to a world stage would erode its ceaseless marketing attempts at being the greatest nation of freedom and democracy in the world.

The powder keg that is the race problem in the U.S. was bound to explode in the front lines of law enforcement, because it's where the U.S. race problem is most blatant, most raw and most naked. When the police are able to capture the likes of James Egan Holmes, who went on a shooting rampage in a movie theater in Colorado, or

Dzhokhar Tsarnaev, the suspected Boston marathon bomber, both of whom are white, it is a glaring example of the racism in the U.S. If these white suspects of atrocious crimes can be apprehended nary a scratch, then why can't the police apprehend unarmed black and brown people without killing them? I think the answer is plain and simple.

Incidents of racial bias by police, harsh treatment of a black and brown citizenry by police and police shootings in questionable circumstances are continuing to generate protest and investigation across the U.S. Many critics of contemporary law enforcement cite the continued dominance of police departments by whites, often in cities that have become majority black and brown, as a significant cause of continued problems between police and the communities they serve. While police departments across the country are quick to point out they are having a difficult time recruiting people of color due to the pay scale, in reality, it is the racial bias and police brutality that has hindered any interest from the black and brown citizenry joining the police department. And even if they did join, it is highly unlikely they will buy into "blue supremacy" in order to keep their jobs or build their careers at a cost they are not willing to incur.

Amid the growing prominence of the Black Lives Matter movement, police brutality cases have become much harder for the police and the public to ignore. The resurgence of the racial justice movement and the sustained activism against police brutality is turning the tide on police culture, and the public's demands for increased accountability and transparency has already forced a number of forces throughout the country to overhaul and reform their departments.

The paradigm shift in the U.S. in recent years against this blue supremacy has the potential to be the catalyst that the nation needs to face its racist history and all that it's wrought. Law enforcement in this country have a fundamental obligation to protect human life and reserve deadly force as a method of absolute last resort. The fact that no state laws conform to this standard is deeply disturbing and raises serious human rights concerns. Amnesty International[14] recently released a report that found each of the fifty states have failed to comply with global standards on police use-of-force and engage in "a widespread pattern of racially discriminatory treatment by law enforcement officers and an alarming use of lethal force nationwide."[15]

If that dialogue and the work that surely must come after it is done, then there's a chance we can make substantial changes that is too long in coming. All of this provides a strong case that the problem with policing isn't actually the police, but us – the police are merely enforcing our "democratic" will. It's good that Americans – both whites and people of color – are beginning to recognize the reality of police brutality and the need for police reform, which also includes instituting community oversight, equality, decriminalization, and a commitment to reducing prison populations. Certainly, Black Lives Matter has made a tremendous difference in how Americans view police brutality, but we need to do more. In order to make some kind of meaningful impact, it needs to start at the top level, with law enforcement officials and politicians, but it also needs to be sustained at the grassroots level with black, brown and white communities coming together to eradicate police brutality and blue supremacy once and for all. ∎

ENDNOTES

1. Gary Potter, "The History of Policing in the United States, Part 1," accessed December 12, 2016, http://plsonline.eku.edu/insidelook/history-policing-united-states-part-1.

2. "The Rise of the African-American Police State," May 4, 2015, *Counterpunch*, by GARIKAI CHENGU accessed December 12, 2016, http://www.counterpunch.org/2015/05/04/the-rise-of-the-african-american-police-state/

3. Spencer Ackerman, "The disappeared: Chicago police detain Americans at abuse-laden 'black site'," *The Guardian*, February 24, 2015, accessed December 12, 2016, https://www.theguardian.com/us-news/2015/feb/24/chicago-police-detain-americans-black-site.

4. The USA PATRIOT Act, accessed December 12, 2016, https://www.justice.gov/archive/ll/highlights.htm.

5. Allen McDuffee, "NYPD Commissioner Says Snubbing Mayor de Blasio Was 'Inappropriate'," *The Atlantic*, December 28, 2014, accessed December 12, 2016, http://www.theatlantic.com/national/archive/2014/12/nypd-commissioner-says-snubbing-mayor-bill-de-blasio-was-inappropriate/384076/.

6. Kim Barker and Al Baker, "New York Officers' Killer, Adrift and Ill, Had a Plan," *The New York Times*, December 21, 2014, accessed December 12, 2016, http://www.nytimes.com/2014/12/22/nyregion/new-york-police-officers-killer-was-adrift-ill-and-vengeful.html?_r=0.

7. Ryan Sit, John Annese, and Dareh Gregorian, "Cops suing NYPD say police use quotas, and it's making the subways more dangerous," *New York Daily News,* March 1, 2016, accessed December 12, 2016, http://www.nydaily-news.com/new-york/nyc-crime/cops-suing-nypd-police-quotas-arrests-article-1.2549579

8. Saki Knafo, "A Black Police Officer's Fight Against the N.Y.P.D.," *The New York Times Magazine,* February 18, 2016 accessed December 12, 2016, http://www.nytimes.com/2016/02/21/magazine/a-black-police-officers-fight-against-the-nypd.html?_r=0.

9. Patrik Jonsson, "Anti-police violence as hate crime: Do officers need more legal cover?" *Christian Science Monitor,* January 6, 2015, accessed December 12, 2016, http://www.csmonitor.com/USA/Justice/2015/0106/Anti-police-violence-as-hate-crime-Do-officers-need-more-legal-cover.

10. Elahe Izadi, "Louisiana is the first state to offer hate crime protections to police officers," *The Washington Post,* May 26, 2016 accessed December 12, 2016, https://www.washingtonpost.com/news/post-nation/wp/2016/05/26/louisi-anas-blue-lives-matter-bill-just-became-law/?utm_term=.e1d517a8792d.

11. Josh Robin, "When the Only Crime Is Resisting Arrest, *The Daily Beast,* March 29, 2015, accessed December 12, 2016, http://www.thedailybeast.com/articles/2015/03/29/when-the-only-crime-is-resisting-arrest.html.

12. Matt Agorist, "Americans Killed by Cops Now Outnumber Americans Killed in Iraq War," Free Thought Project, December 12, 2013, accessed December 12, 2016, http://thefreethoughtproject.com/americans-killed-cops-outnum-ber-americans-killed-iraq-war/#k7CyEoHGRzSHYeqK.99

13. Ryan Gabrielson, Ryann Grochowski Jones and Eric Sagara, "Deadly Force, in Black and White, A ProPublica analysis of killings by police shows outsize risk for young black males," ProPublica, Oct. 10, 2014. accessed December 12, 2016, https://www.propublica.org/article/deadly-force-in-black-and-white.

14. "Amnesty International Report Finds That All 50 States Fail to Meet Inter-national Standards on the Use of Lethal Force by Police," June 18, 2015, accessed December 12, 2016, http://www.amnestyusa.org/news/press-releas-es/amnesty-international-report-finds-that-all-50-states-fail-to-meet-interna-tional-standards-on-the-us.

15. Nadia Prupis, "To Prevent Police Brutality, Overhaul Police Culture: Report," *Common Dreams,* August 20, 2015, accessed December 12, 2016, http://www.commondreams.org/news/2015/08/20/prevent-police-brutality-over-haul-police-culture-report.

Kwaku O. Kushindana

From Babylon to Alkebulan[1]:
Where Black Lives Really Do Matter

The Overview

IT IS THE BASIC CONTENTION of this article that for black lives to really matter, there has to be an expansion of the scope of thinking about being "black" or "African." Tragically, for keen observers, the link to the historical aspect of African heritage has been severed, largely downplayed or outright omitted in the current popular struggle. The only perspective by which black lives do matter is by way of a cultural continuity, and the historical reality that our existence did not begin on slave plantations.

The international reggae star Bob Marley's classic song "War," popularized the idea of "world citizenship." The song was inspired by Ethiopian Emperor Haile Selassie's speech before the United Nations General Assembly on October 4, 1963, calling for action against racial inequality, international injustice and world peace at the U.N. Conference in New York City. This historical speech was spoken a few weeks after the Organization of African Unity (OAU), founded in the Ethiopian capital Addis Ababa where Selassie chaired a summit meeting gathering of almost every African head of state. As an additional footnote, Selassie, who was born Tafari Makonnen Woldemikael, was given the Ethiopian title "Ras" (which means "prince" or "chief")[2]. It was the combination of Selassie's first name and his title that created the term "Rastafari," which gave rise to the Rastafarian movement. For me, I find the connections of Marley and Selassie relevant to my discussion:

---

[1] A note of thanks is due Yosef "Dr. Ben" Jochannan for giving us a popular understanding of Alkebulan, or the African continent.

[2] The reference to Haile Selassie simply highlights a historical moment and there is no attempt to deify him.

their shared discourse of peace and violence; the Rastafarian doctrines of the dualism of Babylon/Zion, and the divinity of Selassie through the use of Jah's words and teachings; and more importantly, at least to me, was their desire to unite and equate Africans with all Rastafarians and all blacks worldwide.

Sounding so very contemporary (the song first issued in 1976), Marley inserted sections of Selassie's speech into "War," and wrote lyrics that assert, "Until the philosophy which holds one race superior and another inferior/is finally and permanently discredited and abandoned/everywhere is war." In analyzing and listening to "War," and Marley's lyrics intermingled with Selassie's powerful speech, they provide clues and a probable foundation of the importance of African people (both continental and diaspora) becoming "world citizens," free from the appendage of being "obscene caricatures of Europe" as Frantz Fanon once described.[3]

By including Selassie's speech, what Marley was proposing in "War" was Pan-Africanism, a worldwide intellectual movement that aims to encourage and strengthen bonds of solidarity between all people of African descent. At its core, Pan-Africanism is a belief that African peoples, both on the continent and in the diaspora, share not merely a common history, but a common destiny, stressing the need for collective self-reliance. Selassie, Julius Nyerere, Ahmed Sekou Toure, and Kwame Nkrumah, grassroots organizers such as Marcus Garvey and Malcolm X, and academics such as W. E. B. Du Bois, and others in the diaspora were advocates of this cause. What I am proposing is that in order to establish Pan-Africanism, we must move towards world citizenship. And in order to truly become world citizens, African Americans and people of African descent must move beyond provincial, parochial and limited ways of thinking by using critical study and international travel as a springboard for internal transformation, in order to acquire cultural appreciation of one another. As the revolutionary poet, political organizer and international figure Amílcar Cabral of the PAIGC[4] once noted when paraphrasing Karl Marx, "theory in the hands of the masses becomes a material force."

---

[3]   Frantz Fanon, Chapter 6. "Conclusion," *The Wretched of the Earth* (1961)

[4]   Amílcar Cabral (1924-1973) of Guinea-Bissau and Cape Verde Islands in West Africa, founded in 1956 the PAIGC or Partido Africano da Independência da Guiné e Cabo Verde (Portuguese for African Party for the Independence of Guinea and Cape Verde), which was instrumental in promoting the independence causes of the then Portuguese colonies.

Much like the Black Lives Matter movement, which is a decentralized organization that challenges heteronormative thinking, the idea of world citizenship simply compliments an existing ideology of Pan-Africanism that can link African people in a non-essentialist way towards better understanding. Working at Washington Dulles International Airport (IAD) in Northern Virginia, each day I witness various languages spoken by many nationals from a vast array of countries. I find it both tragic and amusing that many people of African descent fail to realize that the African population spans the globe, beyond the United States and Africa, who speak different languages and have varied cultural backgrounds. In fact, I find it depressing to witness the vast hatred and misconception between African Americans and African people while simultaneously worshiping all things European and Western.

While it is true that Africans (from the continent) do not harbor the same fear of rootlessness as African Americans who have ached for acceptance in a culture where pronounced whiteness is the only acceptable beauty, they both share a background that reveals cultural and historical factors (such as colonialism and imperialism). Yet despite our shared circumstances and conditions, a clash exists between the two groups. Tragically, too many African Americans think that Africa is one country with one language. I wish this were not true, but I have heard this so often that I am no longer shocked when I hear it. Or as one person I ran into on an HBCU campus once told me, I could not have possibly been in Africa, because she received an email from me, and there is no email in Africa. Sadly, these firsthand accounts of misunderstandings are not one-sided, there also exists a deep misunderstanding and a failure from the African population to appreciate African Americans' contributions to the African diaspora. Regardless of what people from places like Nigeria, Uganda or Jamaica may think of African Americans, were it not for the Civil Rights and Black Power movements (from which Black Lives Matter evolved), it is more than likely that the African world would still be suffering from some form of institutional apartheid today.

What I have found truly fascinating among every segment of the African world is that next to none, an infinitesimal amount of people have put the conditions of African Americans in its proper social and historical context. This does not include the intracountries misconceptions and rivalries, the deep-seated tribalism, and the acceptance and perpetuation of age-old myths, which have zero limits. Mind blowing is that people from various African countries, the United States, the Caribbean, and other parts of the world have absolutely no grasp of an international Pan-African connection. With many experiences in mind, I have become utterly exhausted at the way people speak about various aspects of the African world by floating ideas on specific myths and stereotypes amplified by the "white power structure" and the media, but have little to no understanding of themselves, not to mention the larger African world. This is why I am proposing critical study and travel to obtain world citizenship.

These ideas evolved from traveling to sixty-nine countries (with hopes to make Cuba my seventieth country now that there are no longer restrictions). These countless adventures were planned out of a necessity, a curiosity to learn, to expand my horizons. I've learned languages, people, and cultural traditions, but more importantly, I learned more about myself and my place in the world. When I share this knowledge with other people, they are baffled. They see international travel and self-directed critical study as absurd and out of reach, regardless of their education, socio-economic status, or gender. But things are looking up.

There's a "Black Travel" movement going on, a growing band of travel agents and social networks that celebrate and promote travel by people of color. There is a sense of awareness that's heightened when African America people travel. If you're reading this with a defensive edge, understand that this is for anyone who is interested in world citizenship, and how traveling abroad can enhance one's experiences, this is why travel is so vital because visiting new places, especially beyond clichéd and commercial tourist traps, is enlightening.

Do we bring the same colonial sense of superiority that people of color have had to endure to other people? Are we even aware of our attitude toward other cultures? The best antidote for decolonizing the mind, is critical self-directed study. This is why international travel goes hand-in-hand with a desire to learn new things: reading, exploring the library and Internet, the tools for obtaining world citizenship status. Why is this so important? We are an enigmatic and multi-faceted group of people who can learn a great deal from the other side of the world. The flagship of the new world citizenship movement is a cross-cultural one that can allow us to see the world from a different perspective.

Finally, if you have any fears about "traveling black," take a deep breath. For the most part, your Americanness will probably be more notable than the color of your skin. Most people in different countries can spot Americans a mile away. And, because American culture is pervasive worldwide, any stereotypes they might have about our race has been likely formed by our own popular culture. The good news is that the Obama presidency has also informed the way people think about African Americans, which has left a mostly positive impression around the world. The first step, of course, is that in order to gain access, you have to gain confidence in yourself, and be willing to step out of your immediate surroundings. The question is, "Are you willing to take a chance to gain world citizenship?"

Moving Towards Praxis

RATHER THAN AN EXHAUSTIVE LIST of things that can be done to make it concrete that black lives really do matter in an international context, and that obtaining World Citizenship status is key to opening a door into this world, here are a few suggestions:

1. A great way to get instant access to the international communities is by listening to radio. Several apps like TuneIn Radio, now gives us the ability to listen to hundreds of radio stations and podcasts from around the world, with some programs broadcasting in the English language. You can access categories of radio stations as well as by counties and music genre.

2. Use your passport, and if you do not already have one, get one. They are good for ten years and even if you are not planning a trip now, when you do, you won't have to deal with the hassle of getting one at the last minute. Get out and explore!

3. Use your library card, and if you don't have one, get one. The library still remains one of the best sources of information that can lead to knowledge. And if you have kids, bring them too. Let's finally put to rest that "the best place to hide something from black people is to put it in a book."

4. As was one of the basic themes for the cult classic book, *To Heal a People: Afrikan Scholars Defining a New Reality*[5] get out and read the print versions of both mainstream and alternative newspapers to acquire varying viewpoints of what is happening in the world.

5. Learn a second and possibly a third language. I have learned basic Spanish and speak survival French (very limited) and have gained fluency in German. It is utterly amazing how learning new languages greatly expands your cultural understanding of the world around you, and surprisingly gives you greater insight into your own native language.

Conclusion

COMING BACK TO AMÍLCAR CABRAL, let us remember to "tell no lies, claim no easy victories,"[6] which in essence reminds us that in order to overcome the obstacles to achieve world citizenship will require external vigilance, and should not be thought of as a part-time vocation, but a lifetime endeavor.

It is my eternal hope that your travels will not be limited to the familiar, like the Caribbean or Europe, and that as you dip your toe in the water, you will let the ripple widen to other places in the world, leading you to a better understanding of the African diaspora, and a taste of Pan-Africanism. When you are ready, "jump bad" (thanks to Haki R. Madhubuti for this expression), and make the move. And when that happens be sure to smile when you hear Bob Marley's song "War," and know that you are fulfilling a prophecy. ∎

---

[5] Erriel Kofi Addae, *To Heal a People: Afrikan scholars defining a new reality* (Kujichagulia Press, 1996)

[6] Amilcar Cabral, *Revolution in Guinea*, stage 1, London, 1974, pp 70-72

Emmanuel Harris II

"Vidas negras voces negras:"
A Spanish Caribbean Perspective of
Celebrating Black Lives

THE IDEA THAT BLACK LIVES MATTER transcends borders, nationalities, the continental United States, regions, gender and even chronological and special considerations is well accepted. Indeed, the lives of Africans and people of African descent merit celebration, vigilance as well as personal, political and social safeguarding. We need only to look at the initiatives established with the Pan-African Congresses to see that for generations activists, politicians, scholars and common folk worldwide and of various racial classifications have fought for, defended and celebrated black lives. Included in the black diaspora are the struggles and contributions of our Spanish-speaking brothers and sisters in the Caribbean and surrounding areas. As our neighbors, understanding and recognizing the transgenerational importance of black lives using the Caribbean as an example further illustrates the depth and breadth of movements to preserve lives too often jeopardized. In this investigation, I look at some of the key contemporary figures from the Spanish-speaking Caribbean whose activity in such movements exemplifies efforts in the struggle for black self-preservation, political freedom and artistic recognition. I highlight contemporary means to remain vigilant and insure that no stone remains unturned and no injustice unreported or underreported especially when it pertains to people of African descent. These are *vidas negras voces negras* or black lives, black voices.

■ ■ ■

IN THE CARIBBEAN, a region renowned for centuries of the mixing of mostly indigenous, African, and European ancestored peoples, the area's racial makeup has been described as consisting of everything from a completely heterogeneous conglomeration of people, to a highly segregated and racially stratified region not unlike the United States. It is no accident that many of the racial terms still in use today in varying degrees come to us from the Spanish language – *negro, mulato, sambo, mestizo,* picaninny (from *pequeña niña* or little girl). Race or skin color form the basis of a documented social hierarchy in which Europeans (Spanish) held the highest social positions, and blacks the lowest (*Africa in the Americas*).

In Latin America, race constructions are as inconsistent as in any other geographic region, if not more so. Scholars often speak of how individuals may change how they classify themselves according to their class standing. Thomas Mathews presents the issue rather clearly in his essay regarding race matters in Puerto Rico: "It is well-known that the racial classification of the people in Latin American countries, and of course Puerto Rico, can change as they move up the social ladder" (317). Franklin Knight suggests that, in contrast to the United States, places with predominantly black and mestizo populations tend not to stress race in terms of color, but rather these areas "emphasize notional race, in which cultural identification is more important than blood or family" (*African Dimension* 72). Because race categories depend on culture rather than bloodlines, as Knight argues, such classifications can be much more fluid. Nevertheless, race, as incorrectly as we might employ the term, does matter and does have meaning to people. And a disproportionate number of black people fall victim to discrimination, sociopolitical injustice and sometimes death. Especially in the Caribbean, where the critical role and importance of individuals of African descent has not been emphasized sufficiently.

The Puerto Rican writer José Luis González argues that, of the island's indigenous, African, and European roots, the African cultural elements provide the core of Puerto Rican identity. González defines the country as being composed of four different tiers or stories, which in many instances correspond to racial divisions. He also argues that because blacks and mulattoes were forcibly cut off from Africa as a result of slavery, and because they tended not to feel any particular loyalty to the European nations, African-ancestored peoples were the first to accept Puerto Rico as their home (39). Throughout the first three centuries of the country's post-Columbian history, he argues, popular culture was essentially Afro-Antillean in character, which consequently made the island similar to other Caribbean nations (11). According to González, the first story of Puerto Rican society consists of blacks and mulattoes, descendants of slaves, while the second tier is composed of people who immigrated into the country in the early nineteenth century. Many question his categorization of the other two stories in the island's history; the third level he describes occurred as a result of the 1898 war and the United States' invasion; and the fourth level a still forming rising class of former lower strata dwellers. However, let us not forget that the ethnic and culturally identifying foundation of the populous rests firmly on African ancestored shoulders.

Meanwhile, in Colombia, Manuel Zapata Olivella has done more than any other erudite to raise the public consciousness of the black experience in Hispanic America. An anthropologist, medical doctor, folklorist, essayist and novelist, he traveled the world to engage in activities as diverse as promoting Afro-Colombian dance, espousing the socialist philosophies of China's Mao Zedong, and investigating the culture of areas such as the United States' deep South and the African continent. Much of the artistic impetus for his fiction – where he often presents the multiethnic and multiracial perspectives of the lower or oppressed segments of society – derives from these travels and his own experiences. Throughout his prolific literary career and especially evident in his later works, the author grants particular emphasis to African ancestored and racially mixed (*mestizo*) populations in the Americas. His last novel, *Hemingway cazador de la muerte* [Hemingway Hunter of Death] (1993), diverges from this trend only because it takes place exclusively in Africa.

Topics relating to African people or people of African ancestry and their struggles for social, ideological, and/or political liberation constitute a thematic foundation in Zapata Olivella's writing. The writer's response to the conditions suffered by the oppressed sectors of society often appears in some form of physical resistance or ideological subversion demonstrating how black lives matter. A mere cursory glance at the titles of some of his texts reinforces the struggle he undertakes and advocates: *Cuentos de muerte y libertad* [Stories of Death and Freedom](1961), *Caronte Liberado* [Caronte Freed] (1972), *Changó, el gran putas* [Changó, the Biggest Baddass](1983), *El fusilamiento del diablo* [The Execution of the Devil] (1986), *¡Levántate mulato!* [Rise Up Mulato!] (1990), "Los ancestros combatientes" [The Combative

Ancestors] (1991), and *Rebelión de los genes* [Rebellion of the Genes] (1997). *Changó, el gran putas,* a novel which marked the fruition of twenty years of investigation and elaboration by the author, is considered to be Zapata Olivella's master work (Rebelión 27).

Changó incorporates a myriad of Pan-African historical figures and cultural elements into an epic that celebrates the heroes and struggles of the black African diaspora in the Americas. The title refers to Changó (also known as Shangó), the god of fecundity, fire, and war within the Yoruba pantheon of gods. According to Zapata Olivella, the domain associated with Changó, also constitutes a vital part of black folks' lives ("Conversación" 30). The book traces African ancestored peoples' efforts for survival – with the surveillance and intervention of Yoruba gods – from early man in Africa to their arrival in the Americas to the civil rights conflicts in the United States. Within such parameters and with the use of African words in poetry and narrative, the text includes deities like Changó, Esu-Elegbara, and historical figures such as Benkos Bioja, Toussaint L'Ouverture, Harriet Tubman, Nat Turner and Zora Neale Hurston to name just a few, and references among other items to Birmingham's four little girls and Tuskegee. That a Columbian author would be well-versed in black history and African American struggles in 1983 – much better than many of us are today unfortunately – should not be overlooked.

Similarly, of the most preeminent Costa Rican writers and arguably one of the most recognized living Afro-Hispanic writers, Quince Duncan is a black man of Jamaican heritage who was raised in Costa Rica's Caribbean coast. He re-released a collection of his short stories which he titled *Cuentos escogidos* [Selected Stories]. The collection, which includes four previously unpublished works, contains a variety of stories that while set in Costa Rica, underscore the blight of African-ancestored peoples around the world. Yet his lyrical, gripping, quotidian portrayal of the human experience renders his fiction both timeless and quite timely. Nevertheless in today's world, the fiction and the stories they depict are too often underappreciated, overlooked or inadvertently or expressly ignored and marginalized. A closer examination of Duncan's writings belies pertinent and relevant representation of race, race relations and love in his native land and in the Americas as a whole.

Duncan's work has spanned decades and has included a variety of genres, for example novels (*Espejos* [Mirrors], *La paz del pueblo* [Peace of the Pueblo]), short stories "Dawn Song;" "La rebellion de Pocamilla" [The Pocamilla Rebellion] and essays (*El negro en Costa Rica* [Blacks in Costa Rica]). Additionally, he has published a collection of Afro-Costa Rican folktales and travels extensively both nationally and internationally, and is seen as a true public scholar. Dellita Martin Ogunsola describes him as the "granddaddy of the word." Similarly, Dorothy Mosby, in her extensive research into his work, highlights the intellectual, creative and humanitarian contributions he offers in the area of Afro-Hispanic letters, world literatures and the story of the African Diaspora in a region such as Costa Rica, a country not known for a significant black presence. The history of people—black people—becomes the focus and subject of his writings. The study and distribution of his works helps to better understand and appreciate the many hues of the black experience especially in terms of race, race relations and love.

Furthermore in Puerto Rico, Yolanda Arroyo Pizarro is a young, prolific writer who has been published worldwide and translated into English, French, Italian and German. Her novel, *Los documentados* [The Documented Ones] was awarded the Pen Prize in 2006. She also has various collections of short stories such as *Orgami de letras* [Orgami of Words] (2011) and *Ojos de luna* [Eyes of the Moon] (2007); poems such as *Saeta* (2011), and essay collections like *Las negras* (2011); in addition to appearing in numerous noteworthy journals. She has been recognized throughout the world for her literary talent, and is also fervently active in the writing and artistic community on the island. Her deeply personal works unabashedly enlighten the plight of the oppressed and oftentimes display sensual and sexualized themes and events centered around black folks in the Caribbean.

Likewise, the Caribbean, and more specifically Cuba, is the native land of a literary titan in terms of her activism and writing: Inés María Martiatu (affectionately known as "Lalita"), who unexpectedly passed into the realm of the ancestors in July 2013, is profoundly missed in many ways. She was an ardent advocate of African culture and narrative throughout Latin America, and as an Afro-Cuban, Lalita was a courageous voice for black causes and perspectives. She confronted conflicts about race, identity, discrimination, and marginalization of women in her thought-provoking books and essays.

Lalita's written legacy of scholarly and literary works consists of fifteen books, countless articles and essays, and a number of academic and social contributions. Her publications have appeared throughout Cuba as well as the United States, Canada, Mexico, Colombia as well as several other countries. Among the numerous awards and recognitions she received were the Critics Prize from the journal *Tablas* (1984); the Short Story Prize in "Women's Themes" given by the Colegio de México and Casa de las Américas (1990); the Razón de Ser grant for literary and artistic creation from the Alejo Carpentier Foundation (2002). In 2002, she also received the prestigious "Recognition of Distinction for National Culture" conferred by the Cuban Ministry of Culture and the Commission of the State. And most recently her article "¿Y las negras qué? Pensando el afrofeminismo en Cuba," [And Black Women? Thoughts on Afro-Feminism in Cuba] was the finalist for the Casa de las Américas' "Prize for Extraordinary Studies on the Black Presence in America and the Caribbean" (2012). Lalita was also an honored member of UNEAC (Unión Nacional de Escritores y Artistas de Cuba). The Cuban poet, essayist and theatre critic, Waldo González López, praised her "as an intellectual in her unique and important literary production...in essays and narrative creations and her investigations into Afro-Cuban culture and its connection with the setting, the arts, women and society." (*Afromodernidades,* July 13, 2013).

Cuban scholar, Daisy Rubiera explains: "We had a number of projects, and we were always aware of the need to include the voice of black women, not only in the debate about racial conflicts currently taking place within the country, but also those that arise as a counter-discourses opposed to the voices that historically have been recognized. *Afrocubanas: historia, pensamiento y prácticas culturales* [Afro-Cuban Women: Cultural History, Thought and Practices] is an example of this (inclusion)." (*Afromodernidades,* July 14, 2013)

For those that knew her, Lalita's affability, compassion, patience and wisdom were quickly apparent. Never one to judge, she possessed the knowing gaze of the elders and the unhurried calm of the wise. Always giving of her time and attention, she had an impeccable memory and abundance of knowledge. She was known to speak at length without notes or outlines, and yet recall places and names that only the most learned could fully appreciate. She loved Cuba and her people immensely, and took a great amount of pride in her homeland. She celebrated the Cuban spirit and what some deemed as her own cultural *cimarronaje* – escaping slavery or bondage – while she advocated

for the most marginalized sectors of society, and her willingness to take risks that go beyond being a social critic, but always a critic with compassion and understanding on several levels.

Later in life she was physically impeded by rheumatoid arthritis limiting her to a wheelchair and equally complicating the ease in which she corresponded. When I interviewed her in 2011 while in Cuba, at one point she mentioned to me that fifty-four steps were how many she had to climb to get to her government issued apartment. Wheelchair bound and no elevator, yet she had to go up or down fifty-four steps whenever she wanted to leave or return home. She explained that most times her second son, Ernesto, would carry her—and Lalita was not light by any means. Other times she would pay a neighbor a small fee to lift her down the stairs. She said she had to thoroughly plan for trips out of the house to ensure she had a means to navigate those fifty four steps. The thought of this world-renowned ideologue and matriarchal black woman being carried up and down three flights of stairs on the back of her thirty-year-old son is bothersome in a plethora of ways. One has to question whether she would be treated accordingly if she were white—even in Cuba. Thankfully, soon after the U.S. publication of her collection *Over the Waves and Other Stories/Sobre las olas y otros cuentos,* she was moved to a first-floor unit.

More and more of her time was dedicated to what would become her passion, Afro-Cubans and especially, the plight of black Cuban women. She participated in various conferences and seminaries around the world dedicated to themes relating to the African Diaspora as it pertained to her native land. From Cuba, she contributed to two blogs, afrocubana.wordpress.com and *Teatro Afroamericano.* And recently, she began to write about hip hop and socially conscious rap music, which further exemplified the breadth of her cultural interests and knowledge.

It is through the use of the Internet, social media and email grass-roots movements, that local and regional awareness have taken shape in remote areas such as Cuba, but communication with the outside world remains difficult.

■ ■ ■

ON JUNE 11, 2016, ORGANIZERS ABRUPTLY CANCELED Cuban ballet dancer and choreographer Carlos Acosta's groundbreaking auto-biographical presentation of *Sin mir atrás.* Perhaps the closure of a given

production would not have received substantial notice; however, due to the thematic elements as well as the subject of the internationally recognized dancer's work, it received a considerable amount of attention in Cuba, the country in which the production took place. Then on July 23 of that same year, Alberto Abreu Arcia posted an essay in his blog *Afromodernidades* titled, "La censura de Carlos Acosta o los rostros ocultos tras el emblem de nación mestiza" [The censure of Carlos Acosta or the *Hidden Remnants Behind a Mestizo Nation*] in which not only does he shed light on the background to this event, he postulates on the reasons behind what on the surface appears to be an extremely arbitrary decision to cancel the show. Abreu Arcia writes the following in his blog:

> Not only was it a despotic act of censure committed against the glory of international ballet, but without doubt, the motives for the cancellation had to do with the depiction of anti-black racism (a burning topic in contemporary Cuban society). And as if that weren't enough, the decision involved one of the most legendary figures and cultural institutions of post-revolutionary Cuba. (July 23, 2016) [My translation—all translations are my own]

Upon continuation, he quotes Maykel Paneque's article published in the *Havana Times* in which he questions the authorities' motives,

> Once again the official censure has exercised it dominion. While at the same time the rumors and not-so-anonymous voices abound to suggest an explanation that counters the official statement or in this case, its uncomfortable silence.

Thus, Abreu Arcia's voice in the written form of a blog, fills a void that has been silenced in a public arena. In this case, it pertains to the life story of an accomplished artist of African descent being arbitrarily censured.

The issues confronting people of African descent have taken a multiplicity of forms. The role of the writer and the power of the pen can be seen in the groundbreaking investigations and expositions of scholar-authors like Arroyo Pizarro, Duncan, and Lalita, as well as Carlos Guillermo Wilson in Panama, and Lucía Charún Illescas in Peru. Addressing race, racial categorizations, phenotypical prejudice in addition to the omission, suppression or destruction of black lives, the Internet and social media constitute a worthwhile point of departure to assess social and cultural realities for example in the Caribbean. Writings by people of African descent, like other ethnic groups, have a rich

and varied history that have explicitly and implicitly influenced others' world views. Emotionally charged writings bring to the forefront the plight of the oppressed in our geographic and ideological neighbors while showing the human aspect of social activism. Further analysis of the digital writings of Cuban author and scholar Abreu Arcia and particularly his blog, *Afromodernidades,* is a case study on how contemporary Afro-Hispanic writers circumvent established norms to underscore the importance of black lives in order to foment social change. Furthermore, upon closer examination and reflection, we see not only the sociopolitical importance of his writings, but also the literary and scholarly value of his and similar writers' postings.

As stated in his web profile, Abreu Arcia is a renowned essayist, novelist and born in Cardenas, Matanzas, Cuba where he still resides. He is the author of several books and important studies on contemporary Cuban culture among which *Virgilio Piñera: un hombre una isla; Los juegos de la escritura o la (re) escritura de la historia,* which received the Dador Award from the Cuban Book Institute and the Casa de Américas Prize for Essay in 2007; an anthology with Isnalbys Crespo, *Campos cruzados: Crítica cultural la latinoamericanismos y saberes al borde,* and 2014 book publication of *La cuentística de El Puente y los silencios del canon narrativo cubano.* He celebrates his African heritage and writes on topics such as race, identity, and LGBT issues; and is a member of the Articulación Regional Afrodescendiente de América Latina y el Caribe (ARAAC). He has given presentations throughout the United States and Latin America and his blog, *Afromodernidades,* is just one of the many ways he is involved with the Afro-Cuban community.

Afromodernidades merits significant attention for a number of reasons. However, it is important to first understand the context of blogging in Cuba. As one can imagine, the use of the Internet and in particular a blog, presents numerous opportunities to be heard for those with something to say. The situation in Cuba, contrary to popular belief, is rather peculiar. According to Anna Cristina Pertierra in her article, which appeared in *Boletin del mundo,* the information sharing that occurs in Cuba is quite ample:

> It is certainly true that all telecommunications and media infrastructure in Cuba is state controlled and that access to such technologies and media is determined by political rather than commercial considerations. Furthermore, much state-produced

Cuban media is dedicated to news and current affairs and closely connected to the viewpoints and objectives of the socialist government. Consequently, media such as newspapers, television and radio broadcasts, and more recent media and communication technologies such as mobile phones and the Internet have been central and visible platforms upon which the cold war politics of the United States and Cuba have been staged in recent years.

The high cost of Internet connections prohibits the overwhelming majority of the population to have access. A press release from the World Briefings in July of 2015 stated that in Cuba Internet use would decrease from $4US to $2US for households. Additionally, the increased availability and implementation of cellular phones further facilitates surfing the web to a certain extent. Nevertheless, Cubans tend to readily have more access to email. Herein, the blog fits well and becomes a means if not to connect with the masses, provides a mechanism to connect to the Cuban diaspora and its sympathizers.

Research on blogs and bloggers has increased recently though most have focused on the sociopolitical and mass media perspectives. I propose we additionally heed the contents of social media such as blogs like Abreu Arcia's *Afromodernidades* to provide a more global perspective outside of what mass media might choose to provide. At times, greater truths can be found from alternative sources—eyewitnesses for example—than perhaps the "alternative truths" that local, state or national governments present. The examples are too numerous to name completely but the social media outcries to the killing of blacks at the hands of police in Ferguson, Cincinnati, Charlotte led to sustained intense investigations.

We must keep in mind that Abreu Arcia is a recognized and accomplished writer and intellectual, and a Casa de Americas award recipient *who writes and lives in Cuba*. Marie Laure Geoffray's article which provides analysis of the sociopolitical realities of Internet use by Cubans corresponds especially well with *Afromodernidades*, and helps contextualize the blogs objectives to create change. Geoffray categorizes blogs into three areas:

I propose to name those arenas: the dissident, contentious, critical and diaspora arenas. The classification I propose here

is based on an analytical distinction I make between these arenas' political positions and strategies vis-à-vis the Cuban government. Dissidents directly confront the government, find the socialist regime to be illegitimate, and call for free and fair elections. Contentious voices accept the socialist heritage as legitimate, but they disagree with the current socialist rule. Critical voices remain within authorized boundaries and do not question the government's legitimacy.

Abreu Arcia would fall somewhere between the second and third groups in that while he is critical of the government especially in terms of its treatment of African-ancestored peoples, women, and the LGBT community, he does not advocate its overthrow or complete subversion. And it is unclear as to whether or not he disagrees with the socialist rule. Nevertheless, the writings that appear in his blog are often brazenly critical of the government, yet at no time does Abreu Arcia call for a new revolution.

According to Stafani Vicari's conclusions, which she postulates in her article, "Blogging politics in Cuba: the framing of political discourse in the Cuban blogosphere," Abreu Arcia's entries become even more salient. According to Vicari:

> Overall, research on blogs and blogospheres has shown that blogging eases the renegotiation of public and private discourse practices, where popular and unpopular topics differently spread from blog to blog in dynamics of concentration and isolation. . . In line with these considerations, [her] study considers bloggers as social agents who blur argumentations in support or against normative politics via the extensive use of personal narratives and cultural knowledge. (1002)

At times, Abreu Arcia's writing ranges from dynamic isolation to spheres significantly more public. In his blog index, he includes what could be called his vision statement in which his postings counters the dominant discourse in Cuba which is white, male, heterosexual and pedantic. Abreu Arcia states, "*Afromodernidades* aspires to be a bridge that permits the introduction and reflection to a subaltern modernity. It is about those that from this vantage point raise their voices attempting to place their claims in the political sphere of debates that are not only Afro-Cuban but also Afro-Caribbean and Afro-Latin American. We

reclaim appeals and inquisitions that speak of cimarronajes, utopias, cultural and historic reclamations." (*Visuales*). A cursory glance at the blog demonstrates that dating back to 2010, there are approximately 240 entries. They are indexed into eight categories, which include cultural criticism, interviews, the (re)writing of history, Afro-cultural debates and reviews. The majority of the entries fall under the "uncategorized" group and, as one would imagine, addresses a wide range of topics such as feminism, black theology, the Cuban artistic scene, Afro-Cuban dignitaries, and advocacy for racial equality.

While a few of the *Afromodernidades* entries are re-posts, such as articles by others that speak to issues relevant to Cuba, many of the entries or profound investigations of up to 2,000 words in length with references, quotations and a solid theoretical foundation. Without question, Abreu Arcia's writings merits reading, analysis and inclusion in Afro-Hispanic debate. In his most recent publication, *Por una Cuba Negra: Literatura, raza y modernidad en el siglo XIX* [Towards a Black Cuba: Literature, Race and Modernity in the Nineteenth Century] we are privy to the insight and uplift from Cuba by a Cuban about black lives in this digital age.

As Abreu Arcia concludes, he refuses to remain silent "Nor am I going to feign a tranquil gaze at the horizon with the internal passivity of someone contemplating the future of the birds in flight. Meanwhile the gray seas roar unsettlingly along with the wind at his back and raise a dust storm of garbage to the sky." It has been said that the pen is mightier than the sword. Today, in an ever more cosmopolitan world, the hope is that the keystroke is more powerful than the gun, or perhaps the assault rifle. This time around the Revolution may not be televised, but perhaps it will be podcasted, broadcasted or posted online so that the multitude can be informed, alternative truths laid bare, corrupted political so-called leaders exposed and that the lives of black men, women and children forevermore protected under the watchful eyes of the ancestors. ■

WORKS CITED

Abreu Arcia, Alberto. https://afromodernidades.wordpress.com/bienvenidos.

González, José Luis. *Puerto Rico: The Four Storeyed Country and Other Essays*. Trans.

Gerald Guinness. New York: Markus Wiener, 1993.

González Lopez, Walden. https://afromodernidades.wordpress.com/5 July 2013.

Geoffray, Marie Laure. "Transnational Dynamics of Contention in Contemporary Cuba" *Journal of Latin American Studies*. Cambridge UP 47. 223-249.

Harris II, Emmanuel D. and Antonio Tillis. *The Trayvon Martin in US: An American Tragedy*. Rutledge: New York, 2015.

Knight, Franklin W. *The African Dimension in Latin American Studies*. Macmillan: New York, 1974.

Mathews, Thomas G. "The Question of Color in Puerto Rico." *Slavery and Race Relations in Latin America*. Ed. Robert Brent Toplin. Westport: Greenwood, 1974. 299-324.

Martiatu, Inés María. *Sobre las olas y otros cuentos/ Over the Waves and Other Stories*. Chicago: Swan Isle Press. 2005.

Martin-Ogunsola, Dellita. Introduction. *The Best Short Stories of Quince Duncan*.

Mosby, Dorothy. *Quince Duncan Writing Afro-Costa Rican and Caribbean Identity*. U of Alabama P, Tuscalusa, 2014.

Pertierra, Anna Cristina. "If They Show Prison Break in the United States on Wednesday, by Thursday It's Here. Mobile Media Networks in Twentieth Century Cuba." *Television & New Media*. 13 (5) 2012 p 399-414.

Reid, Andrew. *Afro-Latin America, 1800-2000*. Oxford UP, 2004.

Rubiera, Daisy. https://afrocubana.wordpress.com/2013/07/08/fallecio-ines-maria-martiatu-una-afrocubana-de-conviccion/.

Vicari, Stafania. "Blogging politics in Cuba: the framing of political discourse in the Cuban blogosphere" *Media, Culture & Society*. Vol 36 (7) 2014. p 998-1015.

World Briefings. "Cuban Internet Users Get More Access" *Los Angeles Times. Tribune Publishing*. 19 July 2015

Zapata Olivella, Manuel. "Conversación con el doctor Manuel Zapata Olivella." With Yvonne Captain-Hidalgo. *Afro-Hispanic Review* 4.1 (1985): 26-32.

---. *La rebelión de los genes: El mestizaje americano en la sociedad futura*. Bogotá: Altamir, 1997.

Sean K. Conroy

The Fear

THE WHITE MEN ARE SCARED. It was a slow development. It grew over time, decades in fact, to where we are now. The white men are scared, and they are acting out against anyone trying to challenge their privilege. The white men are scared. I know firsthand, because I am a white man. Although I am not scared, I live among them, and I see their fear and hear their words of hatred every day. They are riled up because the rest of society is not going to take it lying down anymore, so they are fighting back.

It was among these people that I was raised. In a small town, surrounded by small minds, in an environment with little tolerance for others. A casual, not overtly racist mentality, yet with subtle influences. A slow conditioning to view outsiders with suspicion, certainly when their differences are outwardly visible. When your hometown is almost completely Caucasian the outsiders are easily identified, and cautiously dealt with. The question is, how do you "unlearn" these ideas and traits? How do you get past the fear of "other" and become a fully functional human being that's willing to make a difference in the world?

■■■

GROWING UP IN SOUTHWEST NEBRASKA, I did not see a black person in my hometown until I was in junior high school and that's only because a black family had moved to town, and they enrolled their son at my Catholic school. I later learned there were a few children at the public school who had been adopted by one of the community college professors, but as you can see, there were few black people in McCook until the late 1980s. It's not that there were no black people in Nebraska; they lived primarily in the big cities, like Omaha and Lincoln, although I never really understood why. My father led me to believe that small town Nebraska had nothing to offer them. Were they afraid of tractors? Averse to corn, to jobs in agriculture? I never really figured it out. The best he could offer was that they liked basketball, and only came to McCook on athletic scholarships, then got the hell out, leaving what he described as "half breed babies" behind. My father added as an aside to my sister, "The worst thing you could do to your children is to marry a black man, and they come out half black." Living in a small white town in Nebraska, it's not easy to be seen as different; even worse when there are few like you to offer support.

In grade school I learned about the civil rights movement, how blacks fought for equality as if it was a done deal. However, as I became older, I realized these gains were merely a foundation for the years that would follow, because full equality has not yet been achieved.

One of the things that had a tremendous impact on white people who lived in a primarily white environment was rap and hip hop. Out of the late 1970s into the early 1980s black artists emerged with an entire new genre of music that quickly grew in popularity. They spoke out against police brutality, racial inequality, and the poverty they suffered as a result of the government slowly turning its back on them. White America did not know what to make of these rappers and their hip-hop lifestyles; and in time would use their white imagination and turn these black individuals into demons and criminals.

By the 1980s, President Reagan perfected a sophisticated and subtle appeal to the prejudices and resentments that motivated whites in both the South and the North by channeling anti-black prejudice into a broader anti-government politics. He accomplished this by cultivating the impression that federal social welfare programs were mostly wasted on "undeserving" black people, building support for the anti-government ideology that exists today. While it's hard to state definitively that Reagan was himself racist, the president did make a deliberate decision to reach out to the minority of white American voters who were motivated by anti-black sentiment. And that decision has had significant political and social consequences ever since. A new mindset now greatly embedded in our society. *Fear.*

Although the density of blacks in southwest Nebraska was very low, I learned both through observation as well as from the newspaper articles coming out of Omaha that the population in the big cities of eastern Nebraska included many African American and Hispanic residents. The most visible black Nebraskan, and the bane of my father's existence as far back as I can recall was State Senator Ernie Chambers. It seemed like every time Chambers was in the news, my father became irate. Based on the interactions I had with my father growing up, it was easy to assume it was because Ernie is a black man. I wanted to give my father the benefit of the doubt though, perhaps it was because he is not a Republican, and so he must be a Democrat, which was akin to Satanism, but Chambers turned out to be an Independent, aligning himself with neither major party. Well, then, maybe it is a big city versus small town sort of thing. Yet, that was not it either, for no other big city representative in the news seemed to set my father off. My father seemed to think that if we gave in to the black senator in Omaha, the state was doomed. And so an "us" versus "them" mentality quickly developed as my father responded to the latest news out of eastern Nebraska. This mindset was not far off from what most mid-westerners felt about blacks in politics, even on a national level: When a black man speaks up for black rights, then "white rights" will be affected. In other words, for them to gain, "we" must lose, which makes no sense. Just because someone gains equality, does not mean you lose yours. The fear that somehow black people were trying to take something away from white people has become the focal point of white people protecting their white privilege and white power.

Because I was isolated from diverse groups, my familiarity with black people was limited to the media. *The Cosby Show* was the gold standard in my household, and Bill Cosby was a guy to look up to. It seemed that black people were acceptable as long as they "acted" like us, but more often than not, they were judged if they acted "too black." If they weren't of the highest upward mobility, like doctors or lawyers, they were gang bangers and cocky athletes – no middle ground there. An impossible standard was created that did not apply to white people. My father believed the civil rights movement was over, and that black people needed to assimilate and accept what had been given to them, and "act like civilized individuals" instead of tainting society and dragging everyone down.

The 1990s were arguably the most tumultuous, controversial, and racially charged decade since the 1960s. It was also an important time for me because I was coming of age and beginning to make my own decisions about race. In 1991, I remember watching in horror as a group of Los Angeles police officers faced trial for beating a man nearly to death during a traffic stop. The video evidence showed the gruesome handling of another human being who had not acted violently, had never been a threat, and could not defend himself. I was old enough to understand what was happening, and I was appalled. At first, I was thankful that the justice system would at least punish the assailants for what they did, but that didn't happen. Instead, those monsters were acquitted, which provoked the Los Angeles Riots in 1992, and in time grew to symbolize the sorry state of race relations in America. My father, on the other hand, shook his head, dropped a few "N" bombs, and turned the channel. I fully understood what was happening, but I couldn't understand why my own father could not.

The names and name calling. My family used some phrases that were common at the time, and I didn't think much of it. I grew up hearing them and initially thought they were just other words for black people. The descriptors in society evolved to be more respectful: colored became Negro, later became black, and then African American. As far as I knew, "nigger" was just another word for Negro, an antiquated but acceptable term. I remember my mother finding my sister's cassette tape of herself singing novelty Christmas carols, "Deck the Halls with Poison Ivy" and the like. My mother was appalled when she got to the "Jingle Bells" parody and heard my sister use that word in the song. When she grilled my sister, she stammered with tears streaming down her face, "I thought it was just another word for black people, daddy says it all the time." In time, we both learned better. We slowly began to realize that our father did not see the world the same way we did, and that the words and name calling were inappropriate. The Rodney King incident was our wake-up call. Something was wrong with America and we were part of the problem.

When I began to attend public high school, a much larger population of students would introduce me to people from different backgrounds. It was my first chance to figure out on my own how to interact with people dissimilar to myself. I have to believe that education was one of the strongest factors that changed my trajectory about race and took me away from the household I grew up in. Even when I attended Catholic grade school, I recalled messages of tolerance and acceptance, taught in the words of Jesus of course. In addition, interacting with my peers at such a young age influenced me as well. On the playground when we were not discussing the latest Michael Jackson video, we were fighting over who got to be Jerry Rice, Emmett Smith, Joe Montana, or John Elway. To us they were all the same, great football players who were worthy choices to emulate in our sandlot football games.

I escaped my small hometown to a college town in Nebraska where minds are further opened and diverse groups of people come together where athletic and foreign scholarships drew diverse students from across the country and around the globe. The more I learned, the more my mind expanded. As my beliefs grew, my desire to serve my fellow man as a physician who never turned anyone away based on race, creed, or orientation grew stronger and stronger. I eventually graduated college, and moved to Omaha to work in a medical laboratory. I became entrenched in a more diverse population, in the neighborhood I lived and worked in, and the patients I helped to provide care for. It was on a rare evening shift when I looked up from my microscope to see CNN reporting on a race in Illinois. A new senator had been elected, and they kept pointing out that he was African American, only the fifth ever elected as senator. I just recall how poised and professional he looked. For some reason I knew he was going to do well. So when he ran for president, before even finishing his term as senator, I was not surprised that he was already moving on to bigger things. The color of his skin didn't matter to me. I listened to him speak about change and hope for a better country, so I voted blue in a red state, wondering if all of that other stuff even mattered. In fact, Mr. Obama managed to snare one (out of the five) electoral votes my state offered, and I felt more than a little proud to have contributed to his election to the presidency.

Some time later, my mother and I were discussing President Obama's policies: I was disappointed he had not pulled out of Iraq as soon as he had promised, and had reservations about how he planned to overhaul healthcare. During our discussion, I confided to my mother, "I voted for him hoping he would do the one thing, and forget about the other, but he has gotten it backwards so far." My mother gasped and in a hushed voice responded, "You voted for him? You can never tell your father. Obama is ruining our country, and if he knew, he might never speak to you again." I again had to wonder, as I did with Ernie Chambers, is this a black thing? Is it a Democrat thing? But then I heard, "Barack Hussein Obama was born in Kenya, and is a Muslim terrorist," and his words stunned me. After years of not living under his roof, I was no longer accustomed to my father's casual racism. It seemed to have grown more overt now that a black man was the president of the United States. "He is going to take our guns and give them to his buddies in the Taliban." In the next eight years, my father and his friends saturated my Facebook feed with this and other sentiments, every day without fail. Calls for his birth certificate, calls for impeachment, Photoshopped photos of the president in Arab garb, devil horns, lynched from a tree, you name it. As I felt the shift, I hoped it was just an isolated hatred shared by only a few people in the middle of the country where intolerance seems to simmer the strongest. Surely this could not be the mindset of an entire country?

Obama's second election was a result of a backlash against a backlash. As people witnessed the fierce intolerance of Obama's detractors erupting out of the woodwork, they also witnessed how he helped navigate the country out of the recession, and how he used his office as a bully pulpit on social issues. Given another four years, I clung to the hope that he could continue to heal the divide in the country, even though progress was coming slowly.

Then George Zimmerman shot Trayvon Martin, and the racism seemed to surge higher, becoming glaringly apparent in everyday life. Social media blew up with hateful messages, with Zimmerman the white hero brave enough to protect his community from the "black gang bangers that terrorize us all." And just as I had witnessed in 1992, racial tensions grew stronger and stronger. When Obama spoke of the tragedy, remarking that as a younger man, he too could have been Trayvon, white people became even more incensed and the racial driven hate in America grew even stronger.

In addition to this, the police shootings began to grab our attention. Unbeknownst to white people, these shootings had been happening all along, but now every day we were hearing about young black men and women dying at the hands of police, courtesy of videotaped evidence of systematic racism that had become viral on the Internet. Walking down the street black. Driving while black. Detained by police because you are black. Getting shot because you are black. When Black Lives Matter emerged from Ferguson, it affected citizens from all cultural backgrounds who rallied to support this movement. It affected me. What do we do to make change happen? How do we stop this?

But white men doubled-down with their vitriol remarks. My father and his kind called these protesters black thugs, ignoring the diversity of the demonstrators who had come together. "If they had jobs they would be too busy to protest." He called it a problem created by criminals, ignoring police profiling based on the color of their skin in a system of permissive racism. "If you aren't a criminal you won't be stopped by the police. If you are stopped, put your hands up, and follow instructions. These thugs are getting shot because they deserve to be shot."

What many of these people, including my father, failed to understand is how pervasive racism really is. When the police had the gall to respond with "Blue Lives Matter," I thought about what the comedian Dave Chappelle quipped, "What, was you born a police? That is not a blue life. That is a blue suit. If you don't like it, take that suit off, find a new job, because I'll tell you right now, if I could quit being black today, I'd be out the game." (*Saturday Night Live,* November 12, 2016) The police are not being systematically murdered in the streets, nor are they being violently assailed by their own city government, yet they continually cry out as if they are being violently victimized. As far as white middle aged men are concerned, they will continue to lay the blame on black victims, simply because they are black. And as long as the system protects "us" from "them," they will continue to support a system that works for them. Why? *Because they are scared.*

Where I live, in the middle of Red America, it feels as if racism has always worked to benefit white people. And when the people being oppressed by these benefits (along with their open-minded allies) challenge the systems and institutions that are responsible for this oppression, they are attacked. Why? *Because the white men are scared.*

They felt like no one was really paying attention to them. No one was listening to them cry out that they did not want equality, they did not want the police to hesitate to shoot and kill black people in order to protect their communities. They wanted protection regardless of cost, to them another dead black body in the street is of no consequence, at least not to them, as long as they can feel safe at night.

They felt like they had put up with enough to get to where they are in life, and they were not going to let anything or anyone threaten their station. First it was the blacks. Then the gays. Blame it on the Mexicans taking jobs they never really wanted. Muslim extremists attacked our country, so all Muslims must go. The white men have had enough. So what did they do? They embraced the most racist, xenophobic, sexist, homophobic man they could find, and elected him president of the United States.

At first it seemed like a joke, like it could not really come to fruition. What I do know is that the white men had grown scared. And when it came time to vote for continued progression toward racial harmony, for continued safety of all Americans, for equal rights for everyone regardless of race, sex, or orientation, the white men voted against it. They recruited their sisters and daughters, their wives and coworkers, and aligned behind the candidate of hate. Build a wall. Create a Muslim registry. Stop and frisk. Ban brown foreigners from America. They lobbied to make America great again by making it white again. They didn't even bother to hide their white supremacist beliefs. They made their voices loud and clear. *Frightening.*

I am a white man, and I am scared too. *I am scared of them.*

Challenging our country's racist institutions is something black people and other people have been struggling to do for generations. Freedom movements, like Black Lives Matter, have taken different shapes and forms. And while there hasn't been one particular objective, what has been consistent is the resistance of society at large – the nation in general – to transform society. White men aren't necessarily the enemy here; fear is, and we need to continue to come together to defeat fear.

There is nothing extraordinary about my story, it is probably more common than many of you would believe. It is an experience cobbled together from education, from family, from friends and from society, and for the past fifteen years, I've been slowly reprogramming the backwards logic that I was taught. It hasn't been easy, and some days are easier than others but I continuously struggle for change because I want to learn from and respect others.

We have come too far as a country to turn back. Black lives matter. They have always mattered, they always will. Brown lives matter, gay lives matter, and female lives matter. I hope we can get back on track as a country, and continue to make great strides toward defeating racism in our country. The path is there, we just need to stay on it, and fight any forces that try to derail us. *And this I am not scared to do.* ■

George Cassidy Payne

The New Double Consciousness: Race in a Post-Obama America

OUBLE CONSCIOUSNESS is a term coined by W. E. B. Du Bois. In *The Souls of Black Folk,* the author and philosopher was referring to the political and existential challenge of "always looking at one's self through the eyes" of a racist white society, and "measuring oneself by the means of a nation that looked back in contempt."

The double consciousness that Du Bois wrote about is a particular response to the horrific legacy of slavery on generations of African American families. This same legacy has given birth to a new type of double consciousness that is prevalent in America today. Every citizen – whether they know it consciously or not – is expected to hold two diametrically opposed truths at the same time. On the one hand, they are taught to understand that race is one of the most significant factors in any room. Yet, on the other hand, they are told that race is essentially a baseless and perhaps even dangerous idea to believe in.

This bipolar view creates tremendous angst and confusion in society. At the same time while people are told that race is not grounded in biology and genetics, it becomes vividly real once people talk about it and live their lives as if it were real. Ultimately, the failure to see the world through the lens of race often blinds people to the suffering caused by personal and institutional bigotry.

However, as one narrows their focus to better see the world through the lens of race, they often fail to see how every human being is designed to be a unique individual. Every human being is a collection of experiences, thoughts, and dreams. To be human is to be shaped by environmental conditions, educational influences, and religious exposure. It is to be moved and transformed by forces outside the willful control of our autonomy. To confine a person to their particular shade of pigmentation is a gross simplification of who they are as a being in evolution.

That being said, there is not a single vocation that a person of color does not have access to. They have been teachers and professors, authors and composers, inventors and engineers, astronomers, architects, CEOs, Oscar winners, head football coaches, presidential cabinet members, Joint Chief of Staff officers, Supreme Court Justices, and a President of the United States of America.

If we are honest with ourselves, we can see that people of color have always had these positions. In fact, they have held these positions thousands of years before white people. The reason we have architecture and mathematics is because of black and brown people. The reason we have organized religion and jurisprudence is because of black and brown people. The reason that we have a formal educational system is because of black and brown people. The reason that we have civilization is because of black and brown people. Where were the first laws of human beings crafted? Where were the first instruments made? Who engineered the first tools?

Despite this remarkable history, from the quality of a woman's prenatal care to the likelihood that someone will experience police brutality and mass incarceration, race still impacts everything. Did you know that the average African American male lives five years less than the average white American male? Did you know that one in every fifteen African American men and one in every thirty-six Hispanic men are incarcerated in comparison to one in every one-hundred and six white men? Or that unarmed black people were killed at six times the rate of unarmed whites in 2015? Or that for every level of educational attainment, black Americans have unemployment rates that are similar to or higher than those of less educated white Americans?

Du Bois said: "Strange, is it not, my brothers, how often in America those great watchwords of human energy – 'Be strong!' 'Know thyself!' 'Hitch your wagon to a star!' – how often these die away into dim whispers when we face these seething millions of black men? And yet do they not belong to them? Are they not their heritage as well as yours?" Today, in accordance with Du Bois' vision, citizens must see with the eyes of unconditional equality without hidden racial assumptions. All of us must learn to see two worlds: one in color and one in black and white. We must see them as equally real and equally valid. ■

Layla D. Brown-Vincent

This Ain't Yo Daddy's Civil Rights' Movement: A Generational Analysis of the Movement for Black Lives

I AM, PER GENERATIONAL DESCRIPTORS, a millennial. What it means to be a millennial can differ depending on who you ask, but for our purposes it may be useful to understand that the term is often used to describe a generation of lazy, entitled folks who have the benefit of far too much technology. You should now forget this depiction of millennials and attempt to understand us from an alternative perspective. Some argue that millennials, Black Millennials in particular, will not, as a generation, by multiple measurable standards, experience the financial stability and hope for generational improvement promised those preceding us. Social security will likely be an unviable source of income in our elder years despite our paying into it; many of the gains of Civil Rights/Black Power and enslaved ancestors fought and died for are being systematically walked back. And, to make matters worse those histories are constantly being distorted.[1]

As "elder millennials," many of our parents, mostly baby boomers and a few early Gen Xers, were born and came of age during a time of mass social upheaval. Their politics and world views largely shaped by the Civil Rights, Black Power, antiwar and feminist movements. The South African divestment campaigns were equally influential in shaping their early adulthoods. Black baby boomers are sometimes understood as the first generation to generally experience more financial precarity than their parents. My paternal and maternal grandparents purchased homes and sent multiple children to college as a Chicago city sanitation/domestic worker and army soldier/school teacher, respectively. Without academic

---

[1] Like the notion that our ancestors died for our right to vote for any old candidate rather than the right to be presented with viable candidates that represent our communities and take our needs seriously.

scholarships, my parents would not have been able to accomplish the same with less than a quarter of the children their parents birthed. I am certain there are members of these generations who will dispute these characterizations, but the glue that holds a social generation together is the least common denominator among them across space and time. Those inescapable social realities that shaped the lives of hundreds of thousands of people at the same moments in time are the ties that bind a generation.

Which brings us back to prevailing classifications of millennials, a generation most noted for coming of age during a technological boom and also referred to as the "me generation," that is until Ferguson became "our Civil Rights Movement," "our Black Power Moment," and more. On the heels of the Occupy movement, faced with increasingly visible state sanctioned genocide of black bodies seen in the murders of Trayvon Martin, Jordan Davis, Renisha McBride, Mike Brown, Tamir Rice, Freddie Gray, Sandra Bland, and more; on the heels of massive upheavals across North Africa and the Middle East like Tahrir Square and the ramping up of the Palestinian Genocide by the state of Israel; this generation, my generation, millennials, decided to take to the streets in a loud and highly visible demand for recognition and radical change.

Many of us turned the corner of adulthood in the wake of the massive social and racial disaster otherwise known as Hurricane Katrina. We came of age shaped by, but removed from the bloody struggles of the 1960s and 1970s. Many of us romanticized being alive in those times. We came of age waiting for our next charismatic, brilliant, unapologetically black leader. Many of my peers who have studied our histories as a fighting people came of age "waiting for Malcolm." But we also came of age critiquing, though not always fully understanding, the magnitude and the specificity of the battles our ancestors fought. As Ferguson gained momentum, so too did the declaration that "This Ain't Yo Daddy's Civil Rights Movement."

I remember the first time I heard this war cry in the streets. I heard it referenced in smaller organizing spaces but not so much as a call to my millennial sistren and brethren to form a collective imagination of ourselves in opposition to those who had come before us. I was in St. Louis, Missouri for the #FergusonOctober demonstrations. The crowd had gathered after a day of marching the streets of St. Louis not far from where Dred Scott was reminded that no person of African descent, slave or free, had the rights of a citizen in the United States of America. Local rapper Tef Poe was closing his speech, attempting to get the crowd hyped for the rest of the day when he made the proclamation. I remember battling a mixed bag of emotions when I heard the declaration. I was excited because I had grown exhausted by what I considered the liberal, white, donor chasing, and often apologetic rhetoric of organizations like the NAACP and their peer institutions like the Urban League, the Congressional Black Caucus, etc., I was aware of the ways Tef Poe's declaration alluded to the reality that the non-violent demonstrations our predecessors showed up to in their Sunday best, weren't going to suit my tatted-up, natty-dread wearing, profanity using, unapologetically black and queer peers vanguarding our twenty-first century movement for black lives. But the movement baby in me, the one that was nurtured by the very generation of activists being critiqued in that bold declaration, a generation who encouraged me to travel to Florida in order to occupy the state capitol with the Dream Defenders, to protest outside the Ferguson Police department with HandsUpUnited, who bailed me out of jail and encouraged me to start my own youth organization in North Carolina after Moral Mondays, knew that my Daddy's Civil Rights Movement had so much more to teach us than we seemed to have learned.

My Daddy's Civil Rights Movement encouraged me to chart my own paths without reinventing the wheel, sound advice for anyone in it for the long haul. The same generation rallying behind the cry that this wasn't our Daddy's Civil Rights Movement had grown up idolizing it and in many ways inadequately understanding the intimate relationship between the Civil Rights and Black Power movements, which have all too often been pitted against one another by liberal white activists and academics. One would be hard pressed to find a young black activist in the United States who had not, at least once in their lifetimes, daydreamed about being a Black Panther, meeting Malcolm, Martin or Assata. In fact, my generation continues to flock to Angela Davis speaking engagements because of her civil rights era persona, and has utilized the words of Assata as a mantra, a battle cry in the streets, a daily reminder of our responsibility to one another, a way of being in this world that never loved us.

Early Twenty-First Century Rumblings

I REMEMBER THE FIRST TIME I saw his youthful, smiling, brown face against a white backdrop, floating above a deep red Hollister T-shirt, flash across the television in my parents' living room. Trayvon Martin had been murdered almost a month before his name became a nightly-news sound bite. We had no way of knowing then, that hoodies, Skittles, and Arizona Tea, would become symbols of struggle for a new generation of black youth. His murder had not yet been questioned when the local police chief declared there was no reason to believe George Zimmerman had acted inappropriately. In the days that followed, the ensuing public outcry over the refusal to arrest Trayvon Martin's murderer set the stage for a defiant opposition that would lead an entire community of youth to occupy public streets from Tallahassee, Florida to Ferguson, Missouri for nearly a year, declaring they had had enough of the brutal state sanctioned slaughtering of black and brown bodies. The names of the men, women and children who have become martyred are shamefully numerous. This ever-growing list of names, tragic and senseless as it is, has become the catalyst for one of the most wide-spread and longest sustained periods of visibly organized black resistance/rebellion in the belly of the imperial beast since the 1960s and 1970s.

Frantz Fanon declared that "Each generation must, out of relative obscurity, discover its mission, fulfill it, or betray it" (Fanon 1969, 206). Every generation creates new movements, organizations, and associations to address the specificities of the problems they confront. Movements that speak their language, express their style, and articulate their analysis of the path forward: The NAACP in the early twentieth century, the National Negro Congress during the Great Depression, the Southern Christian Leadership Conference (SCLC) in the 1950s, the Student Non-Violent Coordinating Committee (SNCC), the Black Panther Party and the All African People's Revolutionary Party of the 1960s and more. Our generation, in this moment, is no different than our Daddy's Civil Rights Movement in that regard. In an era that compels us to virtually, if not personally, witness the snuffing out of black lives, repeatedly, in real time, on individualized, portable devices, black youth of today, just as our predecessors did, are struggling daily to mitigate, respond to and ultimately terminate that trauma.

I remember the significance of the trial verdict for myself and a small community of folks in Durham, North Carolina. Myself, my husband, Reverend Curtis Gatewood of the Durham NAACP and a few local organizers in the Durham area were gathered at Professor Timothy Tyson's house for dinner, drinks, and lively conversations, but the house fell still as the verdict was announced. The murder of Trayvon Martin and the subsequent acquittal of George Zimmerman marked a significant turning point in the lives of many American millennials. The aftermath of the murders of Mike Brown, Eric Garner, Tamir Rice, and countless others represents a tipping point in the consciousness and anger of American youth. So many of us knew that the verdict would not turn out in favor of the people, yet and still so many of us wanted to hold on to the hope that we might be wrong, just this once. The relatively peaceful and unassuming anger that grew out of the acquittal of George Zimmerman just barely kept the flame going, but the death and subsequent non-indictment of Darren Wilson would blow up like a bomb, a bomb that would smolder and reignite for months following Mike Brown's murder.

In Florida, where Trayvon Martin was murdered, one group of young people decided to respond to the trauma they faced. In April 2012, friends and students at Florida Agricultural & Mechanical University, a Florida HBCU, including Chicago native, Umi Selah (then known as Phillip Agnew who would become executive director), and East Jerusalem, Palestine native Ahmad Abuznaid (the current legal and policy director), and a host of other Florida students created a Facebook invitation for a conference call to organize against the racially motivated murder of Trayvon Martin. More than 150 people participated in the call and threw out ideas for how best to organize in the wake of Trayvon Martin's death. The call resulted in the organization of a 40-mile, three-day protest march from Daytona Beach to Sanford and ultimately marked the birth of a group of black and brown youth that would come to be known as the Dream Defenders, who in 2017 are commemorating five years of sustained organization, despite their present lower profile.

When asked about the march, Ahmad reflected on what they were thinking at the time, "we thought we'd like to start a movement reminiscent of the civil rights movement of the past, but in our generation," he said. He recalled a young woman on the call that spoke up and said, "You all are defending the dream. You should call yourselves the dream defenders." And so it was. For the better part of a year and a half, they organized, grew and prepared for their next major move. By August 2012, they were a formal organization with funders, a logo, T-shirts, a website and a social media presence, however public attention waned in the months leading up to Zimmerman's trial. His acquittal in July 2013, however, brought the Dream Defenders back into the media limelight.

Umi remembers hearing reports on the news claiming black folks "were going to destroy our communities in the wake of the verdict." Having successfully organized the 2012 march, Umi believed, at the time, they had proven they could be disciplined, smart, energetic, real, strategic and ultimately help present a way forward. In the national uproar following the trial verdict the group took a different tactic. From all over the state, black and brown youth flocked to the Tallahassee Capitol building in July 2013 to push for an alternative to Florida's "stand your ground" law. During a thirty-one-day sit-in of Governor Rick Scott's office, they demanded a review of stand your ground and presented their version, "Trayvon's law," which would effectively repeal it. They asked for an end to racial profiling and the school-to-prison pipeline. For a month (more or less), they slept on the Capitol's marble floor under the Florida Civil Rights Hall of Fame wall. Nearby churches provided them with places to shower, local friends offered their homes during the day, and at 5:45 a.m. every day, the Dream Defenders would wake up, move their things from the lobby floor to the third floor and occupy the capitol.

Moral Mondays

THE SUMMER OF 2013 WAS SIGNIFICANT in North Carolina for its own reasons. Despite having been raised in and around various political communities, I was twenty-six years old the first time I made an autonomous decision to participate in a political action, one that my parents supported morally but for which they would not be present. In 2013, during the same summer we watched as black youth rallied all over the country to have George Zimmerman arrested, charged and tried for Trayvon Martin's murder, North Carolina was gaining national attention for a weekly series of grassroots led demonstrations that would come to be known as Moral Mondays. Moral Mondays was a response to the NC Republican party's 2012 rise to power in the form of majority control of both state houses and the election of Republican Governor

Pat McCrory. For the first time since 1870, fiscal and social conservatives had enough control to begin enacting legislation that threatened voting rights, educational access, employment and housing opportunities, environmental justice, tax reform, along with a myriad of other concerns. In an effort to combat the draconian changes being implemented by the Republican legislature, the NC-NAACP declared the citizens' right to claim their "moral majority" and stop the regressive legislation before it was too late. In a statement titled "Why We Are Here Today," Reverend William J. Barber II of the NC-NAACP declared the following:

> (W)e have no other choice but to assemble in the people's house where these bills are being presented, argued, and voted upon, in hopes that God will move in the hearts of our legislators, as he moved in the heart of Pharaoh to let His people go. Some ask the question; why don't they be quiet? Well, I must remind you, that it has been our collective silence that has quietly opened the city gates to these undemocratic violators of our rights.

The first Moral Monday's demonstration took place towards the end of April in 2013 with a total of seventeen people being arrested. By the end of the summer nearly one-thousand people had been arrested in weekly protests at the North Carolina legislature. After the first few weeks of demonstrations and arrests, a North Carolina based conservative policy think tank called the Civitas Institute began compiling and publishing a database of the Moral Monday's arrestees with important demographic data like each protester's name, city and county of residence, sex, race, age, arrest date, occupation, employer (and whether it's in the public, private or nonprofit sector), interest group affiliations, and mug shot. The database has since been deactivated, but it was created in an attempt to create a climate of fear for those being arrested and for many, it also meant the possibility of workplace hostility or worse, unemployment. Each week thousands of diverse supporters turned up to the demonstrations to support those being arrested, however, a look through the Civitas database revealed that the people being arrested were primarily older, retirement age, politically liberal, white citizens. At the time my husband Joshua had recently stopped working for the NC-NAACP but still had many close ties to the organization, so he had been supporting the demonstrations as well. I was working an awful summer job for the city that paid $8.50 per hour, so my work schedule prevented me from attending demonstrations. However, when I saw the movement gaining momentum, I decided I wanted to go see what it was about.

The week I decided to go also happened to be the week they were going to vote on House Bill 589 in the NC legislature. HB 589 was essentially a voter suppression bill, which we only began to see the true effects of for the first time during the 2016 presidential primary season when hundreds of people were turned away from the polls for failure to have a "proper" form of identification. The bill effectively shortened the early voting period by a full week, eliminated same-day registration, required strict forms of voter ID, prevented out-of-precinct ballots from being counted, expanded the ability to challenge voters at the polls, and terminated a preregistration program for sixteen and seventeen-year olds, all changes which disproportionately affected black, brown and young voters. This bill presented a prime opportunity to increase the participation of black and brown youth in the Moral Mondays movement. On July 24, 2013 more than twenty young people, including myself, showed up to observe and protest HB 589 in the legislature, which they essentially filibustered on the floor in anticipation of a protest demonstration. As a result of the filibuster, several of us decided to stage a demonstration in the office of Representatives Thom Tillis to demand they kill bill 589.

It was during planning and preparation for our occupation of the representative's office that I first encountered and became close to Bree Newsome. During our occupation of the representative's office, my husband Joshua Vincent and Bree Newsome (the young woman who would later scale the flag pole outside of the South Carolina legislature to take down the confederate flag), read statements of our demands and within less than five minutes we were arrested. We had only discussed the possibility of being arrested the day before as this demonstration was not the typical Monday demonstration with thousands of supporters. We were arrested on what the movement had termed "Witness Wednesdays," referring to the process of sitting in and witnessing the Wednesday legislative sessions. Ultimately six of us were arrested, though in our discussion the day before Joshua and Rob Stephens, who at the time was a field organizer for the NC-NAACP, were not supposed to be arrested because they had already been arrested during a prior Witness Wednesday and the legal advisors were unsure of the ramifications of multiple arrests during the Moral Monday process. The decision the day before had been that we would all occupy the representative's office, fully aware that the legislative staff was required to give a series of warnings to disperse before they began arrests. Once the final warning to disperse was issued, those who were unwilling to be arrested would leave and the rest would stay. On that Wednesday when the final warning to disperse came, most people in the room left so Joshua and Rob made the last-minute decision to stay and be arrested along with myself, Bree, and two other young people, leaving a total of six.

I cannot say that I was particularly fearful of being arrested because I knew I had the support of the NAACP as well as my parents in the process, but I was nervous because I had no idea what to expect. One by one they began cuffing us with plastic zip-ties and escorting us to the cafeteria in the basement of the legislative building were they did preliminary searches of our persons and belongings before they loaded us in the police van and drove us to the Wake County detention center. Most of the arresting officers were white men, though I do remember one female officer being present to perform the body search on the women arrestees. We all remained together for those initial hours, so the mood was relatively light and we were able to talk and debrief a little as we waited. When we arrived at the detention center our handlers transitioned from white male police officers with buzz cuts to predominantly black and Latino correction officers. By this time in the summer they had been processing Moral Movement arrestees for several weeks, so when they discovered what we had been arrested for the correction officers were quite talkative and friendly, with some even covertly expressing support for our acts of protest. After the second round of body searches, finger printing and mug shots we sat in a common area where the men were required to sit on one side of the room and women on the other, waiting to be assigned to cells. This common area had TVs displaying live news so footage of our arrests was flashing before us. Many of the other people who had been arrested and were also waiting to be assigned to cells recognized us from the TV and asked who we were and what the demonstrations were about. These conversations resulted in all of us being treated relatively well by both the corrections staff and the people being booked that night. I must admit that I was impressed that so many people not only cared but, seemed to be supportive of our decisions to be arrested for such a cause even as they were upset and questioned their personal circumstances.

The bail bond process was probably the most stressful portion of the process. I knew we had the support of the NAACP but I wasn't exactly sure what the bail process would be. So when we were allowed to make our phone-calls, I did what most people do, I tried to call my parents. It was at this moment I became painfully aware of my status as a millennial specifically, the fact that my cell phone had made me lazy about remembering the phone numbers of people I needed to contact in that moment. At this point, all my belongings including my cell phone had been confiscated so when I started trying to make phone calls I realized the only numbers I had memorized were my parent's house phone, both their cell numbers, Joshua's cell and my sister's cell number. Joshua was in jail with me so his number would do me no good, my sister lives in Washington, D.C. so she was only of limited use. My mother was out of town and I couldn't get through to my father for well over an hour. I would later discover that his cell phone was dead but he was already waiting for me at the jail in the release area. None of the women and I had any prior arrests or incidents on our records so our bonds had been set at $1,000 and we were each required to pay $100 to be released. Of the three men, Joshua and Rob still had pending charges from an earlier Moral Movement arrest and the other young man had prior unaffiliated charges, so their bonds were set at $10,000 and they were each required to pay $1,000 to be released. Most of us were released before midnight but Joshua was not released until 1:00 a.m. We were worried that they would require him to spend the night in jail; and later found out that they required him to strip while they performed a cavity search, and forced him to change into a prison orange jumpsuit. We are still unsure to this day exactly what happened to hold up his processing, but we were all eventually released on the same night.

Though I knew my arrest was highly likely, I still don't think I was entirely prepared for what I was about to undertake as the arrest took place. I certainly did not anticipate that I would still be dealing with the charges more than a year later. This arrest however, marks for me, a turning point in my own radicalization process. Being arrested for civil disobedience, is yet another of those rites of passage for political organizers. Presently, I question the utility of arrests as a political mobilization strategy when numbers and resources are limited, however, one of the strategies of the Moral Monday's demonstrations was to overwhelm the state with the arrests to highlight the amount of money the state spends on such practices, so while I am happy to have been a part of that movement, I don't have plans of being intentionally arrested in the near future. I realize now though, that my involvement in Moral Mondays and my subsequent arrest opened doors to communities of political activists that I did not have before that moment. From the summer of 2013 on, my husband Joshua, Bree and I developed a friendship based on our shared interest in social justice and radical change. In our quests to find causes and organizations we could commit to, we developed strong relationships with the Dream Defenders in Florida, various chapters of the NAACP and later Black Lives Matter contingencies, the Ohio Student Association, the Youth Organizing Institute, and Ignite NC, both based in Durham. In that regard, my arrest and how it was interpreted by my peers made me a person of interest in my own right, rather than simply because of my familial affiliations. My desire to interrogate the haphazardness of the process helped develop the very questions that fueled this research project, i.e., how did I end up getting arrested? Why did I decide to do it? Is it always this haphazard? Where do I go from here? Ultimately, how I can learn from my own process of political development helps me to better understand how to generate more contribution to and participation in mass movements for social change.

Black Millennial Organizing Practices

IN DECEMBER OF 2014, Umi sent my husband Joshua and I a message that read: "Hey family, I hope you are well through these times. I'm extending an invitation to our Congress [in Central Florida] this year. I want you there... It will be an opportunity for Dream Defenders around the country to discuss and build towards collective revolutionary aims..." After more than ten hours of driving through the night we arrived at the Congress. We learned that representatives from other organizations such as Students for Justice in Palestine, Black Alliance for Just Immigration, Florida Immigrant Coalition, United We Dream, Malcolm X Grassroots Movement, #itsbiggerthanyou, Coalition of Immokalee Workers, USSA (United States Student Association), Homestead Equal Rights for All, The California Afrikan Black Coalition, Friends of the Congo, Hands Up United, MST (Brazil's Landless Workers Movement), and NUMSA (National Union of Metal Workers of South Africa) had also been invited. The Dream Defenders' annual national congress offers Dream Defenders from all over Florida an opportunity to congregate, discuss the successes and failures of the year, and determine an organizational direction for the following year. In the wake of a surge in national and global activism among youth of 2014 and to connect those both leading and impacting that wave, the Dream Defenders invited people from several organizations to be in the same room with one another to collaborate and build our collective organizing strategies.

The Congress took place in central Florida in a city called Fruit Land Park. This city caters to Florida's relatively wealthy retired community. According to the 2010 census this city is almost 90 percent white. The Dream Defenders secured a Christian retreat center called the Life Enrichment Center. It was a three-day long event packed full of seminars on Mass Incarceration, Capitalism, Patriarchy, White Supremacy, Imperialism, Movement Ecology, Cop Watch, Cooperative Economics, Movement Strategy and Campaign Building, and Storytelling. Some of these seminars were more fruitful than others. Still others could even be problematic at times, to be expected when young folks are charting a path of great resistance. Grappling with what it means to try to be involved in a level of organizing beyond mainstream politics, but simultaneously being reliant upon your proverbial enemies for funding and meeting space is a major issue to which I don't think young black organizers in the U.S. have given enough thought. This could possibly be a testament to our lack of intricate interrogation of the way money or funding operates as a mechanism for control. Additionally, it speaks to a level of political underdevelopment and a general lack of resources and infrastructure in our communities. Increasingly, public scholarship, like that of the various scholars who write for the *Black Agenda Report* have called attention to the potential dangers posed by the growth of the non-profit industrial complex, and the ways in which millennial activists are strapped by donor dollars; not unlike the struggles SNCC and the Black Panther Party faced with their own liberal white donors. The question Black Millennials must ask ourselves is what mistakes can we avoid, and which we are doomed to repeat.

We arrived to find that the Congress was structured with three concurrent sessions where attendees were randomly assigned to attend as they checked-in at the Center. These sessions were in the same building, which consisted of a big sanctuary like room in the middle with red pews, and a series of smaller breakout rooms, all of which were adjacent to the sanctuary. We arrived very tired but ready to see what the conference had to offer. As we walked up we saw a smattering of people outside talking, taking smoke breaks, and listening to music. When we walked to the check-in area, we were given our name tags and Congress packets with two sets of colored sticker dots. The colors represented the sessions we were supposed to attend and that we would rotate with our group for the duration of the day. My first impression of the conference was that it felt like a space led by young people, there were no elders hovering offering their input, directing us or lecturing us with rhetoric. Often, invisible or hovering elders heavily direct these spaces for "young people," which is certainly useful at times. However, young people also need opportunities to sit with the thoughts, dreams and critiques of our peers to push our own agendas and understandings forward. I'm not sure who the invisible elders might have been, but it certainly felt like a space that was at least on the surface, controlled by my peers.

Toward the end of the first day, an interesting, pivotal and emotional moment occurred when the conference attendees were asked to take a picture in solidarity with the contingency from Ayotzinapa, a group of young people who had been mobilized by the disappearance of forty-three students in training to become radical educators in Mexico. As the photo was being organized, one of the women from the delegation read a statement of solidarity from the students in Mexico, in Spanish and then translated. The entire group was then asked to be recorded chanting a slogan in Spanish, in solidarity with the disappeared and their families in Ayotzinapa. The slogan was *"¡Ni Perdon, ni olvido! ¡Castigo a los asesinos!"* Apparently, someone in the group was complaining about being asked to chant the slogan in Spanish without knowing what it meant. As the photo-op was wrapping up, a young Dream Defender named Daniella, who is originally from Margarita Island, Venezuela with tears in her eyes and trembling in her voice asks for the attention of everyone in the crowd. She proceeded to reprimand the group for their impatience and insensitivity, reminding us that we were supposed to be in a collaborative political space, and that folks were displaying imperialist attitudes about the languages being spoken. She then asked us to think for a minute about the endless number of immigrants who must navigate American terrain being treated as less than, and struggling with having no one willing or able to translate English into Spanish for them. The group seemed to receive her criticism without much opposition. While I do not think it unreasonable to want to understand what you are being asked to chant and record, I also did not actually hear the original complaints about the Spanish language. As a person who speaks and understand Spanish I personally was not uncomfortable with the request. I do see however, the ways this relatively simple gesture sheds light on the difficulties of doing solidarity work. For black millennials more specifically, we must interrogate our particular brand of Americentric xenophobia, and focus on decolonizing our minds as well as our political practice.

For the final sessions of the second day, Congress participants were asked to propose and pitch ideas for "unplugged sessions" (impromptu sessions inspired by conversations and issues that had arisen during the conference in the more informal sessions), and other attendees would be allowed to pick and choose two sessions they would like to attend. There were over twenty unplugged sessions proposed, one of which was a session on Pan-Africanism which drew a primarily international group of participants and facilitators. The session was facilitated by a young woman with a Black American Mother and a Nigerian father who was based in Arizona. Other participants were a Congolese organizer with Friends of the Congo who had been based in North Carolina, but recently moved to Ferguson to work with Hands Up United.

There was also an Eritrean student who was based in Oakland, but had also studied in Cape Town, South Africa whose father had fought in Eritrean liberation struggles. There was a young Ugandan man who had been raised primarily in the Bahamas but was now based in Florida, a young Haitian man based in Miami, one of the women from the Ayotzinapa delegation, a Peruvian immigrant woman, Sofia Campos who is a lead organizer with United We Dream, a white Brazilian American citizen, a self-identified Hebrew Israelite from Atlanta, Mazuba, a Zambian immigrant by way of South Africa, and myself, a North Carolina native.

After introductions, we began discussing ways of moving discussions and understandings of Pan-Africanism into the present rather than only viewing the movement as something that peaked with African independence and died with Kwame Nkrumah, and how to effectively live Pan-Africanism in our daily lives. Kambale, the Congolese organizer began to tell this magnificently woven story, essentially a parable for both the necessity and inevitability of Pan-Africanism. He asked us, "Do you know how the Congo is connected to the very issue of state sanctioned violence and terrorism that has brought us all together here at this conference?" He continued by telling us that Sanford, Florida, the city where Trayvon Martin was murdered in cold blood, is named after Henry Shelton Sanford. In 1861, President Abraham Lincoln appointed Sanford as the ambassador to Belgium. In 1876, he was named acting Delegate of the American Geographical Society to a conference called by King Leopold II of Belgium to organize the International African Association with the purpose of opening equatorial Africa to "civilizing" influences. Leopold II used Sanford to convince Henry Morton Stanley to explore the Congo basin for Belgium in 1878. He then hired Sanford in 1883 as his envoy to the United States to try to gain American recognition for his colony in the Congo Basin, which became known as the Congo Free State. In 1886, Sanford organized in Brussels and dispatched to the Congo and its tributaries, the Sanford Exploring Expedition in the name of scientific and commercial discovery and for the opening of an interior trade. His steamboats "Florida" and "New York" were the first commercial steamers to penetrate the waters of the upper Congo. From September 1886 to February 1888 Sanford worked for the Expedition on river transports. King Leopold II of Belgium led one of the most ruthless genocidal campaigns and his endeavors to control the landmass that would come to be known as the Congo, would become recognized as the sole possession of King Leopold by the United States of America. I remember all of us being amazed at his ability to link the connectivity of our present struggles against state violence with histories of imperialism and colonization.

If nothing else that day, Kambale made it abundantly clear that we must go back and fetch the stories of our past to understand the intricacies of our present oppression and exploitation, and envision a more free future. When speaking of state violence and how these issues are connected globally, the Congo is perhaps one of the more pertinent historical examples. As laid out earlier, the Congo and the United States of America are intricately linked from their births, births which both required significant amounts of bloodshed. Just as the United States is a country founded on the blood of Native Americans and the backs of enslaved Africans, the slaughter led by King Leopold of Belgium that brought the Congo Free State into existence is perhaps one of the largest African genocides to take place in the nineteenth century. It is in understanding connections like this that we can begin to articulate a living breathing Pan-Africanism of the twenty-first century. If, as Henry Sylvester Williams argued, "Pan-Africanism is something we must define in struggle" we must keep our eyes and ears open for wherever revolutionary struggle is taking place. In the U.S., protests, demonstrations and full-scale uprisings have taken place in direct response to the increasing visibility of genocidal tendencies on the part of the U.S. government. If we had a camera that could take a panorama of the worlds uprising by dispossessed peoples, we would also have to look at the Palestinians long struggle, and interrogate how our oppression interlocks with theirs.

It was this session that prompted Mazuba and I to begin to discuss how useful it would be to have this conversation about Pan-Africanism with the folks we had been working and organizing with over the previous six months. We decided that we would figure out a way to invite some of these people to Durham for a few days of brainstorming and sharing ideas. At the time, we had no idea what bringing these people to North Carolina would entail. And we certainly had no vision of what exactly we would do once they arrived, but what we did know was that it was incredibly important to continue the work of building community amongst like-minded people who are trying to do good work. We floated the suggestion to the group and everyone was excited about the possibility. It would only be in mid-February that we would really begin to have a fleshed-out vision for the visit and that we started making the weekend happen. To some degree, I want to say this is typical of millennial organizing. I have not observed that we utilized study circles in the same way that our parents' generation read and studied Marx, Du Bois, and other critical black thinkers of generations past. Despite our ability to be connected in ways previously unavailable to us, there seems to be something about our ability to congregate in spaces together and across differences that fuels our mobilizing strategies. I believe that we are still learning the ways in which we need to think past our ability to mobilize and discover what it means to organize over long periods of time and realistically deal with major setbacks.

In a 1991 documentary entitled, *A Place of Rage,* the black feminist poet June Jordan called upon young black activists to reclaim "rage" as a tool for social justice. Nearly a quarter of a century later, it is precisely this notion of collective, unapologetic black rage, coupled with the equally unapologetic love of ourselves and freedom that has been the catalyst for the new movement condemning police violence against black people. More importantly, a movement that declares Black Lives Matter. Central to the Pan-Africanist project as personified by the late Kwame Ture, was a deep and enduring commitment to African peoples. We see this enduring commitment in the organizing trials and triumphs of black millennials. This commitment is based most fundamentally in a revolutionary love of the people which is concretely expressed through work and struggle for and with the people. Kwame had "an undying love for our people" (2003, 632), and called upon us as African peoples to share in that love for ourselves and one another as a part of what it means to be African, to be revolutionary and ultimately, to be human. Revolutionary love for Kwame was at the same time a call to struggle to clear free space and empower ourselves to do so. We have continued to witness this work as the larger Movement for Black Lives umbrella has worked to articulate a political platform, maintain visible resistance of the daily violence we endure at the hands of the state, and as it has forced its members to grow, stretch, and understand what it means to place the struggles of the most vulnerable among us, those of us who are poor, who are women, who are minors, who are queer, who are trans, at the center of our theorizing and resisting our oppression and most importantly for envisioning a new future. Perhaps these are the ways the Movement for Black Lives isn't quite our Daddy's Civil Rights Movement, but a forward progression on the same continuum.

Kwame goes on to say, "The society we seek to build among black people, then, is not a capitalist one, but a society in which the spirit of community and humanistic love prevail." But he cautioned, "We can build a community of love only where we have the ability and power to do so among Blacks" (2000, 613). In our love of the people, Kwame maintained, we are compelled to be revolutionary and struggle for total liberation on every level. And this, he argues, can only be done by organizing them around their own emancipatory interests. Thus, he says, "the job of the revolutionary is, of course, to overthrow unjust systems and replace them with just systems (and) a revolutionary understands this can only be done by the masses of the people. So, the task of the revolutionary is to organize the masses of the people." For through this process of organization and struggle, they become self-conscious agents of their own life and liberation. The cry Black Lives Matter is above all a cry of self-love. To declare that black lives have always mattered is a reminder to be patient with ourselves despite the fierce urgency of now. To continue to struggle for our liberation is the ultimate act of revolutionary self-love. It is ultimately from this place of revolutionary self-love that black millennials in the Movement for Black Lives are both declaring that black lives have always mattered and are responding to Fanon's call to discover our mission, fulfill it, or betray it. ■

Charlie R. Braxton

Election 2016: An Assessment

there are no noblemen here
no giant gallant knights
no pale males
with armor glistening white
atop a herd of alabaster steeds
descending from clouds
of ethereal cotton
down to this bitter, bitter earth
scurrying across the
wide white plains
to rescue us
in the nick of time
no
there are no
hipster-looking
bearded saviors here
it's just us
poor black, brown, red, yellow
others
and us
has got to love
and do
for us

Felipe Luciano

Matter-Blackness-Our Lives

LYING DORMANT BENEATH the cynical nihilism of gangster rap and black crime, beneath the urban topsoil of broken dreams and shattered families, lie some crystal shards reflecting what we used to be, some golden seeds of prayer, faith and genius that have survived the American holocaust of the last hundred years, waiting to blossom past the attitudinal perceptions of too many white Americans and the in-a-me of our own apathy and disinterest. Those seeds are sprouting today. Those seeds represent triumph over the brutality of slavery and Jim Crow, and resistance in the face of an American contradiction that lauds the history of its founding fathers, and ignores the suffering of the shackled black human beings they owned brought over from Africa to work the land and make them rich. Those seeds that survived are Black Lives Matter.

If we don't read and learn history, we will repeat it. After President Lincoln's Emancipation Proclamation, after the Civil War, after the Thirteenth, Fourteenth and Fifteenth Amendments came Reconstruction. Black businesses, black schools, and black churches were formed in the twelve years following the Civil War, as well as the election of black senators. The defeated South couldn't bear black voting rights or equality so they forced Lincoln's successors, Andrew Johnson and Rutherford Hayes, into removing Federal troops from the South, to back-track and renege on black citizenship including the promise of 40 acres and a mule, and turned a blind eye to state sponsored Klan terror and voter suppression (sound familiar?), now known as Jim Crow.

One-hundred and forty years later, while some things have changed, most things have remained the same. A black president is elected in 2008 to save America from its own greed and subsequent financial depression and economic crisis. As soon as President Obama accomplished that herculean task and created an Affordable Care Act for all Americans, disaffected whites decided modern "Reconstruction" is too threatening and elected an ignorant amateur as president to protect their rights and push back civil rights through police-sponsored murders of young black men, and the deportation of Latinos and Muslims.

But this time, young black people rise and scream and demonstrate. This time, white children join in. This time, America's hypocrisy is visible worldwide. But if we, as a people, have not learned that appealing to the dominant culture's sense of morality and compassion by claiming that Black Lives Matter is an exercise in futility, we have learned nothing. Power is what forces change. Organized resistance demands leadership, discipline, militancy, financial support, solid organization, and a clearly outlined ideological manifesto, with achievable goals. Black lives will matter when we start to respect ourselves, our traditions, our culture, our parents, and yes, our God, in whatever manifestation we choose.

We started losing our lives when we decided that money was more important than love and family; when we drank the elixir of materialism, of buying the lie that "bangles, baubles and beads" was the criteria for self-worth; when we ignored those elders who weren't famous and only recognized OG's who survived jail and shoot-outs. Elders are now afraid of their own youth, their own grandchildren, fearful that any well-meaning criticism will result in a beating or death. So we are demanding and marching for a system based on white skin privilege to accord us humanity and justice when we don't have it for ourselves. We have not taught our children that contradictions will always exist in American politics; they exist in politics, in the church, in the schools, in the workplace, in our families and on the streets.

You don't reject your father because he's a number runner; he's still your father. We've got loads of Christians who get high, swear and sleep around. You don't blame Christ for their foolishness and decide the entire church is to blame. You can't throw the baby out with the bathwater. We must start with ourselves; that's when black lives really begin to matter.

We must teach our children that, for now, voting is as important as hanging out, that education is as vital as making love, that staying in a marriage provides the foundation for morality and black codes of conduct, that saying "Yes, ma'am, no ma'am," is black regardless of the color of the other person. Our culture is experiencing extreme moral climate change. We either abandon our kids, setting up the conditions for them to drop out of school and go straight to jail, or we murder our infants because we see the "demons" in them.

Black Lives Matter because we matter; Black Lives Matter because our ancestors matter; because Duke Ellington and Miles Davis and John Coltrane matter; because Malcolm and Martin and Fannie Lou Hammer and Rosa Parks matter; because your momma matters.

And once we center ourselves in the love of ourselves and manifest that love through service and commitment, people will come running to our banner: Puerto Ricans, Dominicans, Asians and young whites. They will see the strength, the unity, the determination, the loyalty of a united black community, and it won't be just the music they'll be seeking, it'll be the faith that black lives matter. ■

Shirley Bradley LeFlore

Healing

Bear my wind cracked song
Wounded on the second bar
In the throat of your silver trumpet
Play me a getting up morning
A full heart melody
Fold my broken wing inside your bosom
With a healing score
Dance me upstream
A golden salmon sonnet
An angel overture
On a long silk-tome
Make the music honey sweet
A clear note
And let me soar...

APPENDIX 1

■ ■ ■

Glossary

AFRICAN AMERICAN: A racial classification specifier that was advanced in the 1980s to give Americans of African descent a title equivalent to Euro-Americans. While the term peaked in popularity during the 1990s and 2000s, today it is often perceived as carrying a self-conscious political correctness that is unnecessary in an informal context, yet is rarely considered offensive. Nevertheless, many blacks do not embrace the term "African American" because it denotes a connection to a country far removed from their American ancestry. Interestingly and according to a recent study in the *Journal of Experimental Social Psychology*,[1] it found that among white Americans, the term "black" elicits a more negative association than "African American." Immigrants from some African, Caribbean, Central American, and South American nations and their descendants may or may not identify with this term because land and resources were not stolen from them in this space, and their ancestors were not brought to America as slaves.

BLACK: A racial classification specifier of Americans with total or partial ancestry from Africa. "Black" replaced the derogatory terminology applied to African Americans such as "Negro" or "nigger" because it was turned into a positive designation during the Black Power movement.

BLACK ARTS MOVEMENT: Also known as the Black Aesthetics movement or BAM, is the artistic outgrowth of the Black Power movement that came about by a group of politically motivated black poets, artists, dramatists, dancers,

---

[1] Erika V. Hall, Katherine W. Phillips, Sarah S.M. Townsend, "A rose by any other name? The consequences of subtyping 'African Americans' from 'Blacks'" *Journal of Experimental Social Psychology* 56 (2015), 183-190.

musicians, and writers. The movement, which emerged in 1965 after Malcolm X's assassination, began in the New York/Newark area, with poet and activist Amiri Baraka widely credited as its leader. As the movement spread to other large black populated cities like Chicago, Detroit, Los Angeles and San Francisco, it called for the creation of poetry, books, visual arts, dance, music, and theater to reflect pride in black history and culture. This emphasis was centered on an affirmation of the autonomy of black artists to create black art for black people as a means to awaken black consciousness and achieve liberation. It inspired black people to establish their own publishing houses, magazines, journals and art institutions. It led to the creation of African American studies programs at colleges and universities, and in time, it inspired Latinos, Asian Americans and Native Americans to create art on their own terms. Although the creative works of the Black Arts movement were often profound and innovative, they sometimes alienated both black and white mainstream culture with its raw shock value and black hyper-masculinity, usually at the expense of black female voices. By the mid-1970s, the movement began to fade when many of its leading members shifted from black nationalism to Marxism, a shift that alienated many who had previously identified with the movement. However, the Black Arts movement left behind an incredible legacy. It helped African Americans openly celebrate their culture, and gain social and historical recognition in the arts. It also spurred activism in black communities through the arts. And through different forms of media, African Americans were able to educate others about the expression of cultural differences and viewpoints within the black community. The Black Arts movement has had a lasting effect, which continues to motivate new generations of poets, writers, and artists of all nationalities.

BLACK CODES: In the United States, white-dominated southern state legislatures passed Black Codes, modeled after the earlier slave codes in 1865 and 1866 (after the Civil War) that successfully suppressed emancipated African American slaves and freed people. These laws had the intent and the effect of restricting and heavily regulating the activities and behavior of blacks. One of the defining features of the Black Codes was "vagrancy laws," which allowed local authorities to arrest black people for minor infractions, and then commit them to involuntary labor and a convict lease system, forcing them to work in a labor economy based on low wages or debt. Mississippi was the first state to pass Black Codes. Its laws served as a model for those passed by other states, beginning with South Carolina, Alabama, and Louisiana in

1865, and continuing with Florida, Virginia, Georgia, North Carolina, Texas, Tennessee and Arkansas at the beginning of 1866, whose laws were crafted to effect a similarly racist regime. The Black Codes largely remained on the books until the U.S. Supreme Court's *Papachristou v. Jacksonville* decision in 1972. Although the laws were defended as preventing crime, the Court held that Jacksonville's vagrancy law "furnishes a convenient tool for 'harsh and discriminatory enforcement by local prosecuting officials, against particular groups deemed to merit their displeasure.'" Many scholars and activists have concurred that today's harsh and discriminatory enforcement by local police and prosecuting officials is a conspicuous legacy of the Black Codes.[2]

BLACK LIVES MATTER: An international activist movement that surfaced on social media with the hashtag #BlackLivesMatter in 2013 after the acquittal of George Zimmerman, and became nationally recognized for its demonstrations and protests following the 2014 deaths of Michael Brown and Eric Garner. The originators of the hashtag as a call-to-action, Alicia Garza, Patrisse Cullors, and Opal Tometi, expanded their project into a national network of over thirty local chapters between 2014 and 2016. Black Lives Matter campaigns focus on systemic racism toward black people by regularly having protests against police killings of black people and broader issues of racial profiling, police brutality, and racial inequality in the United States criminal justice system. The Black Lives Matter movement is a decentralized network and has no formal hierarchy.

BLACK PANTHER PARTY: The Black Panther Party or the BPP (originally the Black Panther Party for Self-Defense), was a revolutionary black nationalist and socialist organization founded in 1966 in Oakland, California by Huey P. Newton and Bobby Seale. The party's original purpose was to patrol African American neighborhoods to protect residents from acts of police brutality. The Panthers eventually developed into a Marxist revolutionary group that called for the arming of all African Americans, the exemption of African Americans from the draft and from all sanctions of so-called white America, the release of all African Americans from jail, and the payment of compensation to African Americans for centuries of exploitation by white Americans. In addition to challenging police brutality, the Black Panther Party launched more than

---

[2]   Gary Stewart, "Black Codes and Broken Windows: The Legacy of Racial Hegemony in Anti-Gang Civil Injunctions," *The Yale Law Journal*, Vol. 107, No. 7 (May, 1998), pp. 2249-2279; and Douglas Blackmon, *Slavery by Another Name: The Re-Enslavement of Black Americans from the Civil War to World War II* (Anchor, 2009).

thirty-five Survival Programs and provided communities with legal aid, transportation assistance and ambulance services, and the manufacture and distribution of free shoes to poor people. Other programs included clothing distribution, classes on politics and economics, free medical clinics, and lessons on self-defense. Of particular note was the Free Breakfast for Children Program (1969), which spread to every major American city with a Black Panther Party chapter. The federal government had introduced a similar pilot program in 1966 but, arguably in response to the Panthers' initiative, extended the program and then made it permanent in 1975. At its peak in the late 1960s, the Black Panther Party grew from an Oakland-based organization into an international one with chapters in forty-eight states in North America with support groups in Japan, China, France, England, Germany, Sweden, Mozambique, South Africa, Zimbabwe, Uruguay, and elsewhere. The organization also found itself squarely in the cross-hairs of the Federal Bureau of Investigation (FBI) and its counterintelligence program, COINTELPRO. By 1969, J. Edgar Hoover, who perceived the Black Panther Party as a terrorist organization and considered the organization the "greatest threat to national security," devoted the resources of the FBI through COINTELPRO to destroy it by using agent provocateurs, sabotage, misinformation, and lethal force. This attack led to infighting, expulsions and defections that decimated the membership. By 1972, most Black Panther activity centered on its national headquarters and a school in Oakland, where the party continued to influence local politics. Though under constant police surveillance, the Chicago chapter remained active and maintained their community programs until 1974. The Seattle chapter lasted longer than most, with a breakfast program and medical clinics that continued even after the chapter disbanded in 1977. By the 1980s, the party had all but disappeared from the public eye, however, its influence assumed a transnational character that went beyond its initial creation. The Black Panther Party also managed to successfully infuse abstract nationalism with community programming that brought attention to the police brutality that had come to characterize life in black urban communities. More importantly, many of the radical ideas the Black Panther Party initiated in the 1960s have been adopted by today's progressives as part of their social justice platform.

BLACK POWER MOVEMENT: Ignited by the 1965 assassination of Malcolm X coupled with the urban uprisings of 1964 and 1965, the slogan, "Black Power" was first used by Stokely Carmichael in June 1966 during a civil rights march in Mississippi. In time, Black Power emphasized racial pride, the creation of political and social institutions against oppression, and the advancement of black collective interests led by a new generation of leadership that called for self-determination, self-respect, and self-defense for African Americans. One of the most misunderstood and understudied protest movements in American history (Jeffries 2006), many white people believed that Black Power was synonymous with violence and black racism, but it was in fact a logical extension of the struggle waged by the civil rights movement.[3] Some black leaders viewed the movement as separatist; some blacks believed that by closing ranks, they could challenge and rectify white-dominated institutions that would bring them closer to a fully integrated society. There were also others who had grown weary of Martin Luther King Jr.'s non-violent tactics, and were eager to adopt a more nationalistic approach; while many saw Black Power as a way of emphasizing black pride and African American culture. While the differences between these currents were explicit – and hotly debated – the idea of Black Power exerted significant influence in black communities. It helped organize community self-help groups and institutions that did not depend on white people. It articulated the cultural, political, and economic programs proposed and developed not only by such vehicles as the Black Arts movement, but also the Student Nonviolent Coordinating Committee (SNCC), the Black Panther Party, the Black Women's United Front, the Republic of New Afrika, the Nation of Islam, the Organization of Afro-American Unity, the Young Lords Party, and the League of Revolutionary Black Workers, among others. Together, these cultural and political formations galvanized millions of black people in the broadest movement in American history. It helped create black and other ethnic studies programs at colleges, mobilized black people to vote, and encouraged greater racial pride and self-esteem. However, by the mid-1970s, the movement was for all intents and purposes over. Government repression, which included the assassinations of Black Panthers Bobby Hutton in Oakland, Mark Clark and Fred Hampton in Chicago, and Carl Hampton of Houston; compounded by raids, arrests, and harassment of many of the movement's members, received much of the credit for the Black Power movement's demise. By 1973, activists began to concentrate their efforts on getting blacks and progressive whites elected to public office as a significantly less dangerous enterprise. The movement's legacy is that it encouraged black people to define their aims and goals

[3] *International Encyclopedia of the Social Sciences* (Thomson Gale, 2008). http://www.encyclopedia.com/topic/Black_power_movement.aspx.

in terms of their own heritage and cultural aspirations, and to become more assertive and confident in what they could achieve in social and racial justice.

CIVIL RIGHTS: Civil rights are the rights of individuals to receive equal treatment (and to be free from unfair treatment or discrimination) in a number of settings, such as education, employment, and housing, and is based on certain legally-protected characteristics. Most laws guaranteeing and regulating civil rights originate at the federal level, either through federal legislation, or through federal court decisions (such as those handed down by the U.S. Supreme Court). States also pass their own civil rights laws (usually very similar to those at the federal level), and even municipalities like cities and counties can enact ordinances and laws related to civil rights.

CIVIL RIGHTS MOVEMENT: The civil rights movement (which was initiated in the nineteenth century and peaked during the late-1960s) was a nonviolent series of events to secure full civil rights to African Americans in the United States of America. African Americans along with whites, organized and led the movement at national and local levels, which marked a sea-change in American social, political, economic and civic life. They pursued their goals through boycotts, sit-ins, negotiations, petitions, marches, and nonviolent protest demonstrations. It promulgated court battles, landmark Supreme Court cases, and federal legislation. It brought with it bombings, murders, assassinations, and other violence; prompted worldwide media coverage and intense public debate; forged enduring civic, economic and religious alliances; and disrupted and realigned the nation's two major political parties. It also influenced the Native American, Latino and Asian American movements of the 1960s, as well as launched the LGBT and modern women's rights movements of the 1970s.

COLONIALISM: Colonialism is the establishment of a colony in one territory by a political power from another territory, and the subsequent maintenance, expansion, and exploitation of that colony. The term is also used to describe a set of unequal relationships between colonial powers and colonies, and often between the colonists and the indigenous people of those territories.

CULTURE: Refers to the cumulative deposit of knowledge, experience, beliefs, values, attitudes, meanings, hierarchies, religion, notions of time, roles, concepts of the universe, and material objects and possessions acquired by a group of people in the course of generations through individual and group striving.

Culture guides people how to perceive, feel, think, act, and discern what is acceptable or unacceptable, important or unimportant, and right or wrong.

DIASPORA: A Greek term that means "to scatter," diaspora was used exclusively to describe the dispersion of the Jewish people following their expulsion from the Holy Land. Today it is used to describe a community of people who live outside their shared country of origin or ancestry, but maintain active connections with it. Whether one is aware of his or her heritage, nearly every American is part of at least one diaspora. Many of us come from mixed heritages, and, therefore, claim multiple diaspora communities.

DISCRIMINATION: The practice of unfairly treating a person or group of people differently based on specific characteristics such as race, nationality, religion, ethnic affiliation, age, sexual orientation, marital or family status, and physical or mental disability. Discrimination usually leads to the denial of cultural, economic, educational, political or social rights of members of a specific non-dominant group.

EQUALITY: It means that every person enjoys the same status, and should be treated the same way so that everyone can realize their full potential. Often the discourse of equality is used to perpetuate discriminatory practices because there is a focus on same or equal treatment, which is perceived as fair by the dominant culture. If the focus remains on the treatment (which is a form of denial that ignores how dominant institutions do not meet the needs of racialized people) and not the result, then equality will never be achieved.

HUMAN RIGHTS: Human rights are inherent to all human beings, whatever our nationality, place of residence, sex, national or ethnic origin, colour, religion, language, or any other status. We are all equally entitled to our human rights without discrimination. Universal human rights are often expressed and guaranteed by law, in the forms of treaties, customary international law, general principles and other sources of international law. International human rights law lays down obligations of governments to act in certain ways or to refrain from certain acts, in order to promote and protect human rights and fundamental freedoms of individuals or groups.

INSTITUTIONAL RACISM: A form of racism that occurs when institutions, such as corporations, governments, colleges and universities discriminate either deliberately or indirectly, against certain groups of people and limits their rights. Race-based discrimination in housing, banking, education, employment and health are also forms of institutional racism. Institutional racism is more subtle, less visible, and, therefore, more difficult to identify than individual acts of racism, but no less destructive to human life and human dignity. For example, the people who manage or work in these institutions may not be racist, but by simply carrying out their job are unaware that their role contributes to a discriminatory outcome.

INTEGRATION: Integration is the process of ending systematic racial segregation. When the U.S. Supreme Court declared in its landmark unanimous decision, *Brown v. Board of Education of Topeka* (1954) that separate schooling of black and white children was inherently unequal, it marked the beginning of the modern civil rights movement. Over the next twenty years, the civil rights revolution put in place laws that attempted to guarantee (essentially for the first time since our nation's founding) that no one should be restricted in their access to education, jobs, voting, travel, public accommodations, or housing because of race. For most people, this is what integration means. Although people of color have achieved some success as a result of integration, race remains one of the most intractable problems in America. This is due in large part to personal biases and racial stereotyping, which cannot be altered by legislation or lawsuits. Desegregation is a legal matter, integration a social one.

JIM CROW: Named after the plantation song, "Jump Jim Crow" (a song-and-dance caricature of blacks performed by white actor Thomas D. Rice in blackface, which first surfaced in 1832), Jim Crow refers to a series of racist laws and measures against African Americans and other people of color that enforced racial segregation primarily in the South at the end of Reconstruction in 1877. It was codified on local and state levels and most famously with the U.S. Supreme Court in *Plessy v. Ferguson* (1896), in which the Court ruled that "separate but equal" facilities were constitutional. It was the rise of the civil rights movement in the late 1950s combined with a series of significant landmark cases brought before the Supreme Court (*Korematsu v. United States* (1944); *Brown v. Board of Education of Topeka* (1954); *Loving v. Virginia* (1967)), which helped eradicate Jim Crow. While *de jure* segregation was not brought to an end until the passage of the Civil Rights Act of 1964 and the Voting Rights Act of 1965, many laws (often Black Codes) remained on the books in primarily Southern states as late as the 1990s. Inasmuch as Jim Crow was a milieu that permeated culture and ideology historically, the struggle against American racism continues, and in that regard, the effects of Jim Crow remain relevant today.

MAJORITY: When we're talking about race, ethnicity, gender, religion, or any other socially meaningful group of people, the majority refers to the social group considered to have the most power. In the United States, white people are considered the majority.

MELTING POT: A term used to refer to an American monocultural society in which there is a conscious attempt to assimilate diverse peoples into a homogeneous culture, rather than to participate as equals in the society while maintaining various cultural or ethnic identities used to describe the assimilation of immigrants to the United States. The exact term "melting pot" came into general usage in 1908, after the premiere of the play, *The Melting Pot*, by Israel Zangwill.[4] This term is often challenged, however, by those who assert that cultural differences within a society are valuable and should be preserved.

MICROAGGRESSION: The everyday verbal, nonverbal, and environmental slights, snubs, or insults, whether intentional or unintentional, which communicate hostile, derogatory, or negative messages to target persons based solely upon their marginalized group membership.[5]

MINORITY: A minority is any category of people distinguished by either a physical or cultural difference that society has subordinated. The differentiation can be based on one or more observable human characteristics, including ethnicity, race, religion, caste, gender, wealth, health or sexual orientation. In the social sciences, the term "minority" is used to refer to categories of persons (such as African Americans, Native Americans, Asian Americans, and Latinos) who hold fewer positions of social power. Most people of color detest being referred to as a "minority" because it implies the not-so-hidden connotation of being labeled as "insignificant."

THE MOVEMENT FOR BLACK LIVES: Created in 2016, The Movement for Black Lives is a coalition of groups across the U.S. that respond to sustained and increasingly visible violence against black communities. The collective is made up of more than fifty organizations, which include members such

[4] Israel Zangwill, *The Melting Pot*, Wikipedia, accessed February 29, 2016, https://en.wikipedia.org/wiki/The_Melting_Pot_(play).

[5] Derald Wing Sue, "Microaggressions: More than Just Race," *Psychology Today*, November 17, 2010 https://www.psychologytoday.com/blog/microaggressions-in-every-day-life/201011/microaggressions-more-just-race.

as the Black Lives Matter Network, the National Conference of Black Law-yers, and the Ella Baker Center for Human Rights. The impetus behind the Movement's founding was in 2015 at Cleveland State University where activists met to strategize how to hold law enforcement accountable for their actions on a national level by establishing an organizational platform that articulates goals, demands, and policies that will help achieve the liberation of black communities across America.

MULTICULTURALISM: A philosophy that became a significant force in American society in the 1970s and 1980s to appreciate ethnic diversity, and encourage people to learn about and respect diverse ethnic backgrounds.

THE NEW JIM CROW: A commonly used phrase that comes from the book, *The New Jim Crow: Mass Incarceration in the Age of Colorblindness* (2012) by Michelle Alexander, a civil rights litigator and legal scholar. The book discusses race-related issues specific to African American males and mass incarceration in the United States, but Alexander notes that the discrimination faced by African American males is prevalent among other minorities and socio-economically disadvantaged populations. Alexander's central premise, from which the book derives its title, is that "mass incarceration is, metaphorically, the New Jim Crow."

OPPRESSION: The socially supported mistreatment and exploitation of a group, category, or group of people or individuals. Oppression is built into institutions like government and education systems. It gives power and positions of dominance to some groups of people over other groups of people.

PEOPLE OF COLOR: The term is an attempt to describe people with a more positive term than "non-white" or "minority" because it frames them in the context of the dominant group. Identifying as a person of color in solidarity with other people of color acknowledges similar or shared oppressions by white people, a willingness to work together against racism and perhaps, a deeper commitment to allyship.

POLITICAL CORRECTNESS: (Also known as "politically correct.") Conforming to a particular socio-political ideology or point of view, especially to a liberal point of view concerned with promoting tolerance and avoiding offense in matters of race, class, gender, and sexual orientation. Commonly abbreviated to "PC."

PREJUDICE: A pre-judgment or unjustifiable and usually negative attitude of one type of individual or groups toward another group and its members. Such negative attitudes are typically based on unsupported generalizations (or stereotypes) that deny the right of individual members of certain groups to be recognized and treated as individuals with individual characteristics.[6]

RACE: Race is a socially meaningful category of people who share biologically transmitted traits that are obvious and considered important, such as facial features, stature and hair texture. But for most cultures, skin color seems to be the most important trait when it comes to race. Although humans are sometimes divided into races, the morphological variation between races is not indicative of major differences in DNA, which has led some scientists to describe all humans as belonging to the same race – the human race. Race is associated with biology, whereas ethnicity is associated with culture.

RACIAL PROFILING: The act of suspecting or targeting a person of a certain race based on a stereotype about their race.

RACIST: A person who believes that a particular race is superior to another.

RACISM: Oppression against individuals or groups based on their actual or perceived racial identity. The use of race to establish and justify a social hierarchy and system of power that privileges, preferences or advances certain individuals or groups of people usually at the expense of others. Racism is perpetuated through both interpersonal and institutional practices.

RECONSTRUCTION: The concept of Reconstruction began to crystallize as early as December 1863, when President Abraham Lincoln announced a plan to establish governments in the South loyal to the Union. Lincoln granted amnesty to most Confederates so long as they accepted the abolition of slavery, but said nothing about rights for freed blacks. Rather than a blueprint for the postwar South, this was a war measure to detach whites from the Confederacy. On Reconstruction, as on other questions, Lincoln's ideas evolved. At the end of his life, he called for limited black suffrage in the postwar South, singling out the "very intelligent" (prewar free blacks) and "those who served our cause as soldiers" as most worthy. Unfortunately, Lincoln did not live to preside over Reconstruction. It was a task that fell to

---

[6] *Institute for Democratic Renewal and Project Change Anti-Racism Initiative. A Community Builder's Tool Kit* (Claremont, CA: Claremont Graduate University). http://www.racialequitytools.org/resourcefiles/idr.pdf.

his successor, President Andrew Johnson. Once lionized as a heroic defender of the Constitution against Radical Republicans, Johnson today is viewed by historians as one of the worst presidents to occupy the White House. He was incorrigibly racist, unwilling to listen to criticism and unable to work with Congress. Over Johnson's veto, Congress enacted one of the most important laws in American history, the Civil Rights Act of 1866. In retaliation, Johnson set up new Southern governments controlled by ex-Confederates, and one by one, the Reconstruction governments fell. They quickly enacted Black Codes that severely limited freed people's rights and sought, through vagrancy regulations, to force them back to work on the plantations, an effort to restore slavery in all but name only. The Ku Klux Klan and other kindred groups began a campaign of murder, assault and arson that can only be described as homegrown American terrorism. As a result, widespread violence, coupled with a northern retreat from the ideal of equality, doomed Reconstruction. After the disputed presidential election of 1876, the Republican Rutherford B. Hayes assumed the Oval Office and disavowed further national efforts to enforce the rights of black citizens, while white Democrats controlled the South. By 1877, when the last federal soldiers left the South and Reconstruction drew to a close, blacks had seen little improvement in their economic and social status, and the vigorous efforts of white supremacist forces throughout the region had undone the political gains that had been made. Reconstruction failed, despite the heroic efforts of African Americans (and their white allies) to re-imagine a new, more inclusive country that had never been in existence.

SEGREGATION: A system that keeps different groups separate from each other, either through physical dividers or using social pressures and laws. Segregation may also be a mutually voluntary arrangement but more frequently it is enforced by the majority group and its institutions. Exclusive neighborhoods and gated communities that are predominantly white are examples of economic segregation and demonstrate how whiteness and middle- to upper-class ideologies are mutually reinforcing.

SLAVERY: Slavery in America began when the first African slaves were brought to the North American colony of Jamestown, Virginia, in 1619, to aid in the production of such lucrative crops as tobacco. Slavery was practiced throughout the American colonies in the seventeenth and eighteenth centuries, where slaves helped build the economic foundations of the new nation.

The invention of the cotton gin in 1793 solidified the central importance of slavery to the South's economy. By the mid-nineteenth century, America's westward expansion, along with a growing abolition movement in the North, would provoke a great debate over slavery and eventually tear the nation apart in the bloody American Civil War (1861-1865). Although the Union victory freed the nation's four million slaves, the legacy of slavery continued to influence American history, from the tumultuous years of Reconstruction (1865-1877) to the civil rights movement that emerged during the 1960s, to the twenty-first century, where the lingering racism and discrimination that began with slavery in America continues to this day.

SOCIAL JUSTICE: It is defined as "promoting a just society by challenging injustice and valuing diversity." It exists when "all people share a common humanity and therefore have a right to equitable treatment, support for their human rights, and a fair allocation of community resources." In conditions of social justice, people are "not be discriminated against, nor their welfare and well-being constrained or prejudiced on the basis of gender, sexuality, religion, political affiliations, age, race, belief, disability, location, social class, socioeconomic circumstances, or other characteristic of background or group membership" (Toowoomba Catholic Education, 2006). Social justice involves activists who have a sense of their own agency as well as a sense of social responsibility toward and with others, and society as a whole.

STEREOTYPE: It is used to categorize a group of people with attitudes, beliefs, and feelings that are widespread and socially sanctioned. These assumptions can be positive and negative, but all have damaging effects. Stereotypes support the maintenance of institutionalized oppression by seemingly validating misinformation or beliefs.

WHITE: A racial classification specifier used for people of European ancestry. The contemporary usage of "white people" as a group contrasts with the terms "black," "colored," or "non-white," which originates in the seventeenth century. Today it is used as a racial classifier in multiracial societies, such as the United States (White American), the United Kingdom (White British), Brazil (White Brazilian), and South Africa (White South African). Various social constructs of whiteness have been significant to national identity, public policy, religion, population statistics, racial segregation, affirmative action, white privilege, eugenics, racial marginalization and racial quotas.

WHITE PRIVILEGE: It implies that being born with white skin in America affords people certain unearned privileges in life that people of another skin color simple are not afforded. There are many different types of privilege, not just skin color privilege, which impacts the way people can move through the world or are discriminated against. It is not something you earned, it is something you are born into that afford you opportunities others may not have.

WHITE SUPREMACY: White supremacy—the belief in the superiority of the white race, especially in matters of intelligence and culture—achieved the height of its popularity during the period of European colonial expansion to the Western Hemisphere, Africa, and Asia stretching from the late 1800s to the first half of the twentieth-century. White supremacists have based their ideas on a variety of theories and supposedly proven facts; the most prominent of these include the claims of pseudo-scientific racist academic research that attempted to correlate inferiority and pathological behavior with categories of racial phenotypes, especially head size in the case of eugenics. There is a direct correlation between the rise of imperialism and colonialism, and the expansion of white supremacist ideology justifying the changing international order, which increasingly saw Europeans assuming political control over peoples of darker skin color through military force and ideological means, such as religion and education. It is important to note that the range of those considered "white" expanded considerably in the twentieth century. For example, in the United States, not all ethnic groups with white skin were initially considered white. It was not until well into the twentieth century that the Irish and Italians, for example, were considered white. By the end of that century, the United States federal government had also expanded its definition of whites to include Arabs. ■

APPENDIX 2

■ ■ ■

Suggested Reading

Alexander, Michelle. *The New Jim Crow: Mass Incarceration in the Age of Colorblindness.* New York: The New Press, 2012.

Aronson, Marc. *Race: A History Beyond Black and White.* New York: Atheneum Books for Young Readers, 2007.

Baldwin, James. *The Price of the Ticket. Collected Nonfiction 1948-1985.* New York: St. Martin's Press, 1985.

Barndt, Joseph. *Understanding and Dismantling Racism: The Twenty-First Century Challenge to White America.* Minneapolis: Fortress Press, 2007.

Barnes, Annie S. *Say It Loud: Middle-Class Blacks Talk about Racism and What to Do about It.* Cleveland, OH: Pilgrim Press, 2000.

Battalora, Jacqueline. *Birth of a White Nation: The Invention of White People and Its Relevance Today.* Durham, CT: Strategic Book Publishing, 2013.

Benjamin, Rich. *Searching for Whitopia: An Improbable Journey to the Heart of White America.* New York: Hyperion, 2009.

Blackmon, Douglas. *Slavery by Another Name: The Re-Enslavement of Black Americans from the Civil War to World War II.* New York: Anchor, 2009.

Bonilla-Silva, Eduardo. *Racism without Racists: Color-Blind Racism and the Persistence of Racial Inequality in America.* New York: Rowman & Littlefield Publishers, 2013.

Brown, Michael K. and Martin Carnoy, et. al. *Whitewashing Race: The Myth of a Color-Blind Society*. Berkeley, CA: Univ. of California Press, 2005.

Chang, Jeff. *Who We Be: A Cultural History of Race in Post-Civil Rights America*. New York: Picador, 2016.

Colby, Tanner. *Some of My Best Friends Are Black: The Strange Story of Integration in America*. New York: Penguin Books, 2012.

David, Gabrielle and Sean Frederick Forbes. *What Does It Mean to Be White in America? Breaking the White Code of Silence, A Collection of Personal Narratives*. New York: 2Leaf Press, 2016.

Du Bois, W. E. B. *The Souls of Black Folk*. Dover Publications, 1994.

Frankenberg, Ruth. *White Women, Race Matters: The Social Construction of Whiteness*. Minneapolis: Univ. of Minnesota Press, 1993.

Fredrickson, George M. *Racism: A Short History*. New Jersey: Princeton Univ. Press, 2003.

Glaude Jr., Eddie S. *Democracy in Black: How Race Still Enslaves the American Soul*. New York: Crown, 2016.

Goad, Jim. *The Redneck Manifesto: How Hillbillies, Hicks, and White Trash Became America's Scapegoats*. New York: Simon & Schuster, 1998.

Gonzalez, Juan and Joseph Torres. *News For All The People: The Epic Story of Race and the American Media*. New York: Verso, 2012.

Goodman, Alan H., Yolanda T. Moses and Joseph L. Jones. *Race: Are We So Different*. Hoboken, NJ: Wiley-Blackwell, 2012.

Hartigan, John. *Odd Tribes: Toward a Cultural Analysis of White People*. Durham, NC: Duke Univ. Press, 2005.

Hill, Jane H. *The Everyday Language of White Racism*. Hoboken, NJ: Wiley-Blackwell, 2008.

Ignatiev, Noel and John Garvey. *Race Traitor*. London: Routledge, 1996.

Ioanide, Paula. *The Emotional Politics of Racism: How Feelings Trump Facts in an Era of Colorblindness*. Palo Alto, CA: Stanford University Press, 2015.

Irving, Debby. *Waking Up White, and Finding Myself in the Story of Race.* Elephant Room Press, 2014.

Isaac, Benjamin. *The Invention of Racism in Classical Antiquity.* New Jersey: Princeton University Press, 2006.

Jacobson, Matthew Frye. *Roots Too: White Ethnic Revival in Post-Civil Rights America.* Boston: Harvard University Press, 2008.

Jensen, Robert. *The Heart of Whiteness: Confronting Race, Racism and White Privilege.* San Francisco: City Lights Publishers, 2005.

Joseph, Peniel E. *Waiting 'Til the Midnight Hour: A Narrative History of Black Power in America.* New York: Holt, 2007.

Katznelson, Ira. *When Affirmative Action Was White: An Untold History of Racial Inequality in Twentieth-Century America.* New York: W. W. Norton & Company, 2006.

Kendall, Frances. *Understanding White Privilege: Creating Pathways to Authentic Relationships Across Race.* London: Routledge, 2012.

Kennedy, Randall. *The Persistence of the Color Line: Racial Politics and the Obama Presidency.* New York: Vintage, 2012.

Kivel, Paul. *Uprooting Racism: How White People Can Work for Racial Justice.* British Columbia: New Society Publishers, 2011.

Lebron, Christopher J. *The Color of Our Shame: Race and Justice in Our Time.* New York: Oxford University Press, 2015.

Linker, Maureen. *Intellectual Empathy: Critical Thinking for Social Justice.* Ann Arbor, MI: Univ. of Michigan Press, 2014.

Lipsitz, George. *The Possessive Investment in Whiteness: How White People Profit from Identity Politics.* Philadelphia: Temple Univ. Press, 2006.

López, Ian Haney. *Dog Whistle Politics: How Coded Racial Appeals Have Reinvented Racism and Wrecked the Middle Class.* New York: Oxford Univ. Press, 2015.

Mills, Charles W. *The Racial Contract.* New York: Cornell Univ. Press, 1999.

Morrison, Toni. *Playing in the Dark: Whiteness and the Literary Imagination*. New York: Vintage, 1993.

Oliver, Melvin and Thomas M. Shapiro. *Black Wealth / White Wealth: A New Perspective on Racial Inequality*. London: Routledge, 2006.

Olson, Joel. *Abolition Of White Democracy*. Minneapolis: Univ. of Minnesota Press, 1994.

Painter, Nell Irvin. *The History of White People*. New York: W. W. Norton & Company, 2011.

Pierce, Jennifer. *Racing for Innocence: Whiteness, Gender, and the Backlash Against Affirmative Action*. Palo Alto, CA: Stanford Univ. Press, 2012.

Roediger, David R. *Black on White: Black Writers on What It Means to Be White*. New York: Schocken, 1999.

Roediger, David R. *Working Toward Whiteness: How America's Immigrants Became White: The Strange Journey from Ellis Island to the Suburbs*. New York: Basic Books, 2006.

Román, Ediberto and Michael A. Olivas. *Those Damned Immigrants: America's Hysteria over Undocumented Immigration*. New York: New York Univ. Press, 2013.

Rothenberg, Paula S. *White Privilege: Essential Readings on the Other Side of Racism*. New York: Worth Publishers, 2015.

Sue, Derald Wing. *Race Talk and the Conspiracy of Silence: Understanding and Facilitating Difficult Dialogues on Race*. Hoboken, NJ: Wiley-Blackwell, 2016.

Tatum, Beverly Daniel. *Why Are All the Black Kids Sitting Together in the Cafeteria: And Other Conversations About Race*. New York: Basic Books, 2003.

Terkel, Studs. *Race: How Blacks and Whites Think and Feel About the American Obsession*. New York: The New Press, 2012

Thandeka. *Learning to Be White: Money, Race and God in America*. New York: Bloomsbury Academic, 2000.

Tochluk, Shelly. *Witnessing Whiteness: The Need to Talk About Race and How to Do It.* Lanham, MD: R&L Education, 2010.

Vilson, Jose. *This Is Not A Test: A New Narrative on Race, Class, and Education.* Chicago: Haymarket Books, 2014.

Walker, Rebecca. *Black Cool: One Thousand Streams of Blackness.* Berkeley, CA: Soft Skull Press, 2012.

Wallis, Jim. *America's Original Sin: Racism, White Privilege, and the Bridge to a New America.* Ada, MI: Brazos Press, 2016.

Waters, Mary C. *Ethnic Options: Choosing Identities in America.* Berkeley, CA: Univ. of California Press, 1990.

Wise, Tim. *Colorblind: The Rise of Post-Racial Politics and the Retreat from Racial Equity.* San Francisco, CA: City Lights Publishers, 2010.

Womack, Ytasha L. *Post Black: How a New Generation Is Redefining African American Identity.* Chicago: Chicago Review Press, 2010.

Woodson, Carter Godwin. *The Mis-Education of the Negro.* Lindenhurst, NY: Tribeca Books, 2013.

Wray, Matt. *Not Quite White: White Trash and the Boundaries of Whiteness.* Durham, NC: Duke Univ. Press, 2006.

Yancy, George. *Look, A White!: Philosophical Essays on Whiteness.* Philadelphia: Temple Univ. Press, 2012.

Zack, Naomi. *White Privilege and Black Rights: The Injustice of U.S. Police Racial Profiling and Homicide.* Lanham, MD: R&L Education, 2015. ∎

ABOUT THE CONTRIBUTORS

■■■

KIMBERLY MARIE ASHBY, born and raised in Philadelphia, is an African American, womanist, fifth-year doctoral candidate in the counseling psychology program at Boston College. She received her MA in counseling theories from Boston College, and her BA in psychology and comparative ethnic studies from Columbia University. Ashby is currently the Diversity and Activism Liaison to the Massachusetts College of Art and Design Counseling and Wellness Center and is a co-coordinator of the Eradicate Boston College Racism Movement, an anti-racist student activist collaborative. Ashby practices psychotherapy and conducts research on Black women's mental health for the Institute for the Study and Promotion of Race and Culture (ISPRC) under Dr. Janet E. Helms. She is also a visual artist and singer-songwriter.

VICTORIO REYES ASILI is an activist, poet, essayist and artist living in Albany, New York. His poems have been published in *Acentos Review, The Mandala Journal, Pilgrimage Magazine, Mobius, Word Riot, The Pine Hills Review;* and the anthologies *It Was Written: Poetry Inspired by Hip Hop* (2017), and *Chorus–A Literary Mixtapea* (2012). His essays can be found at Awst Press and *She Breathes.* Reyes Asili served as the executive director of The Social Justice Center of Albany for eleven years. He is currently pursuing a PhD in English at the University at Albany.

DEDRIA HUMPHRIES BARKER is a member of the Squaw Valley Community of Writers. Her work has appeared in *Redbook, The Detroit News, Sundry: A Journal of the Arts,* and *ABSOLUTE VISIONS: An Anthology of Speculative*

Fiction, and *Literary Mama (2012).* She has been published by the Society for the Study of Midwestern Literature, and the Ohio and Michigan historical societies. A native of Detroit, she earned an MA in English from Wayne State University, moved to the state capital and became a professor of English at Lansing Community College. TWITTER: @dedria_hb.

VAGABOND is a filmmaker and multidisciplinary artist born in Brooklyn to Puerto Rican and Jamaican parents. He is the graphic artist of *Last of the Po'Ricans y Otros Afro-artifacts* (2013), and the author of *Nothing to be Gained Here* (2017). A graduate of Fiorello H. LaGuardia High School of Music & the Arts, he attended The School of Visual Arts but dropped out after his first year to work on independent black films such as Spike Lee's *Do The Right Thing.* He has written, produced and directed the documentary *Ricanstructing Vieques* (2013), and the award-winning feature film, *Machetero* (2008).

TARA BETTS is the author of the poetry collections, *Break the Habit* (2016) and *Arc & Hue* (2009). Her work has appeared in *POETRY, American Poetry Review, Essence, NYLON, ESPNW* and numerous anthologies. She is the co-editor of *The Beiging of America: Personal Narratives About Being Mixed Race in the 21st Century* (2017). Betts holds a PhD in English from Binghamton University and an MFA in creative writing from New England College. She teaches at University of Illinois-Chicago. www.tarabetts.net. FACEBOOK: @tarabettswrites, TWITTER: @tarabetts, INSTAGRAM: @chitownbetts, TUMBLR: http://chitownbetty.tumblr.com.

MELBA JOYCE BOYD is a Distinguished Professor in African American Studies at Wayne State University. She is an award-winning author of thirteen books, nine of which are poetry, including the critically acclaimed books, *Wrestling With the Muse: Dudley Randall and the Broadside Press* (2005), and *Discarded Legacy: Politics and Poetics in the Life of Frances E. W. Harper, 1825-1911* (1994). Boyd's poetry, essays and creative nonfiction have appeared in anthologies, academic journals, cultural periodicals and newspapers in the United States and Europe. She has a PhD in English from the University of Michigan, and BA and MA degrees in English from Western Michigan University.

CHARLIE R. BRAXTON is a poet, playwright and journalist born in McComb, Mississippi. He has published two volumes of poetry, *Cinders Rekindled* (2013), and *Ascension from the Ashes* (1991). His poetry has appeared in a number of literary journals, including, *The Black Nation, Black American Literature*

Forum, Cutbanks, Drumvoices Review, Eyeball Literary Magazine, Shout Out UK, The San Fernando Poetry Journal and *The Transnational.* Braxton's work has also appeared in the anthologies *The African World in Dialogue: An Appeal to Action!* (2016), *Role Call: A Generational Anthology of Social and Political Black Literature & Art* (2002), *Step into a World: A Global Anthology of the New Black Literature* (2000), *Trouble the Water: 250 Years of African American Poetry* (1996), and *In the Tradition: An Anthology of Young Black Writers* (1992). He studied journalism and creative writing at Jackson State University.

LISA BRAXTON is a former newspaper reporter and television reporter and anchor. She was nominated for an Emmy award during her television career. She earned her MFA in creative writing from Southern New Hampshire University, her MS in journalism from Northwestern University, and her BA in Mass Media from Hampton University. Her stories and essays have been published in anthologies, magazines, and literary journals, including *Vermont Literary Review, Clockhouse Review, Northwestern University Magazine, Chicken Soup for the Soul,* and *The Book of Hope.* She received Honorable Mention in *Writer's Digest* magazine's 84th annual writing contest in the inspirational essay category, and was a Top 10 Finalist for the 2017 Still I Rise Grant for Black Women Writers. She has completed her first novel. www.lisabraxton.com.

ALAN BRITT is a professor, editor, translator and poet. He has published fifteen books of poetry, his latest include *Violin Smoke* (Bilingual English/ Hungarian, 2015), *Lost Among the Hours* (2015), *Parabola Dreams* (with Silvia Scheibli) (2013), and *Alone with the Terrible Universe* (2011). He served as judge for the 2013 The Bitter Oleander Press Library of Poetry Book Award, and participated in the Ecuadorian House of Culture Benjamín Carrión in Quito, Ecuador in 2015, for the first cultural exchange of poets between Ecuador and the United States. Britt is book review editor for *Ragazine,* poetry editor for the *We Are You Project* (www.weareyouproject.org), and teaches English and creative writing at Towson University.

KIMBERLY GARRETT BROWN has an MFA in creative writing from Goddard College. Her novel, *Cora's Kitchen,* was a finalist in the 2016 Louise Meriwether First Book Prize, and short listed in the 2015 William Faulkner–William Wisdom Creative Writing Competition. Brown's work has appeared in *Zimball House Anthology, The Feminine Collective, Mused BellaOnline Literary Review, Compass Literary Magazine, Chicago Tribune, Today's Chicago Woman,* and *National View.* She is the founder and editor of Minerva Rising Press. www.kimberlygarrettbrown.com. FACEBOOK: @kgarrettbrown, TWITTER: @kimgarrettbrown.

LAYLA D. BROWN-VINCENT recently earned her PhD in Cultural Anthropology from Duke University. Her dissertation, "We Are the Ones We Have Been Waiting for: Pan-African Consciousness Raising and Organizing in the United States and Venezuela," examines constructions of race, gender and identity in relation to processes through which African diasporic youth become radicalized with an emphasis on emergent Pan-African sensibilities. She recently accepted a Visiting Assistant Professor appointment in the African American Studies Program/Race & Pedagogy Institute at the University of Puget Sound. TWITTER: @PanAfrikFem_PhD.

WANDA EASTER BURCH as a historian, writer, and retired site manager of an eighteenth century house museum. Her published works include, *The Home Voices Speak Louder than the Drums: Dreams and the Imagination in Civil War Letters and Memoirs* (2017); *She Who Dreams. A Journey into Healing through Dreamwork* (2003); and *Dreaming of Home,* a liner-note booklet that accompanies the music CD, *Come Dearest the Daylight is Gone* (2015). Her articles have appeared in several publications, including *New York History, Celebrating Johnstown: A Community Looks Back on 250 Years,* and *Sibyl Magazine: For the Spirit and Soul of Woman.* A long term breast cancer survivor, she is a peer reviewer for the Breast Cancer Research Program sponsored by the Department of Defense; and is a staff member for Creative Healing Connections' Adirondack arts retreats for women surviving chronic illness and for women who have served in the military. She received her MA at SUNY Oneonta, Cooperstown Graduate Program. www.wandaburch.com. FACEBOOK: @wanda.burch.1, TWITTER: @RonWanBurch.

ANNA CHRISTIAN is the author of six books, most recently, *Then Sings My Soul* (2015), *The Newcomer* (2013), *Daniel's Wife* (2010), *The Big Table* (2008), and *Mrs. Griffin is Missing and Other Stories* (2005). She writes book reviews that appear in Goodreads.com, and for her blog, "Celebrating Life" on blogspot.com. Christian has an MA in English from CSULA, and taught Language Arts for LA Unified School District and Moreno Valley Unified School District, and as an adjunct professor at Riverside Community College, from which she retired. She currently resides in Moreno Valley, California where she facilitates a Creative Writing/Life Story class at the Moreno Valley

Senior Center. http://anachristian.com, http://francesplace.org. FACEBOOK: @Anadoodlin, TWITTER: @annachristin9.

JANEL CLOYD is a poet, fiction writer and essayist. She received her BA in journalism from New York University, and is a Watering Hole Fellow and a Willow Books/Willow Arts Alliance Fellow. She has publications with *The Yellow Chair, Poeming Pigeon, Cave Canem Digital* and The Watering Hole Poetry Contest, and her book, *Anthology: Mujeres, The Magic, The Movement and The Muse,* is forthcoming. She is a member of Women's Writer's Poetry in Bloom Literary Salon, and The Poetry & Writer's Network & Exchange. Cloyd has participated in workshops and readings with Cave Canem, Bowery Poetry, Hobart Women's Writers and Women's Writers in Bloom. She is also a mixed media artist with a concentration in collage, paper arts, fiber, poetry, text and images.

ALI D. COLLINS, born in Boston, Massachusetts, resides in Greensboro, North Carolina, and is currently studying creative writing at North Carolina A&T. Collins has been a literary artist for ten years, publishing eight works as a Black Queer Erotica author.

SEAN K. CONROY was born and raised in McCook Nebraska. He matriculated first from Chadron State College in Chadron, Nebraska with a bachelors in Biology. He received a bachelors in Clinical Laboratory Science from the University of Nebraska Medical Center, Omaha, and concluded his studies with a masters in Physician Assistant Studies from Union College in Lincoln, Nebraska. Conroy has practiced medicine in Kansas in primary care including family practice, emergency medicine, and urgent care medicine since 2010, and currently provides medical care at Decatur Health Systems in Oberlin Kansas. He has thus far authored the book: *Through the Eyes of a Young Physician Assistant* (2016), and has published a number of short stories in anthologies, most recently in *What Does It Mean to Be White in America* (2016).

BRITTNY RAY CROWELL, a native of Texarkana, Texas, is a 2007 graduate of Spelman College. A Fulbright ETA recipient, she taught English in Phitsanulok, Thailand, and is a freelance writer for *ALT* and *Four States Living Magazine.* Her work has also appeared on *For Harriet and Education Post,* and *The Aquila Review.* She is currently an MA English candidate at Texas A&M-Texarkana.

FIKISHA LOIS CUMBO, a poet, author, filmmaker, television host and photographer, was born and raised in Houston, Texas. She earned a BA and graduated *magna cum laude* in biology and chemistry at Texas Southern University. She was a research assistant at the University of Southern California, and was an instructor at Brooklyn College (CUNY) biology department. Her photographs have appeared on the Peter Tosh albums, *Equal Rights* (1977) and *Honorary Citizen* (1997); and in the books, *The Life of Peter Tosh, Steppin' Razor* (2013) and *Bob Marley: King of Reggae* (1984). Her published work has appeared in *ATTITUDE Dance Magazine, CIRCUS Magazine, The Daily Challenger,* and *The Afro Times.* Cumbo is the host of the cable program, CACE INTERNAIOTNAL TV, which broadcasts online on YouTube and New York local cable stations. www.caceinternational.com, FACEBOOK / TWITTER / LINKEDIN: @fikishacumbo.

GABRIELLE DAVID is the executive director of the Intercultural Alliance of Artists & Scholars, Inc., a New York-based nonprofit organization that promotes multicultural literature and literacy, and the publisher of 2Leaf Press, an imprint of the organization. www.gabrielledavid.net.

CHRISTINA MARIE DOUYON is a Haitian-American third-year doctoral student and Diversity Fellow, pursuing a degree in counseling psychology at Boston College. She earned her BS in psychology at the University of Florida and an MA in clinical psychology from Teachers College, Columbia University. Prior to obtaining her MA, Douyon taught with Teach for America in New Orleans, Louisiana. She is currently a counseling psychology intern at Wellesley College's Stone Center. Douyon is also a member of the Institute for the Study and Promotion of Race and Culture (ISPRC), and co-leads a student group, The Race Culture Challengers, that informs and encourages conversations on issues of race and culture.

MELISSA DUNMORE is an Afro-Boricua was born and raised in Brooklyn, New York and transplanted to Phoenix, Arizona where she studied at Arizona State University. She is a performing artist and producer for Mujeres del Sol, a collective of women and girls in the arts. Dunmore's bilingual poetry has been published by *Mujeres de Maiz, Fem Static,* and *St. Sucia,* as well as in a forthcoming anthology, *Songs of Yemaya.*

ANGEL C. DYE hails from Dallas-Fort Worth, Texas by way of Milwaukee, Wisconsin, and is currently a senior at Howard University studying English with a concentration in creative writing. She is the author of two poetry collections, *Rhyme Or Reason from 2 Pens & Lint* (2013), and *urban is the new n@&!% (. . . and other names we answer to)* (2015); and the editor of the anthology, *Love Letters to Our Daughters: A Collection of Womanly Affirmations* (2015). Dye's poetry has appeared in *Sixfold Journal* and in Black Earth Institutes' *About Place Journal.* www.edenworkspublishing.com. FACEBOOK: @angeldye2694, TWITTER: @blkgrlpoet, INSTAGRAM: @blkgrlpoet.

CHRISTINE E. EBER holds a PhD in anthropology from SUNY Buffalo, and is Professor Emerita of Anthropology at New Mexico State University. She is the author of *Women and Alcohol in a Highland Maya Town: Water of Hope, Water of Sorrow* (1995), co-author of *The Journey of a Tzotzil-Maya Woman: Pass Well Over the Earth* (2011), and co-editor of *Women of Chiapas: Making History in Times of Struggle and Hope* (2003). Her poems have been published in *Malpais Review, Adobe Walls,* and *Anthropology and Humanism.* Her first novel, *When a Woman Rises,* is forthcoming from Cinco Puntos Press in 2018. She lives in Las Cruces, New Mexico where she is a founding member of Weaving for Justice, a volunteer network that assists Maya weavers in Chiapas to sell their textiles through fair trade. www.weaving-for-justice.org.

GIL FAGIANI is an independent scholar, translator, essayist, short story writer, and poet. A graduate of Hunter School of Social Work, his work has been translated into French, Greek, Italian, and Spanish. He has published five poetry books, which include *Logos* (2015), *Stone Walls* (2014), and *A Blanquito in El Barrio* (2009), as well as three chapbooks. Fagiani's poetry has appeared in twenty anthologies and publications such as *The New York Times, Descant, Skidrow Penthouse, Bitter Oleander, Mudfish, Maintenant, The Paterson Literary Review,* and *The Journal of Italian Translation.* A social worker and addiction specialist by profession, Fagiani directed a residential treatment program for recovering alcoholics and drug addicts in downtown Brooklyn for twenty-one years. He currently co-curates the Italian American Writers' Association's monthly reading series in Manhattan.

KAREN FORD is the author of *Thoughts of a Fried Chicken Watermelon Woman* (2014), and is a contributor to The Professional Woman Network anthology, *The Professional Black Woman,* and the forthcoming anthology, *The Black Woman Leader.* She is a freelancer for *People's World* (peoplesworld.org) and a columnist for *South Side Weekly* (southsideweekly.com), and has published in the *Chicago Tribune, Screen Magazine* and *Lutheran Woman Today*. She served two terms as Third Vice President of the National Writers Union, UAW 1981, and currently serves as treasurer of the Chicago chapter. Ford is the recipient of several awards for her community and labor-related work, and recently an International Women's Award by the Women's Information Network (2011). She received a BA in general studies and an MS in public service management from DePaul University, and resides in Chicago. www.karenfordonline.com.

CLARA B. FREEMAN, born and raised in Mississippi, is an activist, author and former nurse. She is the author of *Unleash Your Pearls Empowering Women's Voices* (2016), and *My Authentic Woman* (2011). Her articles have appeared in *Chicago Magazine, Bronze Magazine, Me! Magazine,* the *Chicago Bulletin Newspapers* and a host of other publications. Freeman is a member of Color of Change, Moms Rising.Org and Food for the Poor, Inc. http://wisewoman2.wordpress.com TWITTER: @ c50something, FACEBOOK: @ clara.freeman.904, LINKEDIN: @clara-freeman.

STEPHANIE FREEMAN is the director of the Arts and Humanities Program at North Carolina Central University in Durham, North Carolina. A long-time educator with over two decades of teaching experience on a collegiate level, she recently co-authored an essay for Oxford University Press' series, *Creativity, A Reader for Writers* (2015). She received a BA in English at North Carolina State University, an MA in from the University of North Carolina at Chapel Hill, and a master of theological studies from Duke University, and is currently a dual major at Apex School of Theology in Durham, North Carolina where she will receive both the master's in Divinity and Doctor of Ministry degrees. Freeman is currently working on her memoir. www.stephieannfreeman.com.

F.I. GOLDHABER, a graduate of University of Washington, won an international award for her non-fiction, and a first place award for her fiction under her pseudonyms, as well as numerous second and third place awards in various literary categories under all of her names. She has published five books of poetry under two names, seven novels/novellas, and fourteen collections of short stories. She also edited the anthology, *Green is the Color of Winter,* a fundraiser for SMART (Start Making A Reader Today). Goldhaber's poetry has appeared in paper, electronic, audio magazines, books, newspapers, calendars, anthologies, and street signs, including publications such as *Windfall: A Journal of Poetry of Place, Gold Man Review, In Our Own Voices, Appleseeds, The Rambler Magazine, New Verse News, Every Day Poets, Poetry for the Masses,* and *Diverse Voices Quarterly.* Her most recent poetry collection, *Food ♦ Family ♦ Friends* releases May 20, 2017. http://goldhaber.net.

EMMANUEL HARRIS II is an associate professor of Spanish, and is also an instructor of African American Studies and Latin American Studies courses at University of North Carolina at Wilmington. His articles have published in various academic journals such as the *Afro-Hispanic Review* and *Palara.* He was awarded Teacher of the Year in Washington University in 1996, and has a service award established in his name in 2000 at Baker University where he formerly instructed. An author and translator, he has translated Malambo by Lucía Charún-Illescas, which was the first-prize winner of *ForeWord Magazine's* Best Translation of 2004. Harris is the English translator of the critically acclaimed collection of short stories, *Over the Waves and Other Stories/ Sobre las olas y otros cuentos* by Inés María Martiatu. He received his master's and PhD from Washington University in St. Louis where he was a Chancellor's Fellow.

WILLIAM HARRIS was raised in Raleigh, North Carolina, and studied at North Carolina A&T State University. He was the first place winner in the Bi-Annual Public Speaking Contest at North Carolina A&T State University (2014), and won first place for his spoken word in the Wake Forest MLK Creative Performance Contest (2009 and 2010). His passions include writing fiction and non-fiction, poetry and spoken word, music, and performing at live events.

SEAN C. HARRISON, born and raised in St. Thomas, Jamaica, is a singer, poet and songwriter. After attending the Edna Manley College of the Visual and Performing Arts, he joined the band, Connected, and performed at prison ministry and Christian events. He began publishing his poetry in 2011 in *The Gleaner,* a local newspaper, and entered a number of literary contests, which led to appearances on local television programs. Harrison recently released the EP, *Gospel and Inspirational Songs,* and has published the poetry collections, *Thee Steps away from Faith, A Deeper Joy, Special Poems for Exceptional Children, The Black in Me,* and *As I Reminisce.* TWITTER: @ antophersean, #poetryseancharrison.

JOEANN HART is the author of the novels *Float* (2013) and *Addled* (2007). Her short fiction, essays, and articles have appeared in a wide variety of publications, including *Orion* and the *Boston Globe Magazine*. www.joeannhart.com.

AMELIA SIMONE HERBERT, raised in Rahway, New Jersey, studied history and African American studies at Duke University. She self-published a chapbook of poems and short stories, *Contagious Acts of Freedom* (2013), illustrated by artist Margaux Joffe. Herbert taught in Newark public schools for eight years, and is currently a PhD candidate in Anthropology and Education at Columbia University, Teachers College. TWITTER / INSTAGRAM / FACEBOOK: @ameliasimone.

MARIA JAMES-THIAW is professor of writing in the Department of English and Communication at Central Penn College. She is the 2014 Catalyst Award winner from the Harrisburg Regional Chamber of Commerce and CREDC, and winner of the 2014 Award of Poetic Excellence from the National Black Authors Tour. She holds an MS in communication from Shippensburg University, and an MFA in Creative Writing from Goddard College. James-Thiaw is the author of three poetry collections, *Talking "White"* (2013), *Rising Waters* (2003), and *Windows to the Soul* (1999), and the spoken word CD, *FREEverse* (2006). She is a poetry editor for *Philadelphia Stories Magazine, The Central Pen* and *The Triangle;* and serves on the board for Nathaniel Gadsden's Writer's Wordshop in Harrisburg. Her poetry, news and reviews have appeared in *Cutthroat Journal of the Arts, New Letters Literary Magazine, Black Magnolias Magazine* and others. She resides in Central Pennsylvania and manages The American Griot Project. http://www.mariathepoet.ink.

ESTHER WHITMAN JOHNSON is a former high school teacher and counselor from Southwest Virginia. She travels the globe volunteering on five continents, often writing about her journeys. Her poetry and prose have appeared in over two dozen publications, including *Artemis, Broad River Review, colere, Connecticut River Review, dirty chai, Earth's Daughters, eno, Lunch Ticket, Longleaf Pine, Main Street Rag, Virginia Writers,* and most recently the anthologies, *Howl, 2016!: Poems, Rants, and Essays about the Election* (2017), and *Forgotten Women: A Tribute in Poetry* (2017). The recipient of numerous awards, Johnson was nominated for a Pushcart Prize in 2016. She received an MA in English, and MeD in counseling from the University of Virginia.

CYNTHIA LEANN JONES is a poet that has published in a number of publications, including *Rhyme-N-Reason,* and *Poetry Art and Justice Slam.* She won first place in the Poetry Competition-Hinds Community College, and second place in the Veterans Civil Rights Movement Student Creative Arts Contest at Touglaoo College.

JE'LESIA M. JONES is a freelance writer, editor and columnist. She has been writing for school newspapers since elementary school through college. She served as press secretary and Communication Director in the administrations of three Massachusetts governors, and remains active in local government. Jones lives in Wellesley, Massachusetts and is working on her first novel.

S. BALTIMORE JONES has self-published two books of poetry, *Brothers of the Damn* (2011), and *Brothers of the Dam II* (2012). He resides in Seattle, Washington.

QUINCY SCOTT JONES is the author of *The T-Bone Series* (2009), and his work has appeared in the *African American Review, The North American Review,* and *The Feminist Wire,* as well as the anthologies *Resisting Arrest: Poems to Stretch the Sky* (2016), *Red Sky: Poetry on the Global Epidemic of Violence Against Women* (2016), and *Drawn to Marvel: Poems from the Comic Books* (2014). He is currently the Coordinator of the Writing Center at Grace Church School.

J. KATES is a poet and literary translator who lives in Fitzwilliam, New Hampshire.

BETTYE KEARSE is a writer and recently-retired pediatrician living in the Boston area. She earned a BA from the University of California at Berkeley, a PhD from New York University, and an MD from Case Western Reserve University. Her essays have appeared in the *Boston Herald,* and *River Teeth,* which was listed for a notable essay in *The Best American Essays 2014,* and nominated for the 2015 Pushcart Prize. She writes children's picture books, and as a descendant of President James Madison, she has completed the memoir, *The Other Madisons: An American Griotte's Quest.* www.bettyekearse.com. FACEBOOK / LINKEDIN / TWITTER: @bettyekearse.

BERNARD KELLER, born and raised in New York City, is an educator and a poet. His poetry has been published in several publications, including

Essence Magazine, African Voices, and the anthology, *Beyond the Frontier: African American Poetry for the 21st Century* (2002). A semifinalist in the McDonald's Essence Awards, he has participated in a variety of competitions and readings throughout the New York City tristate area. Keller received his BA and MA from Hunter College (CUNY).

ERREN GERAUD KELLY has published in numerous publications in online and print publications in the U.S., Canada and around the world, most recently with the Oddville Press, and in *The Eclectic Muse, Convergence, The Haight Ashbury Literary Journal, Torrid Literary Journal,* and *Tipton Poetry.* Kelly is the author of the poetry collection, *Disturbing the Peace* (2012), and his work has also appeared in the anthologies, *The Soul's Bright Home: Collected Poems* (2016), *In Our Own Words, a Generation X Poetry Anthology* (1997), and *Fertile Ground—Memories & Visions* (1996). Kelly has a BA in English and creative writing from Louisiana State University, Baton Rouge, and resides in Los Angeles.

YAEL KENAN is a PhD candidate in the department of Comparative Literature at the University of Michigan, Ann Arbor. Her research focuses on national mourning in Israeli and Palestinian literatures after 1948. She has taught courses on literature and migration, storytelling and textual descriptions of silence.

KWAKU O. KUSHINDANA lives between South Carolina, Louisiana, Alabama and Minnesota. He has traveled to sixty-nine international destinations and hopes for Cuba to be number seventy.

SHIRLEY BRADLEY LEFLORE is a retired professor and oral poet/performing artist. She is the author of the poetry collection, *Brassbones & Rainbows, The Collected Works of Shirley Bradley LeFlore* (2013), and *Rivers of Women, The Play* (2013). LeFlore's poetry and writings have appeared in many anthologies and magazines, including *Spirit & Flame, Anthology of Contemporary African American Poetry,* and *ALOUD: Voices from the Nuyorican Poets Café.* Her play, "Rivers of Women," was at the Missouri History Museum in 2013.

FELIPE LUCIANO is a two-time award winning Emmy recipient, former news anchor and radio personality, poet, speaker, and activist. A native New Yorker raised in East Harlem and Brooklyn, he is a former member of The Last Poets, and a co-founder of the New York chapter of the Young Lords Organization (renamed the Young Lords Party), where he served as Chairman of the New

York group. Following his departure from the Party, he went on to produce and host a number of radio programs at WRVR, WBLS and WLIIB; served as news reporter and anchor for WNBC-TV and WCBS-TV; was the host of *Good Day New York;* and co hosted with Ed Koch the local political affairs show, *Street Talk.* He worked as the Director of Communications for the City of Newark, and recently earned a master's degree from Union Theological Seminary. Luciano lecturers at colleges, universities, unions, and community organizations nationwide.

RASAQ MALIK is a graduate of the University of Ibadan, Ibadan, Nigeria. His work has appeared in various journals, including *Michigan Quaterly Review, Poet Lore, Spillway, Rattle, Juked, Connotation Press, Heart Online Journal, Grey sparrow,* and *Jalada.* He is a two-time nominee for Best of the Net Nominations, and was among the finalists for the 2015 Best of the Net. Recently, *Rattle Magazine* and *Poet Lore* nominated his poems for the 2017 Pushcart Prize.

MICHELLE MANN is originally from the western suburbs of Chicago. She is a graduate of the University of Notre Dame, where she majored in Africana Studies with a minor in Business Economics. Her work has published in *The Notre Dame Magazine,* and she is currently employed in the consumer packaged goods industry.

KIARA MANOSALVAS is currently a second year Mental Health Counseling student at Boston College. She received her BA from the University of Maryland, College Park. She works as a research assistant for the Institute for the Study and Promotion of Race and Culture. Manosalvas interns at South Boston Behavioral Health Clinic, and works with a wide variety of individuals who struggle with mental illness. She currently resides in Boston.

SAMANTHA MCCRORY was raised in Clovis, New Mexico and Warner Robins, Georgia. She received a BA in English from The Fort Valley State University where she is currently working towards a masters degree in the Education of School Counseling Program. She currently resides in Bonaire, Georgia, and works on campus at FVSU's writing lab. McCrory is a freelance editor and this is her first published piece.

RONNIE MCGRATH (aka "ronsurreal") is a socially conscious visual artist, neo-surrealist poet and novelist. He teaches creative writing in a diverse range of educational settings in London. A former creative writing lecturer at The University of The Arts, he is also a founding member of the now defunct musical group The London Afro Blok. In 1993, he was commended for his writing by ACER, which later published and awarded him first place for his writing. He is the author of the poetry collection, *Data Trace* (2010), the novel *On the Verge of Losing It* (2005), and the chapbook, *Poems From The Tired Lips Of Newspapers* (2003). His work has appeared in *IC3* and *The Penguin Book of New Black Writing in Britain*. McGrath has published paintings in *Callaloo: Journal of African American Arts and Letters – The Politics Issue* (Vol. 31, No. 4), and in 2008, appeared on the BBC documentary *Front Room*.

C. LIEGH MCINNIS is an instructor of English at Jackson State University. He is the former publisher and editor of *Black Magnolias Literary Journal,* the author of eight books, including four collections of poetry; a collection of short fiction, *Scripts: Sketches and Tales of Urban Mississippi* (1998); a work of literary criticism, *The Lyrics of Prince: A Literary Look at a Creative, Musical Poet, Philosopher, and Storyteller* (2009); and is the co-author of, *Brother Hollis: The Sankofa of a Movement Man* (2016). His work has appeared in numerous journals including *The Southern Quarterly, The Pierian, New Delta Review, The Black World Today, In Motion Magazine, MultiCultural Review, A Deeper Shade, New Laurel Review, ChickenBones,* and *Journal of Ethnic American Literature;* and the anthologies, *Down to the Dark River: Contemporary Poems about the Mississippi River* (2015), *Black Hollywood Unchained: Commentary on the State of Black Hollywood* (2015), *Black Gold: An Anthology of Black Poetry* (2015), and *Bum Rush the Page: A Def Poetry Jam* (2001). www.psychedelicliterature.com.

MARCIA L. MCNAIR earned her bachelor's degree in English from Dartmouth College and her master's degree in writing from New York University. McNair was an assistant editor at *Essence Magazine* and is currently an Associate Professor of English, Journalism, and Women's Studies at Nassau Community College, and serves as Executive Director and Founder of Long Island Girl Talk, a youth development program. Her non-fiction work published in *Seasoned Women* (2008), and her essays have appeared in *Mothers R Special/Celebrating Momma N'em* (2017), and *Issues in Feminism/ An Introduction to Women's Studies/Fifth Edition* (2001). In 2006 and 2007, she received a grant from the Long Island Council for the Arts for her collaborative performance, *Diary of a Mad Black Feminist,* now known as the award-winning *Sistas on Fire!* An excerpt from her first novel, *E-Males* (2007), was performed at the Schomburg Center for Research in Black Culture in 2009. Originally from New Jersey, she has resided on Long Island for over twenty years. www.sistasonfire.com.

BOB MCNEIL, a writer and spoken word artist, received his MS in media arts and science at Indiana University. His poetry has published in *The 35th Anniversary of Blind Beggar Press Collector's Edition Anthology, Whirlwind Magazine, The Shout It Out Anthology, Brine Rights: Stanzas and Clauses for the Causes (Volume 1), Not My President, A Lime Jewel, Year of the Poet, Writers' World Newspaper, We Cry for Peace (Swords of Words Book 2), Silkworm 9, The Annual Review of the Florence Poets Society, San Francisco Peace and Hope*, and *The Self-Portrait Poetry Collection*. FACEBOOK: @bob. mcneil.16, YOUTUBE: @mcneilbob1.

JESÚS PAPOLETO MELÉNDEZ, one of the original founding members of the Nuyorican Poets movement, has published several volumes of poetry. His most recent publication, *Hey Yo! Yo Soy! 40 Years of Nuyorican Street Poetry, A Bilingual Edition* (2012), consists of three of his earlier publications: *Casting Long Shadows* (1970), *Have You Seen Liberation* (1971), and *Street Poetry & Other Poems* (1972). Meléndez is also the author of *Concertos On Market Street* (1994), and the stage plays, *The Junkies Stole the Clock* (1974), and *An Element of Art* (1978). He is anthologized in numerous publications, notably in *The Norton Anthology of Latino Literature* (2011); *In the Arms of Words: Poems for Tsunami Relief* (2005); *Bum Rush the Page: A Def Poetry Jam* (2001); and *Literature and Integrated Studies – Forms of Literature* (1997). Meléndez has won a number of awards, notably a NYFA Poetry Fellow (2001), The 1st Annual El Reverendo Pedro Pietri Hand Award in Poetry (2006); and The Louis Reyes Rivera Lifetime Achievement Award (2004).

GEORGE CASSIDY PAYNE is an independent writer and photojournalist who reports on politics, religion, and social justice issues. He has published essays, commentary, blogs, poetry, and photography in a variety of regional and national publications including *The Atlantic, Buffalo News, Albany Times Union, Rochester Democrat and Chronicle, Rochester Indymedia, The Minority Reporter, Chicago Crusader, Toronto Star, The South China Morning Post, Ovi Magazine, Moria Poetry Review, The Ampersand Literary Review, KRWG.Org, The Fellowship of Reconciliation Blog*, and more. Payne received a Master of Theological Studies degree from Emory University (Candler School of Theology) in 2009. In 2010 he received the President's Volunteer Service Award. He serves as a Case Manager and residential counselor at Willow Domestic Violence Center in Rochester, New York. www. gandhiearthkeepers.org.

MICHAEL E. REID, a retired Episcopal priest, has published three collections of personal essays, *My Own Skin; Searching for Home; Grand Illusions: The Making of a 21st Century Man* (2011). Other works have been published in *Life in Pacific Grove* (2017), *The LLI Review* (Fall 2011), *CURE* (Summer 2010) and in the Community Foundation for Monterey County blog. Reid received an EdD from Temple University and an MDiv from the Church Divinity School of the Pacific. He currently resides in Monterey, California and is currently working on a book about women who are homeless in that community.

HERBERT M. RICKS JR. is a poet and essayist, and is a winner of the Clark-Atlanta University essay contest with a critique on liberation theology in the works of George Moses Horton. He holds a BA in English/Language Literature from Southern New Hampshire University, and an MA in English/African American Literature from NC A&T University. He is a performance poet who has competed in and won numerous poetry competitions, and served as Artistic Executive Director of Piedmont Spoken & Literary Arts Movement (SLAM), a performance poetry organization. Ricks has facilitated various seminars, workshops and discussions ranging from poetry to cultural studies. He currently works as an Adjunct Instructor of English at Forsyth Technical Community College and NC A&T University, and resides in Winston-Salem, North Carolina.

DEBRA R. RILEY is an aspiring poet who was born and raised in Toledo, Ohio. She currently resides in Houston, TX and spends her time as a volunteer in various community initiatives.

DACHARDAE RONCOLI lives in Belleville, Michigan where she freelanced for the local newspaper years ago. She is currently working on publishing a collection of poems and a collection of short stories while writing for the *Paths2Transformation* website. She's putting her early childhood education degree to good use by currently working as a preschool teacher.

ELLIN SAROT is a poet and editor. Her poems have appeared in *The Main Street Rag, The Paterson Literary Review, The Deronda Review, and Women's Studies: An inter-disciplinary journal,* among other places, and several anthologies, including *Women Writers Resist: Poets Resist Gender Violence* (2013), and *Veils, Halos & Shackles; International Poetry on the Oppression and Empowerment of Women* (2016). In 2014, she was awarded the first Gish Jen Fellowship for Emerging Writers by the Writers' Room of Boston, where she currently serves on the board. Recent prizes include second prize in String Poet's 2014 contest, and the New England Poetry Club's Firman Houghton Award for 2015. Sarot earned her PhD at Columbia University.

JEFFREY A. SCOTT writes poetry, short fiction and personal narratives. He earned a MA in history from the University of New Mexico, and a MFA in writing and consciousness from the California Institute of Integral Studies. He taught African American History at universities in California, Massachusetts, Colorado, Oregon and New Mexico. Scott gives readings of his poetry, talks and workshops on African American history. He has published at wwwpoetsagainstthewar.org (2002), and an article in the African American Studies journal, *Wazo Weusi* (1992), and recently completed an historical novel, *Conjuring Up Freedom*. He currently lives in Silver City, New Mexico.

AMMY SENA is originally from Dominican Republic but currently resides in Rhode Island. She holds a BS and BA from Suffolk University in Psychology and Latin American and Caribbean Studies. She is currently completing her masters degree in Mental Health Counseling from Boston College, where she is a researcher for the the Institute and Study for the Promotion of Race and Culture, and is a college counselor, interning at a local New England university. Sena is also a Graduate Education Diversity Intern at Education Development Center with the American Evaluation Association, learning tools and techniques on culturally responsive evaluation.

HEATHER SIEGEL is the author of the memoir, *Out From The Underworld* (2015), which was named as a finalist in the 2016 *Foreword Reviews* INDIEFAB Book of the Year Award. Her work has appeared on *Salon.com* and in *The Mother Magazine,* as well as in various trade publications and blogs. Siegel is also the founder of several independent businesses, including a coffeehouse, a café, an organic juice bar and a natural beauty bar. She holds an MFA in nonfiction writing from The New School, and lives on Long Island. www.heathersiegel.net.

MARY MCLAUGHLIN SLECHTA is the author of the poetry collection *Wreckage on a Watery Moon* (FootHills), and *The Spoonmaker's Diamond,* a serial game book-style novel for Night Owls Press. A poem was featured in *Rattle's* tribute to African American Poets and she received the Charlotte and Isidor Paiewonsky Prize from *The Caribbean Writer.* Her fiction appears in the anthology *New to North America: Writing by U.S. Immigrants, Their*

Children and Grandchildren (Burning Bush). She earned an MA in English literature from Syracuse University, and is currently an editor with Great Weather for Media.

JOHN WARNER SMITH has published two collections of poetry, *Soul Be A Witness* (2016), and *A Mandala of Hands* (2015). His third collection, *Spirits of the Gods,* is forthcoming from UL Press. Smith's poems have appeared in *Ploughshares, Callaloo, Antioch Review, North American Review, Tupelo Quarterly, Transition,* and numerous other literary journals. His poetry has been nominated for a Pushcart Prize, and for the Sundress Best of the Net Anthology. A Cave Canem Fellow, Smith earned his MFA in Creative Writing at the University of New Orleans. www.johnwarnersmith.com.

SHANNA L. SMITH is a Visiting Assistant Professor in the Department of English and Modern Foreign Languages at Jackson State University, and specializes in African American Literature and Culture. A native of Kentucky, Smith joined the Affrilachian Poets in 1992, and has poems forthcoming in *Black Bone: 25 Years of the Affrilachian Poets* (2017). She has contributed to a collections of essays on Pearl Cleage (2012) and Tyler Perry (2016). Smith received her PhD from the University of Maryland College Park, her MA from the University of Kentucky, and her BA from Kentucky State University.

MARK B. SPRINGER is a multidisciplinary artist from Cincinnati, Ohio. He is a pianist, singer/songwriter, painter, illustrator, and author. He is currently writing a memoir, *Caught in Jim Crow's Scheme,* which is focused around the 1980s prison boom and crack cocaine phenomenon. Springer has served 28 years and counting of a life sentence. His music can be heard on the "Die Jim Crow EP," a concept album about racism in the U.S. prison system. In addition to his musical contributions, Springer is the illustrator of the *Die Jim Crow EP Book* (2016). www.dieartwork.com/mark-b-springer

AYSHIA ELIZABETH STEPHENSON is a playwright, writing instructor and award winning poet. With an MFA in Writing from CalArts and an MA in Sociology; Ayshia uses drama and performance to investigate sexuality, race and gender. Her last play, *Venus Hottentot,* premiered at Jewel Box Theatre's "Midtown International Theatre Festival" in New York City in 2016. She has been published by Boston University Press, *Open to Interpretation, A Gathering of the Tribes, TESOL Review,* and is forthcoming in *Qualitative Inquiry.* She is currently a PhD student in Communication at UMass, Amherst.

ADAM SZETELA is an assistant professor in the liberal arts department at Berklee College of Music, and a lecturer in the English and Media Studies department at Bentley University. His op-eds, peer-reviewed articles, and poetry have been published by *Jacobin, Truthout, Salon, Counterpunch, The Journal of American Culture, James Dickey Review, Pilgrimage Magazine,* and *Grasslimb: International Journal of Art and Literature.* https://berklee.academia.edu/AdamSzetela.

JASON N. VASSER was raised in St. Louis, Missouri, and studied anthropology and later creative writing at the University of Missouri – St. Louis. His forthcoming collection of poems, shrimp, is a look at identity in the post colonial context. Keeping with that theme, his essay "Treading the Atlantic" is published in the *Canadian Journal for Netherlandic Studies'* special issue *Netherlandic Migrations: Narratives from North America.* He also has poems published in *Unveiling Visions: The Alchemy of The Black Imagination* and in other local literary journals and anthologies.

CARLETTA JOY WALKER is a writer, poet, artist, and storyteller. She is a journalist and producer, and has produced, hosted, emceed arts and public affairs programs including *Joy Journal,* a weekly program for writers and readers. She co-wrote the libretto for Smart and Tart Juicing, selected to be part of an international on-line opera project. Walker currently co-edits *And Then,* and has published in *White Rabbit.* She is co-chair of Be Present Inc., also presents in BPI Theater on the Issue conference cultural programs, and is a storyteller at the Sugar Hill Children's Museum for Art and Storytelling. She works in the Boricua College library in New York City.

RAN WALKER is the author of eleven books (six novels, two story collections, two novellas, and a collaboration with Sabin Prentis). His short stories and poetry have appeared in a variety of anthologies. Walker received his BA in English from Morehouse College, his MS in publishing from Pace University, and his JD from George Washington University Law School. He is the recipient of both a 2005 Mississippi Arts Commission/NEA artist grant and a 2006 artist mini-grant, and also served as an Artist-in-Residence with the Commission. In addition, Walker is a past participant in the Hurston-Wright Writers Week Workshop, and is the recipient of a fellowship from the Callaloo Writers Workshop. His novel, *Mojo's Guitar* (2015), was translated by renowned French translator Philippe Loubat-Delranc, and was published in by Éditions Autrement as Il était une fois Morris Jones in 2015. He is an Assistant Professor of English and Creative Writing at Hampton University and lives in Virginia.

JALAYNA WALTON has a BA in Literature from Augustana College in Rock Island, IL. She was the winner of the 2014 Eddy Mabry Diversity Award for her essay "God is Not a White Man." She currently serves as a Community Engagement Specialist (Americorp) for Habitat for Humanity-SKC. She grew up in Bermuda and Ferguson, Missouri but currently lives in the Seattle, Washington area. www.JalaynaWalton.com.

VICKI L. WARD is an author and publisher, and her short stories and poetry have appeared in many anthologies. She is the author of *More of Life's Spices, Seasoned Sistahs Supercharge Your Life After 60; 10 Tips to Navigate a Dynamic Decade* (2017), *More of Life Spices; Seasoned Sistahs Keepin' It Real* (2014) ,*Saavy, Sassy and Bold After 50* (2010), *Life's Spices from Seasoned Sistahs: A Collection of Life Stories from Mature Women of Color* (2005), and *Life's Spices From Seasoned Sistahs; A Collection of Life Stories from Mature Women of Color* (2004). She holds a bachelor's degree in management, and is a retired Superior Court administrator. She lives in the San Francisco California Bay Area. www.vickiward.net/blog. FACEBOOK: @ SeasonedSistahs, TWITTER: @seasonedsistah2.

KIMMIKA L. H. WILLIAMS-WITHERSPOON is professor, poet, playwright, lecturer, director, and performance artist. She is an Associate Professor of Urban Theater and Community Engagement in the Theater Department at Temple. A contributing poet to thirty-one anthologies, and the author of eleven books of poetry, she has performed poetry in over 93 national and international venues. She is also the author of *Through Smiles and Tears: The History of African American Theater (From Kemet to the Americas)* (2011); and *The Secret Messages in African American Theater: Hidden Meaning Embedded in Public Discourse* (2006). Williams-Witherspoon has had over 29 plays produced, and her stage credits include over 20 productions, and 8 one-woman shows. The recipient of a host of awards and citations, she received her PhD in Cultural Anthropology from Temple University. http://Thickdescriptions.blogspot.com, YOUTUBE: @ kimmikawilliams.

TIM WOOD is the author of two books of poems, *Notched Sunsets* (2016) and *Otherwise Known as Home* (2010). He is also the co-editor of *The Hip Hop Reader* (2008). His critical work can be found online at Floorjournal.

com, ActionYes.org and Jacket2.org, and in print in *Convolution* and *Leviathan*. Wood's poetry reviews can be found at the *Colorado Review, The Iowa Review,* and the *Boston Review.* He was a recent Fulbright scholar at the University of Tübingen in Germany, and is currently an associate professor of English at SUNY Nassau Community College in Garden City, New York. www.timwoodwrites.com, https://ncc.academia.edu/TimWood.

DEVA R. WOODLY is the Director of Undergraduate Studies, Politics at The New School in New York City. She has published research papers in Contemporary Political Theory, Institute Letter, and Public Choice, and is the author of *The Politics of Common Sense: How Social Movements Use Public Discourse to Change Politics and Win Acceptance* (2015). She was Research Fellowship, Institute for Advanced Study, Princeton, New Jersey. She received her PhD from the University of Chicago.

THELMA ZIRKELBACH is a multi-published author of memoir, creative non-fiction, poetry and romance. She is also a speech pathologist. An avid reader, Zirkelbach loves to travel, cook, learn and spend time with her granddaughter. ∎

ABOUT ABIODUN OYEWOLE

ABIODUN OYEWOLE is a poet, teacher, and founding member of the American music and spoken-word group, the Last Poets (1968), which laid the groundwork for the emergence of hip hop. He performed on the Last Poets' albums, *The Last Poets* (1970), *Holy Terror* (1993), and *The Time Has Come* (1997). Oyewole rejoined The Last Poets during its 1990s resurgence, and co-authored with Umar Bin Hassan, *On A Mission: Selected Poems and a History of the Last Poets* (1996). He released the rap CD, *25 Years* (1996), published his first poetry collection with 2Leaf Press, *Branches of The Tree of Life: The Collected Poems of Abiodun Oyewole 1969-2013* (2014), and the song albums, *Gratitude* (Sons Rising Entertainment, 2014), and *Love Has No Season* (2014). Oyewole received his BS in biology and BA in communications at Shaw University, an MA in education at Columbia University, and is a Columbia Charles H. Revson Fellow (1989). Over the years, Oyewole has collaborated on more than a dozen albums and several books. He writes poetry almost every day, travels around the world performing poetry, teaches workshops, gives lectures on poetry, history and politics; and holds a weekly salon for artists, poets and writers in his home in Harlem, New York. ∎

OTHER BOOKS BY 2LEAF PRESS

2LEAF PRESS challenges the status quo by publishing alternative fiction, non-fiction, poetry and bilingual works by activists, academics, poets and authors dedicated to diversity and social justice with scholarship that is accessible to the general public. 2LEAF PRESS produces high quality and beautifully produced hardcover, paperback and ebook formats through our series: *2LP Explorations in Diversity, 2LP University Books, 2LP Classics, 2LP Translations, Nuyorican World Series,* and *2LP Current Affairs, Culture & Politics.* Below is a selection of 2LEAF PRESS' published titles.

2LP EXPLORATIONS IN DIVERSITY
Substance of Fire: Gender and Race in the College Classroom
by Claire Millikin
Foreword by R. Joseph Rodríguez, Afterword by Richard Delgado
Contributed material by Riley Blanks, Blake Calhoun, Rox Trujillo

Black Lives Have Always Mattered
A Collection of Essays, Poems, and Personal Narratives
Edited by Abiodun Oyewole

The Beiging of America:
Personal Narratives about Being Mixed Race in the 21st Century
Edited by Cathy J. Schlund-Vials, Sean Frederick Forbes, Tara Betts
with an Afterword by Heidi Durrow

What Does it Mean to be White in America?
Breaking the White Code of Silence, A Collection of Personal Narratives
Edited by Gabrielle David and Sean Frederick Forbes
Introduction by Debby Irving and Afterword by Tara Betts

2LP UNIVERSITY BOOKS
Designs of Blackness, Mappings in the Literature and
Culture of African Americans
A. Robert Lee
20TH ANNIVERSARY EXPANDED EDITION

2LP CLASSICS

Adventures in Black and White
Edited and with a critical introduction by Tara Betts
by Philippa Duke Schuyler

Monsters: Mary Shelley's Frankenstein and Mathilda
by Mary Shelley, edited by Claire Millikin Raymond

2LP TRANSLATIONS

Birds on the Kiswar Tree
by Odi Gonzales, Translated by Lynn Levin
Bilingual: English/Spanish

Incessant Beauty, A Bilingual Anthology
by Ana Rossetti, Edited and Translated by Carmela Ferradáns
Bilingual: English/Spanish

NUYORICAN WORLD SERIES

Our Nuyorican Thing, The Birth of a Self-Made Identity
by Samuel Carrion Diaz, with an Introduction by Urayoán Noel
Bilingual: English/Spanish

Hey Yo! Yo Soy!, 40 Years of Nuyorican Street Poetry,
The Collected Works of Jesús Papoleto Meléndez
Bilingual: English/Spanish

LITERARY NONFICTION

No Vacancy; Homeless Women in Paradise
by Michael Reid

The Beauty of Being, A Collection of Fables, Short Stories & Essays
by Abiodun Oyewole

WHEREABOUTS: Stepping Out of Place,
An Outside in Literary & Travel Magazine Anthology
Edited by Brandi Dawn Henderson

PLAYS

Rivers of Women, The Play
by Shirley Bradley LeFlore, with photographs by Michael J. Bracey

AUTOBIOGRAPHIES/MEMOIRS/BIOGRAPHIES

Trailblazers, Black Women Who Helped Make America Great
American Firsts/American Icons
by Gabrielle David

Mother of Orphans
The True and Curious Story of Irish Alice, A Colored Man's Widow
by Dedria Humphries Barker

Strength of Soul
by Naomi Raquel Enright

Dream of the Water Children:
Memory and Mourning in the Black Pacific
by Fredrick D. Kakinami Cloyd
Foreword by Velina Hasu Houston, Introduction by Gerald Horne
Edited by Karen Chau

The Fourth Moment: Journeys from the Known to the Unknown, A Memoir
by Carole J. Garrison, Introduction by Sarah Willis

POETRY

PAPOLíTICO, Poems of a Political Persuasion
by Jesús Papoleto Meléndez
with an Introduction by Joel Kovel and DeeDee Halleck

Critics of Mystery Marvel, Collected Poems
by Youssef Alaoui, with an Introduction by Laila Halaby

shrimp
by jason vasser-elong, with an Introduction by Michael Castro
The Revlon Slough, New and Selected Poems
by Ray DiZazzo, with an Introduction by Claire Millikin

Written Eye: Visuals/Verse
by A. Robert Lee

A Country Without Borders: Poems and Stories of Kashmir
by Lalita Pandit Hogan, with an Introduction by Frederick Luis Aldama

Branches of the Tree of Life
The Collected Poems of Abiodun Oyewole 1969-2013
by Abiodun Oyewole, edited by Gabrielle David
with an Introduction by Betty J. Dopson

2Leaf Press is an imprint owned and operated by the Intercultural Alliance of
Artists & Scholars, Inc. (IAAS), a NY-based nonprofit organization that publishes
and promotes multicultural literature.

NEW YORK
www.2leafpress.org